The Channel Advantage

The Channel Advantage

Going to market with multiple sales channels to reach more customers, sell more products, make more profit

Lawrence G. Friedman
Timothy R. Furey

OXFORD AUCKLAND BOSTON JOHANNESBURG MELBOURNE NEW DELHI

Butterworth-Heinemann
Linacre House, Jordan Hill, Oxford OX2 8DP
225 Wildwood Avenue, Woburn, MA 01801-2041
A division of Reed Educational and Professional Publishing Ltd

A member of the Reed Elsevier plc group

First published 1999
Reprinted 1999

© Lawrence G. Friedman and Timothy R. Furey 1999

All rights reserved. No part of this publication may be reproduced in any material form (including photocopying or storing in any medium by electronic means and whether or not transiently or incidentally to some other use of this publication) without the written permission of the copyright holder except in accordance with the provisions of the Copyright, Designs and Patents Act 1988 or under the terms of a licence issued by the Copyright Licensing Agency Ltd, 90 Tottenham Court Road, London, England W1P 9HE. Applications for the copyright holder's written permission to reproduce any part of this publication should be addressed to the publishers

British Library Cataloguing in Publication Data
A catalogue record for this book is available from the British Library

Library of Congress Cataloguing in Publication Data
A catalogue record for this book is available from the Library of Congress

ISBN 0 7506 4098 7

Typeset by Avocet Typeset, Brill, Aylesbury, Bucks
Printed and bound in Great Britain by Biddles Ltd,
Guildford and King's Lynn

Contents

Preface

The two authors of this book have at least a hundred sales and marketing books stacked up on the shelves. Some have never been opened. As for the rest, a few have been read cover to cover, but most are bookmarked somewhere between the first and third chapters.

Why is that?

For one thing, we, like our readers, have very limited time for extracurricular reading. There just isn't enough time in the working day to read and digest more than a few books per year. But more importantly, we have found ourselves disappointed by many recent business books. Lots of good ideas and even a couple of gems, but ... too many flavour-of-the-month theories, too many buzzwords, and too few practical ideas that can actually be put to use within an organization. We vowed when we wrote this book that we would avoid that trap – that we would say something important and useful, and that we would get to the point.

In fact, we'll start by getting to the point right now

There are a handful of companies who have completely dominated their markets by using sales channels creatively to grow faster, drive down their selling costs, and establish a larger base of satisfied, loyal customers. Dell Computer comes to mind. Charles Schwab, GEICO, Fidelity Investments – they come to mind too. These companies have a powerful advantage in their markets, one that is often difficult for competitors to copy or emulate. It's an advantage in how they go to market, and we call it a channel advantage.

The rest of us are facing a big problem. Our products don't provide as much differentiation as they used to. Prices, too, are getting more and more difficult to use as a source of advantage. Lower operating costs used to provide a real edge, but today – after ten years of corporate restructuring – whole industries have reached parity in terms of operating efficiency. Even a skilled sales force isn't as much of a differentiator as it used to be: most large companies sport highly-trained, competent sales forces that are about the same as every other large company's competent sales force.

To put it simply, many, many companies do not have a sustainable source of competitive advantage anymore. They have fleeting moments of temporary superiority in their markets, perhaps from a new product feature or from a clever marketing campaign. It doesn't last.

This book is about a kind of advantage that *does* last. It is about reaching more customers by using sales channels to meet them where and how they want to do business. It is about shifting sales transactions to lower-cost channels in order to reduce selling costs dramatically. It is about improving customer retention and satisfaction by giving customers more flexible ways to do business. Ultimately, it is about using sales channels to grow faster – in revenues, profits, and market share. Top-performing companies are doing all this, right now. Throughout this book, we'll give you all the facts on these companies – what they did, how they did it, and the kinds of results they've achieved. Along the way, we'll give you the tools, concepts and ideas we've picked up and tested in our decade or so of working with clients on their channel strategy initiatives.

The time to rethink how you go to market is *now*. In many industries, new channels such as the Internet and call centers are changing the playing field, permanently. They are coexisting alongside traditional channels – sales forces and distributors – that have been fundamentally redesigned to integrate with new technologies and new channels. Who can afford to stand on the sidelines and watch this train go by? The simple truth is that channel innovation is no longer an option. It is a requirement.

This book will help you, the reader, take a step – not a small step, but a big one – toward the use of sales channels for growth, profit, and competitive advantage. That, in the end, is why we wrote this book, and that is what we hope you get out of it.

Lawrence G. Friedman
Timothy R. Furey

Acknowledgements

A book such as this cannot be written in a vacuum. Although the image of brilliant marketing consultants hunkering down to record their pearls of wisdom may be an appealing one (at least to the consultants), it would be a very poor description of how this book was written. Rather, it was a collaborative year-long effort between ourselves, our clients, our staff, and two very significant thought-leaders in sales and marketing, Dr. Rowland T. Moriarty and Neil Rackham.

Row Moriarty, Chairman of Cubex Corporation and a former Harvard Business School professor, is widely credited with the best early research on multiple-channel distribution strategy. His forward-thinking June 1989 article in the *Harvard Business Review* entitled 'Managing hybrid marketing systems' remains to this day one of the best and most definitive works in the field. Row continues to bring shape and substance to the emerging field of go-to-market strategy as a sought-after senior executive consultant and board member for three public companies. Row's contribution to the concepts in this book cannot be overstated.

Neil Rackham, Chairman and CEO of Huthwaite, Inc. and author of numerous best-selling books on sales strategy, has also greatly influenced our ideas. A true giant in the field of sales effectiveness, Neil is recognized worldwide as the pioneer who brought science, fact-based research and substance to the disciplines of large account selling, negotiation, and sales management. His SPIN Selling model has influenced, and is in use at, a vast number of the world's largest and most successful companies.

Row and Neil are rare thought-leaders, whose intellectual capital has greatly influenced our own thinking as well as many of the ideas in this book.

We must also recognize the valuable contributions made by our clients. Our work with senior executives and line managers at companies such as IBM, Lotus, Xerox, Oracle, Marriott and Fidelity Investments has been essential to this book. These and other clients have helped us develop, test, and refine many new concepts and tools, the most successful of which we have tried to capture in this book. Executives such as Fred Fassman, IBM's General Manager of Global Distribution, and Patricia Barron, former Xerox Corporate Vice President, have contributed to the development of our intellectual capital and have been significant channel innovators in their own organizations. In the end, it is executives like these – people who are able to see new go-to-market possibilities on the horizon and take action – who bring shape to the field of go-to-market strategy and create real shareholder value.

Finally, we owe a sincere debt of gratitude to the staff of our two companies. From vice presidents to consultants to administrative staff, they have all supported the development of this book in numerous ways. In particular, Jonathan Wu and Will Stoesser spent many, many hours researching the cases and examples used throughout the book. We must especially thank Kim Dobson, who reviewed and edited every word and illustration in this book for both content and style, from the first page we wrote through to the final submission of the book to the publisher. We were very fortunate to have the assistance and commitment of these colleagues when we took on this project.

Author contact information

Lawrence G. Friedman
President
The Sales Strategy Institute, Inc.
1474 North Point Village Center, Suite 400
Reston, VA 20194, USA
(703) 326-0500
(703) 326-0509 (fax)
lfriedman@salesstrategyinstitute.com

Timothy R. Furey
President and CEO
Oxford Associates, Inc.
7200 Wisconsin Avenue, Suite 710
Bethesda, MD 20814, USA
(301) 907-3800
(301) 907-3282 (fax)
tfurey@oxfordassociates.com

Chapter 1

Introduction: the competitive advantage of sales channels

What do these three companies have in common?

Dell Computer makes personal computers that are about the same as its competitors' products. Aside from the various features provided at different price points, what difference is there, really, between a Hewlett-Packard, IBM, Dell, Gateway, or Compaq PC? Not much, other than an individual customer's preference for a particular brand.

Yet Dell has been the computer industry story for the last several years, with the press having a seemingly endless appetite for news on the company and its billionaire CEO, thirty-three year old Michael Dell. Why? Because Dell's growth is all out of proportion to its competitors' market performance. Almost written off in 1993 after failing in its attempt to launch a laptop business, Dell has come roaring back. Over the past three years, sales have grown fifty-three per cent annually, from $3.4 billion to over $12.3 billion. During the same three years, profits grew eighty-nine per cent per year and Dell's worldwide PC market share doubled. The company's revenue growth is over *twice* that of any of its competitors[1].

How did Dell do it? There's a complex answer, but basically Dell provides a wide range of attractive ways for people to buy their equipment. Customers can configure their own systems and order them over the Internet – which they do, making over one million site visits per week and $4 million in purchases every day[2]. Customers can also buy through efficient call centres linked to Dell's build-to-order system, which eliminates distributors and takes seven per cent out of the cost out of each computer sold. These systems have given Dell significantly higher per-sale profitability as well as the ability to reach dispersed groups of customers in more numerous markets. Competitors, bogged down with expensive direct sales forces or inefficient networks of distributors, are struggling to figure out how to compete effectively against the Dell juggernaut.

Charles Schwab, the discount broker, has the most popular Internet brokerage site, with over 1,200,000 on-line accounts[3]. If you are not an on-line type, Schwab also offers round-the-clock call centres for trading, account information and market data. If you want face-to-face investment advice, Schwab has retail branches in most major cities. Schwab has also emerged in the last two years as a – perhaps *the* – key distributor of competitors' financial products, selling, for example, mutual funds from Fidelity Investments. There is basically no known channel that Schwab doesn't provide to its customers, and no known brokerage product that Schwab doesn't sell through those channels.

The result of this hyperactivity has been stunning. In a hotly contested online brokerage market with dozens of low-cost competitors, Schwab has almost a forty per cent share of the entire on-line brokerage business[4]. The company's revenues are about three times that of its average competitor. Those competitors, who sell the exact same financial products, have been playing frenzied catch-up ball, starting their own web sites, improving their often dismal call centres, entering into partnering agreements to carry other firms' products, and lowering transaction fees. In many cases Schwab's competitors have come up with lower costs, better Internet sites and more extensive services (such as stock picking advice). Schwab, though, loses few customers and is signing up more than two thousand new ones every day. Selling the same products as competitors, sometimes at higher prices, Schwab nevertheless enjoys a commanding position of market leadership. Why?

First Direct is in one of the toughest markets in the world, British retail banking. Deregulation has brought about a wild race among all sorts of companies to see who can become the ultimate one-stop shop for financial services. Banks that used to sell savings accounts and loans are now pitching investment, life insurance and pension products. Insurance companies and 'building societies' (mortgage companies) are fighting back by selling savings and deposit accounts. Supermarkets have their own credit cards. Even the department store Marks & Spencer sells loans and pension products to its customers.

This massive cross-selling and competition has led to a wide-scale industry shake-out. Bank branch offices have declined from 21,000 to less than 15,000 over the past decade. Over ten per cent of the entire banking work force of 274,000 has had to find new jobs as more and more competitors move in on the turf of the retail banks. In the middle of this shake-out, First Direct, in business only eight years, has built a customer base of 760,000 and is adding over 15,000 new customers every month. Two-thirds of its new customers are defectors from the retail banks and building societies. Why the stampede?

Certainly not because of its products, which are the same as those offered by other banks. It's because the company lets customers do business the way they want to do business. Customers interact with First Direct over the phone, through the mail, and over the Internet, as well as through traditional retail branches and ATMs (available through parent Marine Midland Bank). Its telephone operators are available twenty-four hours a day, seven days a week, so customers are never without service. Its range of alternatives, from phones to ATMs to the mail service to the Internet, means that customers do not ever need to make the trip to the bank. In sharp contrast to its competitors, First Direct has a ninety-eight per cent customer retention rate. Having learned something important about customer buying behavior, it is currently adding PC banking and is even looking into television banking.

These successful companies, though in different industries, have at least two things in common.

First, they have all but dispensed with the idea of fighting on the battlefield of product features. They are leaving it to their competitors to tweak this or that gadget in the search for competitive advantage. In terms of what they actually sell, their products are about as good and often about the same as their competitors' offerings. Products, though, are not where they are fighting for competitive advantage. They have all decisively looked elsewhere for competitive differentiation, and specifically on how they *go to market* with their products and services. These companies are achieving strong revenue and market share growth primarily by making it more attractive for more customers to do more business through more convenient sales channels. Put simply, they have all bet big – and so far bet correctly – that they can get more competitive advantage from *how* they sell than from *what* they sell.

Second, these are hugely successful companies, as measured in shareholder value and growth. Dell's stock price has increased 29,000 per cent since 1990, and its price–earnings ratio of fifty-four, the premium paid by investors for anticipated future growth, is nearly twice that of the average company in the S&P 500[5]. Schwab's stock price has increased tenfold over the past five years. First Direct is one of the fastest growing banks in the United Kingdom, and is well on track to reach its target of 1,000,000 customers by the year 2000.

The dramatic successes of these 'channel-centric' companies in highly competitive markets raises an important question. For many years, product differentiation was where companies made their stand. Only recently, perhaps in the last ten or fifteen years, have leading companies begun to look toward *channel differentiation* as a key source of competitive advantage. The question is: what happened?

The challenge facing product-centric companies

For a business to be viable at all, it has to do something well. For it to win in a competitive market, though, it has to do something better than its competitors.

This familiar idea, competitive advantage, says simply that you have to be better than your competitors, at something important to your customers, to make sales. That 'something' could involve better products, or lower prices, or better service, or whatever else matters to customers.

Short-term, modest competitive advantages are not difficult to find and exploit. A small rebate on a Ford Taurus will lead to increased sales; a better cup holder in a Honda Accord will steal some of those sales back[6]. Competitive advantage is constantly in flux as competitors vie back and forth on product features and price. Short-term, small competitive advantages, though, are not the answer for most companies, for the obvious reason that they don't last. The issue is finding and maintaining a *sustainable* competitive advantage: an advantage that has some staying power in a competitive market place.

It's when you think about sustainable competitive advantage that you realize what a fix many companies are in today. When Lotus Development Corporation came out with the Lotus 1-2-3 spreadsheet program in 1982, it had a huge and profitable market largely to itself for a few years. Today, Netscape Communications comes out with new Internet browser software and before you can say 'I'll take one!' Microsoft comes out with a similarly-featured version of its own browser. Millions of dollars in R&D yield fleeting moments of differentiation. Levi's had the denim jeans market to itself for half a century; today popular fashions and fabrics are copied in days and appear in retail stores almost instantly. Do you have a better pizza, video rental concept, or cellular phone to sell? You probably have a few months or less before Pizza Hut, Blockbuster or Nokia figure out what you did, replicate it (if it's a good idea) and get it to market quicker and probably more efficiently. Product competitive advantage isn't measured in years anymore; it's measured in months, or weeks, or sometimes days.

The forces behind this crunching of competitive lead time are well-known. Communication technologies have increased the speed at which companies can find out what competitors are doing and feed back new design concepts into their own product releases. Manufacturing technology has radically lowered the costs, and the barriers to entry, for getting into a market with a high-quality, market-ready product. Today's global corporations have the resources and economies of scale to scour the planet in search of every last customer, leaving perhaps a few desolate islands up for grabs. Advances in distribution and logistics systems have enabled companies to send products all over the world and get them into the hands of customers in a matter of days and, in some cases, hours.

Put all of this together, and you can see why companies are worried about whether a new and better gadget will result in any durable competitive advantage.

If not products, how about competing on lower costs?

For a while companies focused not on producing better products, but on improving business processes to reduce costs. The cost-cutting frenzy and then the reengineering 'revolution' hit the business world like a ton of bricks in the late 1980s, leaving dazed managers with skeleton teams, reduced budgets – and efficient, streamlined business processes. In retrospect, some of the excesses of the reengineering craze now seem a little out of hand, with companies trying to refocus on growth and re-motivate legions of disaffected, bitter employees. Nevertheless, in many organizations productivity increased, costs decreased, and stockholders became millionaires as margins soared.

So far so good. Today, though, many companies have reached parity in terms of cost-reduction and efficiency. How much fat is there really left to cut in the average business, and at what point do you begin cutting into the muscle? Can GM significantly improve some process such that production costs will be substantially lower than what Ford can accomplish? Maybe, but those sources of margin are getting harder and harder to find. The low-hanging fruit has been picked. TQM and its various sibling methodologies have brought parity and equivalence to whole industries in terms of efficiency and cost structure. Even Jaguar, that last holdout of the hand-crafted, spare-no-expense repair shop's dream, has been thoroughly reengineered into the modern age under owner Ford Motor.

Unless you're in an industry that stayed on the sidelines during the cost-cutting, reengineering craze, chances are high that you and your competitors are looking eerily the same in terms of business structure and processes. You've probably worked with the same consultants to streamline or eliminate the same processes and pink-slip the same types of employees. Competing on cost structure is still possible, and for many it's still a little easier than competing on product features, but not by much, and not for long.

Brand: one source of real competitive advantage, with a caveat

In contrast to product and price, one source of competitive advantage that is still alive and well is brand. In fact, globalization and large-scale distribution seem to be bolstering the ability of large, dominant companies to brand their products and leverage that brand for growth and share.

For example, Coke (actually, Coca-Cola) has done quite nicely, to say the least, selling a product, one that's basically about the same as its competitors' offerings, to just about any person on earth who wants a soda. Coca-Cola sold 834,000,000 servings of soda products every day in 1996. As more and more people drink Coke, its brand becomes more and more established, leading to more consumption ... and so on. The same is true for McDonald's. Those Russians and Chinese who stand on lines for five hours to get a hamburger – is it because the hamburger is so inherently good or because McDonald's is, well, McDonald's?

Globalization and economies of scale seem to benefit strong brands and make them stronger. It's enough to make anyone want a strong, global brand. On the other hand, not all brands last forever. It can be a tenuous source of competitive advantage. Coke and McDonald's are making a killing, but what about Adidas or Apple Computer or Montgomery Ward? All were once dominant companies with superior brands, but all have succumbed to savvier competitors and changing consumer tastes. You can take a strong brand to the bank – and companies do, with brand equity showing up on some balance sheets – but you still need a durable competitive advantage to back up and support that brand.

The competitive advantage of a channel-centric approach

All that, in a nutshell, is why many leading companies are putting at least as much effort and creativity into *how* they go to market as into *what* they bring to market. There just are not as many product-based sources of durable competitive advantage as there used to be. At the same time, newer channel technologies such as the Internet, call centres, and database marketing systems have opened up many new options and given companies a wide range of alternatives for crafting and implementing a new kind of advantage: a *channel* advantage.

The theory behind the advantage of a channel-centric strategy is disarmingly simple. Companies generally have a wide variety of options for connecting products with their customers, from sales forces to distributors, from direct mail to the Internet, and everything in between (see Figure 1.1). Each of those channels has certain unique strengths. For example, a direct sales force is usually optimal for complex, high-cost transactions where face-to-face interaction is expected and required. Another channel, the call centre, can reduce selling costs by forty per cent or more, and is also beneficial in terms of customer loyalty, since it can provide twenty-four-hour problem resolution and service. Business partners and distributors can dramatically expand market reach through local access and penetration. The Internet can be used to get the message out to untold millions at an extremely low cost.

On the other hand, each channel has significant limitations and tradeoffs. Sales forces handle complex, lengthy transactions well, but are very expensive. The Internet works well for some types of products, but not for others – and it isn't suitable for sales that require a lot of training or hand-holding.

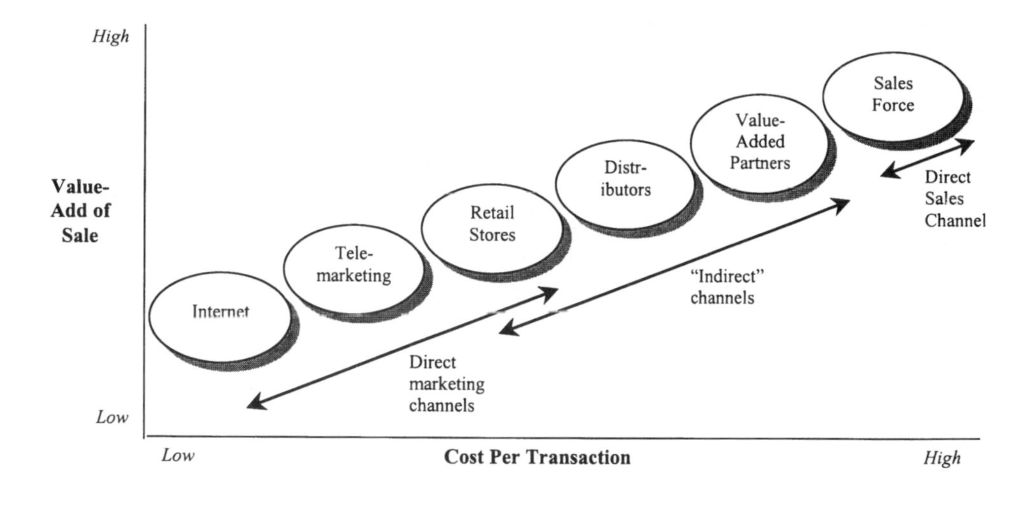

Figure 1.1 Sales channels – connecting products with customers – *Source:* Oxford Associates, adapted from Dr Rowland T. Moriarty, Cubex Corp.

Distributors can dramatically increase market coverage, but can also remove you further and further from the end-customer, whose brand loyalty you need and whose up-to-the-minute requirements you may need to understand.

The bottom line is that use of a single channel limits a company's market performance to whatever that particular channel is able to do well. If you use only a sales force, you may be able to provide good customer service, but you will be at a severe cost disadvantage to any competitor who decides to sell through just about any other channel. If you use only the Internet, you will probably be limited to the sale of simple, low-cost products, and you may have significant challenges in developing loyal customer relationships. No single channel does everything well or competitively.

Companies that choose and cleverly integrate the right mix of channels, on the other hand, can build go-to-market systems that respond optimally to each of the requirements of their products and markets. They can, for example, use expensive sales force reps only to acquire and grow the most important key accounts. They can then use distributors to reach dispersed groups of smaller customers and to provide local sales support. They can use call centres to close simple sales, generate sales leads for other channels, and follow up on direct mail campaigns. They can use the Internet to reach customers who prefer to serve themselves and want to save money. All along the way, they can focus on using the lowest-cost channels that will work best in each type of selling situation. It all can – and does – add up to a huge competitive advantage in terms of revenue growth, market reach, customer loyalty, and higher profits.

The channel advantage – coming soon to a market – and near you!

Channel innovation is separating market winners from market losers, not just in leading-edge technology industries, but even in the kinds of traditional markets where most of us still make a living. Take as an example Amazon.com. Launched in June 1996 by a guy with a web site and a good idea, Amazon.com sells one of the oldest, lowest-tech products known to man – books – over the Internet.

The timing and the concept were perfect. Educated consumers – the kinds of people who buy books – like self-service channels and like using technology too. Books are simple, inexpensive, 'off the shelf' items, the kinds of things that sell well in an efficient self-service channel such as the Internet. The Internet is a cost-effective medium, which has enabled Amazon.com to offer highly-competitive prices. Since there is no physical bookstore to keep stocked with inventory, the company has been able to offer virtually a limitless selection of books, most of which are available on one to two days' notice.

As a result of all these fortuitous circumstances, Amazon.com has emerged from thin air into a market value of about $3.6 billion in three years. That's about the same market capitalization as Border's Group and Barnes and Noble – the established booksellers with real, physical stores and well-branded retail identities – *combined*[7]. Investors have become very wealthy on Amazon.com, and the established industry players in the book business have now – reactively – jumped into the Internet fray.

Here are a few other examples of how channel innovation has seeped into unsuspecting industries:

- People said for many years that personal computers couldn't be sold over the phone. These products are too complex and require too much hand holding; they will always require a local dealer. Dell Computer took a different position, that telesales is an ideal, low-cost medium to deliver what essentially has become a commodity product. Compare Dell's growth to, say, Merisel or Intelligent Electronics. Maybe small PCs really have become commodities that can be sold effectively through low-cost channels. Going further with this idea, though, IBM recently sold a mainframe computer, the most expensive, complicated capital investment most companies ever make, over the phone.
- Pagers were supposedly specialized products, part of a telecommunications 'solution', that could only be sold through a specialty retailer or a direct sales representative. Motorola is selling a ton of them through WalMart.
- Life insurance is a tough product to sell; perhaps no other product requires as much explanation, hand-holding and face-to-face convincing. Unless you're Veritas, one of the fastest growing insurance companies, who is advertising in the media to generate incoming calls and is closing life insurance orders with low-cost telesales representatives.

- The automobile is another product that's tough to sell. You need a dealer to explain the myriad complex options, safety features and different models. You especially need a dealer to keep margins up by talking customers into paying inflated MSRP prices, and helping indecisive people make the decision to part with their hard-earned money. On the other hand, there's AutoByTel, which uses the Internet to connect buyers who already know what they want, and are ready to buy, with dealers who offer no-haggle prices. AutoByTel has been used by over a million customers since its introduction in 1995, and processes over 100,000 requests and sources over $500 million in vehicle sales *per month*[8].
- Merrill Lynch's whole value proposition is based on the idea that it is a high-value-add, high-touch financial services 'partner'. Its well-compensated sales executives manage personal client (never 'customer') relationships. So where does a huge volume of its business come from nowadays? The Cash Management Account (CMA), basically a simple, do-it-yourself checking and credit card account that also handles investment transactions. CMA accounts are advertised in business magazines and processed through inbound call centres; accounts can be opened through the mail with little or no contact between customer and broker.

It sounds so intuitive and easy . . .

So why not just take whatever you sell and throw it onto the Internet or some other new channel, and see what happens? Well, that's exactly what a lot of companies are doing. Whether it's the Internet, direct mail, shopping mall kiosks, or the incredibly annoying call-during-dinner-and-harass-the-hungry-family channel, companies are piling into as many channels as they can, as quickly as possible. The underlying assumption behind this frenzied activity is as follows:

add more channels = make more sales

There is, in fact, some truth in this formula. More channels make it easier for more customers to buy products from more sources, and as a result, sales typically increase. Many leading companies such as Microsoft and Fidelity Investments are adherents of this approach. Microsoft, for example, sells its software through retailers, distributors, application developers, systems integrators and OEMs ('original equipment manufacturers', such as Compaq and IBM). Fidelity has a similarly broad mix of channels, selling and servicing customers through retail branches, inbound call centres, the Internet, other financial service providers, and so on. These leading companies are adherents of the philosophy that the more ways you can reach out to customers, the better.

So what's the problem with just adding a lot of channels? For one thing, not every company achieves the impressive results of a Microsoft or a Fidelity

Investments. For every one of those success stories, there are dozens of companies that struggle year after year to get sales growth and improved profitability out of an ever-expanding go-to-market system – and fail. New channels are added without a clear business purpose, are aimed at the wrong markets or the wrong customers, are under-invested or under-resourced, or are poorly integrated with other channels. Rather than end up with an organized, market-focused, high-performance channel system, many end up with a complex, sprawling mix of channels that looks like some sort of Darwinian evolutionary experiment gone mad.

For example, take a look at Figure 1.2, which shows the recent channel history of a US-based electronic appliance manufacturer[9].

What's the problem here? Actually there are several:

- Every time the company opens a new 'direct' channel, such as a specialty shop or a catalogue operation, business partners see less opportunity for themselves and defect to competitors. The defections that have already occurred have made recruitment of new channel partners extremely difficult. In the US, the company is

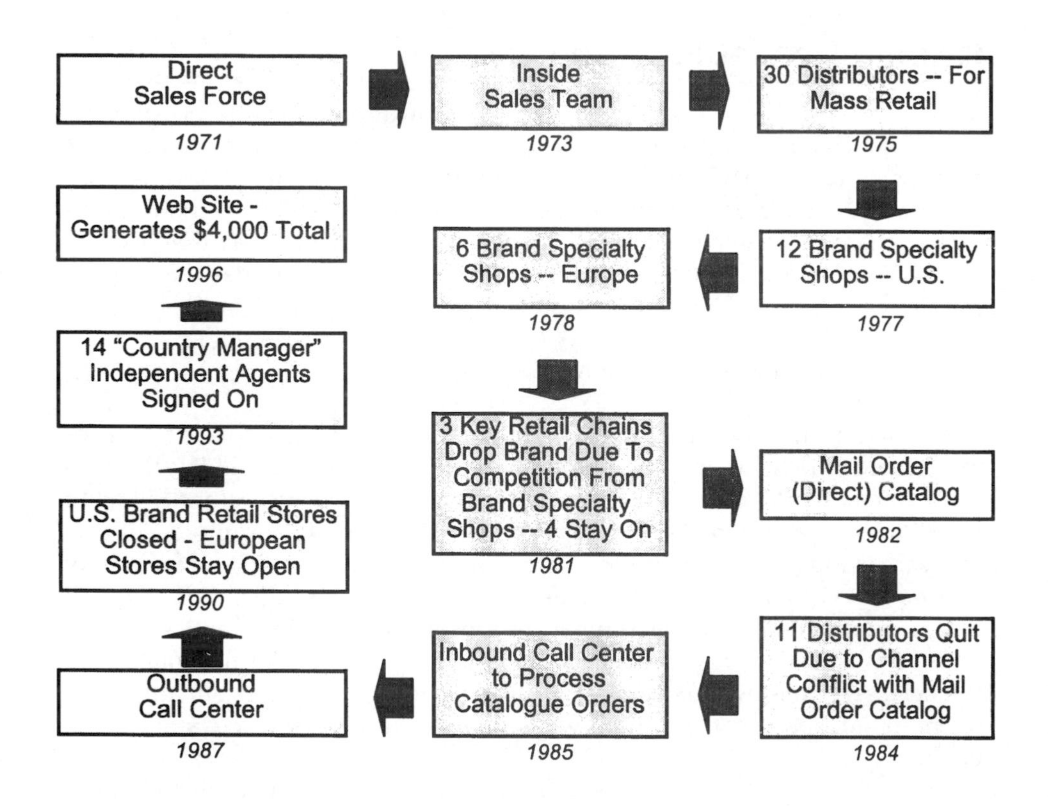

Figure 1.2 Channel progress or channel chaos?

virtually blacklisted from the leading retail chains. Its channel 'innovations,' in short, have created a lot of partner-alienating channel conflict.
- Channel backtracking – such as the closing of its speciality shops in the US – has cost millions in write-offs, and has left customers confused as to where to buy its products.
- The company's newest channel experiment – the Internet – has delivered virtually no sales since its inception. Over a million dollars was spent to design, implement, and maintain this nearly dormant sales channel so far. At its current sales productivity of $2000 per year, it would take until the year 2048 to recoup the investment.
- Selling profitability has been on the decline for years, as the company has struggled to control the costs of its various (and many) channel start-ups and shut-downs.

The list of problems could go on and on, but we won't bore you with the details. There's an important and simple point here. Most companies suffer not from an aversion to new channels or sales innovation, but rather from a lack of experience with bringing the optimal mix of channels together into a coherent, market-focused, high-impact selling system. It isn't enough just to add a web site, hire a few distributors, or build a call centre. The kinds of growth in market share, revenues and profits that leading channel-centric companies achieve don't come from random, chaotic channel experimentation. These kinds of results come from planned, strategic and thoughtful channel innovation.

'Okay, that all makes sense – now what's this book about?'

This book deals with one topic, and it deals with it comprehensively and rigorously. The topic is as follows:

> How to build a channel system that will yield world-class sales performance and durable competitive advantage.

This book will help readers move decisively away from the notion of channel strategy as a sideline to the core business. Building a channel advantage *is* the core business today. The only question is how to build one in an orderly, successful way. This book takes a systematic approach that mirrors the channel strategy development process in leading organizations. It raises – and will help readers answer – three fundamental questions about sales channels:

- Which channels should we be using – and why?
- How should we build those channels to achieve world-class performance?
- How should we manage them together as an integrated go-to-market system?

Enough said! Let's move on to Part One, Choosing the Right Sales Channels.

Notes

[1] Andy Serwer, 'Michael Dell Rocks', *Fortune*, 11 May 1998.
[2] As of April 1998.
[3] As of January 1998.
[4] October 1997. At the time of this book's publication, however, Schwab's online share appeared to be decreasing due to intense industry competition.
[5] As of 6 March 1998.
[6] At least in the United States, where people are fanatical about cupholders.
[7] As of 17 September 1998: Amazon.com market capitalization – $3.64 billion; Border's Group – $2.08 billion; Barnes and Noble – $1.82 billion. It's important to note that although Amazon.com is growing rapidly, the company has yet to turn a profit. Investor enthusiasm may turn south if it doesn't figure out how to do so in the near future.
[8] Source: Auto-By-Tel web site, 28 May 1998 and 18 October 1998.
[9] Companies are named wherever possible. However, as in this case, a number of companies interviewed for this book requested anonymity in return for permission to describe their strategies and experiences.

Part One

Choosing the Right Sales Channels ...

Chapter 2

The starting point: product-market focus

It might seem that a good way to kick off a channel selection discussion would be to look at channel opportunities and choices. Wrong! There is something that has to come first, both in this book and in any channel selection initiative.

It is important to recognize what channels can do – and what they can't do. The role of a sales channel is to connect products with markets, and thereby establish a route through which sellers and buyers can do business. The world's most innovative, best-designed, high-tech sales channel won't do any good, though, if it is given the wrong products to sell into the wrong markets. Think about it this way. If you try to sell armoured troop carriers to monasteries, it won't work – whether you try to sell them over the Internet or through a telemarketing centre. That's a silly and extreme example, of course. Yet even in its silliness it makes an important point: you have to sell the right things to the right people for sales channels to succeed – and indeed for them to matter at all.

Of course, there is no magic answer to the question 'which products should we sell to which customers?' On the other hand, there are some ways of thinking about products and markets that can help a company to focus on its best opportunities. Taking a little time out to ensure that the right product-market opportunities are being targeted is a worthwhile and necessary first step in the design of a channel strategy, and it is the subject of this chapter. We begin by looking at a company that has struggled with its product-market assumptions and, along the way, learned some valuable lessons about product-market selection and focus.

Industrial Products Corporation (IPC) and the challenge of product-market focus

Sometimes, a little bad press can go a long way. Industrial Products Corporation[1], a $250 million manufacturer of plastic components for the automotive and aerospace industries, had meandered along for thirty years. Employees were making a decent living, customers were happy, and the tight-knit community of families that still owned thirty per cent of the shares was wealthy and satisfied. Then, everything changed one day in early 1992. A one-paragraph story appeared in a business magazine questioning the company's management team as well as its growth prospects. The shares plummeted, erasing years of wealth building and converting some multi-multi-millionaires into just millionaires. Things would never be the same again.

Later that year, the Senior Vice President of Business Development stopped by one of the author's offices in the Washington, DC area for some advice. Ten months earlier, he had sat through his CEO's presentation, entitled 'Four Points of Growth'. A very abbreviated version of the plan is shown in Figure 2.1.

Almost a year into the plan, the SVP explained, sales had grown a whopping three per cent and profits had actually *decreased*. The plan was falling flat on every front:

- **New markets** The company had neither the expertise nor experience to sell efficiently and effectively into new markets. The high technology industry, IPC's key new market segment, was fragmented into confusing sub-industries. While high technology presented some good longer-term opportunities, it was hardly a source for immediate sales growth. IPC spent millions training the field sales force to under-

❶	**Expand Into New Markets**	✓ ✓	Slow growth in existing customer base Many untapped markets (e.g. high technology
❷	**Develop New Products**	✓ ✓	Many new products successfully piloted in one or two customer sites Big opportunity to sell these offerings into the broader business base
❸	**Increase Prices 12 Percent**	✓	Reputation for high quality and customized solutions suggests a price premium would be accepted
❹	**Hire 40 New Sales Reps**	✓ ✓	Sales rep productivity is $1.6 million 40 more reps should bring in $64 million

Figure 2.1 Industrial Products Corporation – four points of growth

stand the issues of high technology buyers, and several more millions creating leads and opportunities. Despite all this effort, sales into this new market had totaled less than $4 million, and not a single contract had been profitable.

- **New products** The forty new products that engineering had come up with in the last ten months (to satisfy Point 2 of the Four Points of Growth) had generated just $650,000 in sales. The SVP was hardly surprised by this. He ruefully pointed out that the product catalogue had expanded from 350 products to over 2000 products since 1983 – and yet the original 350 products still accounted for over eighty-five per cent of all revenues! The fact was that most of IPC's new products were specialized applications with very limited portability to new customers. And even when these products were successfully sold to new customers, they tended to be unprofitable for two to three years.
- **Increase prices** IPC had met with fierce resistance in its customer base when it introduced the new, higher prices. Most of its customers were consolidating their suppliers and were only keeping the ones that offered rock-bottom prices. Thus, at a time when its customers were putting renewed vigour on cost-cutting, IPC was presenting a new, more ambitious price list – for no discernible reason other than to make more profit. IPC was forced to make a number of embarrassing pricing U-turns in its key accounts.
- **Hire more sales reps** Thirty had been hired, and sales volume had gone up slightly. However, per-rep productivity had actually *decreased* from $1.6 million to $1.4 million. Sales reps, many of them new and untrained, were being asked to create more leads, close more deals, develop longer-term relationships, and penetrate deeper into existing accounts – all at the same time. Most were thus chasing big and small accounts, new and existing customers, and off-the-rack sales as well as highly customized solutions. There was no focus in the market place or in the sales force. Confusion reigned; a third of the new reps quit, along with eight highly-valued national account managers.

Ironically, with all these problems occurring on so many fronts, the SVP's purpose in stopping by was to look at a channel opportunity. He had concluded that the lower profitability of selling new products into new markets could be countered by utilizing lower-cost channels. His request to us was to evaluate two different types of channels for selling into the high technology industry: independent agents (carrying many vendors products), and exclusive distributors (representing only the client's products).

It took about two minutes to come up with the answer. Neither. It didn't make any sense for the company to be 'channelizing' until its market coverage model – its set of assumptions about which product-markets were worth the pursuit in the first place – was better aligned with its real growth opportunities.

The fact is that the company had barely penetrated its core target markets: automotive and aerospace customers. Within these markets, IPC was a low market share player, and in none of its accounts was it the dominant vendor. The company had complacently existed for years alongside larger competitors who, in just about every situation, were taking the lion's share of the business. Many sales were being lost in existing accounts, where the company already had a home-court advantage. We suggested that even ten per cent sales growth in IPC's largest national accounts would dwarf any opportunity it could exploit by selling new products into new markets for years and years to come. Sales growth in established accounts with familiar products would also be infinitely easier to achieve on a profitable basis than an expensive, risky foray into an entirely new industry. The fact was plain – IPC needed to focus closer to home, on the big opportunities, in existing accounts, that were already sitting on the company's doorstep.

The SVP eventually concurred with this opinion. He and his team went back to the drawing board, crunched some numbers, and concluded the following. Fifteen per cent sales growth per year in its dozen top automotive and aerospace accounts, combined with some targeted, focused new account acquisition, would in fact double revenues in four years and would be the fastest, least expensive and most effective way to achieve the company's growth objectives.

Two years later in 1995, the SVP, not quite having achieved his plan – growth had been in the ten to twelve per cent range – nevertheless felt that IPC had made good progress. The company had refocused sales force efforts toward targeted growth in high-potential existing accounts with tried-and-true products, and it had basically worked. Now, he reasoned, it was time to look at lower-cost channels as a way to reduce costs. This time around, it made a lot more sense. It was now clearer where IPC's growth would come from, and it was appropriate for the company to be looking at how it could use channels to improve efficiency and profits.

IPC's trials and tribulations are important because they mirror the experiences of a multitude of other companies. Many begin with sensible-seeming growth plans that, through lack of sound product-market planning, send the company and its sales force all over the map in an effort to capture new revenues. The resulting internal and market chaos lead to reduced profits and, often, flat sales too.

Rather than trying to be all things to all customers all of the time, most companies are far better off selectively covering a few high-potential product-markets with gusto.

The cure for unfocused market coverage – revenue segmentation

Companies always have to make choices about which product-markets to pursue and which to ignore. There are simply too many market opportunities to pursue all of them with equal fervor. For example, as Figure 2.2 shows, a large company such as a Canon will typically have (at least) four or five different types of customers, as well as (at least) four or five different types of products. Together, these various product and customer types can yield upwards of twenty discrete product-markets – and sometimes many more than that.

Let's imagine, just for a moment, that we are high-level executives within Canon charged with identifying the company's best market opportunities. What's our stratetgy? Should we try to compete like gangbusters in every single product-market? That is probably a little unrealistic. No one can compete profitably in every product-market. So where should we concentrate our efforts? On selling high-volume copiers into large corporate accounts, or on selling networked systems into mid-sized businesses? What is even the basis for making this kind of decision?

To choose the right product-markets, you have to be able to compare them along some meaningful dimension. One very meaningful dimension is *potential growth*: the degree of ease with which future revenues can be captured in large quantities and profitably. *Revenue segmentation* is a technique that can be used to compare product-markets in terms of their growth potential. It is an excellent tool for bringing focus to the selection of product-markets.

As a starting point, revenue segmentation is based on a fundamental principle: revenues in some product-markets are easier to capture than others. Put simply:

- New customers are harder and more expensive to acquire than retained customers.
- New products are harder and more expensive to sell than established products.

While most executives would agree with these two statements, putting them into action is another story. The frenzy of new growth initiatives often pushes

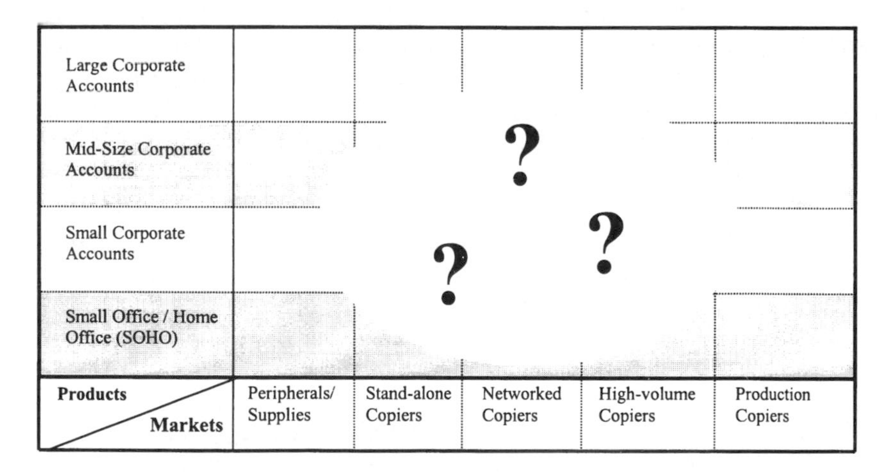

Figure 2.2 Canon – product-market choices

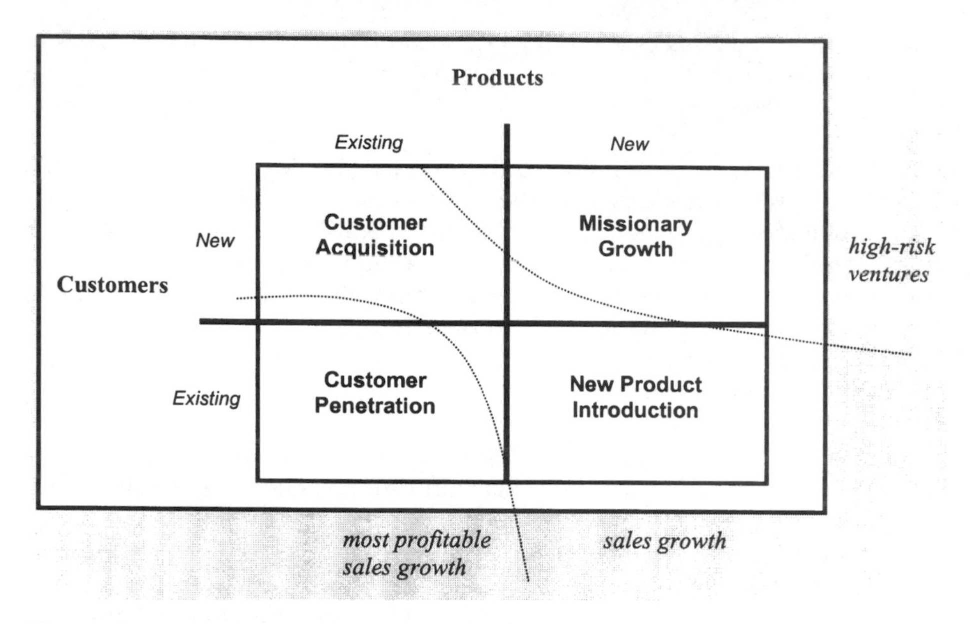

Figure 2.3 Four growth strategies

managers to seek whole new vistas of opportunities, instead of assessing carefully where the bulk of the profitable sales growth really is located. As Figure 2.3 suggests, the further and further a company gets away from its core base of existing products and customers, the more difficult it is to achieve high levels of profitable growth.

- **Customer penetration.** Few companies have anywhere near 100 per cent market share in more than a couple of key accounts. In a typical account, in fact, customers tend to buy comparable products from three to four vendors. The most entrenched vendor may get forty to fifty per cent, the second most entrenched may get another twenty per cent, and the rest of the pack gets the balance. Most vendors in an account will thus have a lot of room to grow. As a result, some of the fastest and lowest-cost growth can come from more rigorous targeting of existing customers with existing products. This is particularly true for companies with low market share (less than, say, thirty per cent) within their top few dozen accounts. A well-executed campaign can often bump up market share within an account by ten or fifteen per cent, leading to substantial revenue growth. In addition, improved customer penetration may also require few incremental selling resources, and the revenues are therefore likely to be some of the most profitable ones available anywhere. Thus:

  Product-markets characterized by partially-penetrated accounts, with low to medium market share, constitute the 'low hanging fruit' in terms of growth opportunity.

- **Customer acquisition** The cost of acquiring new customers is typically three to six times that of retaining existing ones. An office products firm, for example, that might spend $200 (in selling time) to close a sale in an existing account might spend upwards of $1000 or more to sell the same product to an entirely new customer. New buyers must be located, contacted, educated in your products, and convinced of the benefits of doing business with you. All of this costs money. Thus, while new customer acquisition contributes to sales growth, it also drags down overall selling profitability. Of course, every business must find and acquire new customers. But most companies should not be trying to capture the bulk of their revenue in product-markets in which they have very low customer penetration; those that do often fail to turn a reasonable profit[2].

  Product-markets consisting primarily of sales prospects (customers to be acquired) may be good bets for revenue growth but bad bets for profitability. They should be chosen selectively, and should coexist alongside a strong base of product-markets in which accounts have already been penetrated.

  One hidden jewel of customer acquisition is customer 'reactivation.' Every company has dormant customers who have not purchased products for at least two years. These customers are frequently written off prematurely. Reactivation campaigns studied in the high technology, financial services and consumer electronics industries have suggested that, by scouring old order history data bases, companies can identify these accounts, initiate low-cost customer contact, and realize upwards of twenty per cent reactivation rates. These customers – with previous buying history – can reduce the cost of customer acquisition by fifty per cent and provide a quick source of revenue growth. *Product-markets with many dormant accounts can thus provide a more profitable source of growth than those that have not been penetrated at all.*

- **New product introduction** The lifeblood of any sales organization, at least according to its sales reps, is new products. The ability to introduce a new product gives a company a compelling message to generate new customer demand as well as renewed customer interest in the existing product line. New product introductions, however, are very costly. Beyond the development costs and failure rates, the cost-to-sell of new products is substantially higher than existing products. The sales force must be trained, and the customer base must be educated. The sales cycle will be longer, and customers will need higher levels of support. In addition, many companies get stuck in a new product proliferation trap – spending scarce resources on too many new products, most of which have not yet been validated in the marketplace. The key to new product introduction is the careful screening, selection and piloting of new products before they hit the market. In many industries, it is considered risky and unprofitable to rely on new product sales for more than twenty-five per cent of revenue[3]. With respect to product-market selection:

  Product-markets characterized by existing customers buying new, untested products represent a source of growth – at lower margins. These usually only make sense in the context of an accompanying effort to improve the penetration of existing key accounts with familiar products.

- **Missionary growth** The ultimate disabler of a growth strategy is an over-reliance on selling new products to new customers. The costs associated with finding new customers and introducing new products, combined, usually exceed by far the revenue that could possibly be realized from a sale. So profits are the first thing to disappear. It usually doesn't work as a *growth* strategy either; wary new customers will not often buy untested new products from a new vendor. The opening up of whole new product-market vistas is compelling on a visceral level, but the problem is that it rarely, if ever, results in profitable sales growth. Companies that want to pursue this kind of growth should not target more than five to ten per cent of revenues from this type of sale and should be prepared to achieve much less than that. In addition:

  Product-markets that are completely new to a company – that involve new customers buying new products – are best seen for what they are: experimental sidelines to a core business. This may work (on occasion) for Internet entrepreneurs and others on the frontiers of science and technology, but most established, large companies cannot afford to rely on missionary growth as a core sales strategy.

In sum, segmenting product-markets by the degree to which they involve new or existing products and customers is a smart idea. This segmentation can highlight the largest and most profitable growth opportunities. It is also in accord with the behavior of most successful companies. Market leaders tend to focus on product-markets in which they can achieve:

- Deeper penetration of existing accounts with existing products
- Reactivation of 'dormant' accounts
- Selective acquisition of new customers with market-validated products
- Selective introduction of well-screened offerings into the installed base

Leading companies, in short, tend to emphasize and focus on their *core business* – their installed customer base. A strong, growing, profitable installed base is what generates the *entrepreneurial capital* that can later be used to support various forays into uncharted territory: whole new markets, radically new products, and on occasion, both at the same time.

Product-market segmentation can be taken a few steps further, to bring greater specificity to the task of identifying the best product-market opportunities. Two helpful tools to do this are the following:

- customer market share ('share of wallet') analysis
- product-market growth rate analysis

Customer market share analysis

Focusing on the installed base (existing customers and existing products) is almost always a good idea, but the question is: how much focus? Should the installed base be served to the exclusion of new opportunities, or should there be some balance? If it's to be a balance, how much attention should the installed base really get, relative to other sales opportunities? Customer market share analysis can help answer these questions.

It's a simple concept. A company's key accounts – usually, the top twenty per cent of customers, representing about eighty per cent of the revenue – get, and deserve, a lot of selling focus. The question is how much they should get. Understanding the exact extent to which these accounts have already been penetrated is an invaluable guideline for putting resources and money against these accounts as opposed to new selling opportunities. Figure 2.4, for example, shows a sample key account list for a supplier of specialized telecommunications infrastructure equipment.

As suggested in the figure, the company has, on average, about twenty-five per cent market share within its five key accounts. So what does this figure imply? Simple: the company clearly should be focusing on growth in its existing installed base; there is an enormous amount of room to grow through

	1997 Sales (000's)	% of Sales	Estimated Total $$$ (000's)	Share of Account
AT&T	17,500	30.6 %	70,000	25 %
British Telecom	9,500	16.7 %	50,000	19 %
MCI	8,000	13.9 %	18,000	44 %
Nortel	6,200	10.8 %	25,000	25 %
Telefonos de Mexico	4,000	6.9 %	25,000	16 %
All others (26 accounts)	12,000	20.9 %	58,000	20 %
Total:	57,000	100.0 %	256,000	23 %

Figure 2.4 Key account list for 'ComTech' Inc. – $57 million specialized telecom equipment supplier

better and deeper customer penetration. But what if its market share – its degree of penetration – was, say:

- **50–100 per cent** This would suggest that company is the dominant, entrenched vendor and also that future growth opportunities in the installed base will be limited. The bulk of the growth will clearly have to come from elsewhere: new customers, new products, or a combination of the two. The company should limit its target revenue from its entrenched accounts to no more than twenty to thirty per cent of the overall revenue target, with the balance to come from less-well-developed product-markets.
- **25–50 per cent** This typically implies solid, successful account penetration with room for growth in the installed base. Companies with this level of penetration should generally target fifty per cent or so of their revenue from the installed base, with the balance coming from less-well-developed product-markets.
- **25 per cent or less** This suggests that a company is not the dominant player in its key accounts and, in some cases, may be struggling just to show up on its top customers' radar screens. The growth opportunity is clear in these accounts. A minimum of fifty per cent, and as high as 100 per cent, of the overall revenue target should be pursued within the existing installed base.

These guidelines don't apply equally to every industry. As rules of thumb, though, they can help in establishing the right balance between growth in penetrated product-markets versus new product-markets.

Product-market growth rates

Market growth is the force that pulls managers away from a focus on their core business. New and unexplored markets often seem to offer faster growth than the ones a company is stuck with. Sometimes they do in fact offer better opportunities for long-term growth. The key is to make *sure* they do before investing in and relying on them.

To assess whether a market is worth the investment of time, money and energy, one distinction is crucial: the difference between market growth rates and product-market growth rates. For instance, you could encounter an enticing piece of information such as:

> Software companies are predicted to grow twenty per cent per year for the next five years.

That's interesting, but it's hardly the whole story. What if you sell paper clips? The sad truth might be as follows:

> Software companies are going to use about the same number of paper clips in five years as they do today – less, in fact, if they keep replacing paper documentation with new software applications.

Computer software is a market; 'paper clips sold into the software industry' is a product-market.

We will go out on a limb here and say that generic industry growth data is virtually useless as an input to effective product-market targeting. Not everyone would agree. The simple truth, though, is that it really doesn't matter how fast the software industry is growing if you sell paper clips. What matters is how fast their paper clip purchases are growing. Those are two different things.

Although it takes more work, a detailed product-market growth projection is an infinitely more valuable tool for product-market selection than a wistful look out onto the fastest-growing industries. Figure 2.5 shows what this level of detail can look like.

Which is the best industry for the company to pursue? This question is hardly relevant. Companies don't sell to 'industries'; they sell specific products to groups of customers. In this case, what is clear is that there are three distinct product-markets growing like wildfire. If the company is not already competing in those product-markets, it should be. If it doesn't have the products or the established customers to play in the 'office/clerical staffing services for the technology industry' segment, it should go get them – fast. Conversely, if this is where the company already is dominant, it should be focused on further penetrating that product-market. Thus, looking at the relative growth rates of different product-markets is an effective tool when looking for the best sales opportunities.

Market / *Product*	Medical	Technology	Professional (Law, Acctg, etc.)
Specialty Placement	6 %	14 %	11 %
Office/Clerical Staffing	5 %	28 %	21 %
Temp-to-Perm Placement	3 %	22 %	15 %

Figure 2.5 Temporary employment firm industry growth projections – annual

The payoff of product-market focus: the case of Southwest Airlines

Southwest Airlines provides a good example of how a thoughtful definition of, and focus on, the right product-markets can deliver superior business results.

Over the past two decades – in fact for twenty-four consecutive years – Southwest Airlines has been the only US airline to turn a consistent profit. In 1993, for example, Southwest earned after-tax profits of $154 million on revenues of $2.3 billion, while its major competitor, American Airlines, lost $110 million despite being seven times Southwest's size[4]. Southwest has successfully challenged and dominated American Airlines in key markets within Texas and California. The company is now taking its successful model nationwide, entering cities such as Baltimore, Detroit and Oakland.

Founded in 1971, Southwest's first decade was marked by stiff competition and bitter regulatory battles. In 1978, the Texas Aeronautics Commission tried, for example, to force Southwest to move its Dallas flights from the older, more convenient Love Field to the larger Dallas/Fort Worth airport located thirty minutes outside the city. By the time Southwest had won this long legal battle, it had incurred tremendous costs while experiencing little growth. The success of its Dallas–Houston routes, however, fuelled Southwest's growth explosion in the 1980s. Southwest's strategy was simple: focus on short-haul intrastate routes, use less-congested airports, and set prices low enough to fill planes. The company has since grown from those pioneering days, from ten aircraft in 1980 to 243 by the end of 1996.

Southwest's growth strategy has been driven since the company's inception by a thoughtful and smart selection of markets and products (their routes):

- **Market focus** While other major US airlines were pursuing national and international growth strategies, Southwest was 'cherry picking' the market. Southwest ignored the development of expensive hub-and-spoke airport networks and focused, instead, on serving high-volume city pairs. As a result, Southwest was able to achieve high market share in routes such as Dallas–Houston, San Francisco–Los Angeles, Chicago–St Louis, and Baltimore–Chicago. While other airlines bid up the gate fees at larger airports in a frenzy of competition for the best space, Southwest chose less-congested, second-tier airports in cities such as Houston (Hobby Airport), Chicago (Midway Airport) and San Francisco (Oakland Airport). The company's discipline in defining its core markets, and focusing on growth in its installed base, has in fact given it a successful business model that is now turning out to be highly transportable to new markets.
- **Product focus** Southwest's target customer is the price-sensitive local traveller seeking to get from point A to point B as quickly and as conveniently as possible. Its products have been finely honed over time to attract and retain that customer base. Southwest's prices are often fifty per cent or less than prevail-

ing rates at its point of entry into a new market[5]. Even so, the company still has earned a profit every year. The reason is simple. Southwest knows what its product needs to look like to attract its target customers, and every facet of the business is oriented around giving those customers what they want – low-cost, efficient service.

- **No in-flight meals** In addition to eliminating costs, this enables Southwest to increase its on-ground turnaround times substantially.
- **No advanced reservations** Its first-come-first-served policy enables Southwest to run a more efficient boarding process.
- **No computerized reservation systems** By using travel agents only for sixty per cent of its reservations, Southwest avoids the ten per cent agent commission on the other forty per cent. The company saves several dollars per ticket as a result.
- **Smaller airports** Servicing less-congested airports lowers costs and reduces schedule delays, increasing both profits and customer satisfaction.
- **Standardized aircraft** Most other airlines fly six or seven different type of aircraft, requiring specialists for each type. But because of Southwest's emphasis on short-haul routes (most of them under 500 miles), the company has been able to achieve the ultimate product focus in the airline industry – it flies only one type of aircraft, Boeing 737s. This significantly reduces aircraft maintenance costs (parts and technician labour) and training costs for pilots, technicians and flight attendants. This all results in less down-time, lower operating costs, and ultimately higher profits and lower prices.

Despite its low-cost, no-frills strategy, Southwest is the first airline to win the industry's Triple Crown award for a full year, and the company has done it every year between 1992–1997. *No other airline has ever won this award even for a single month.* The Triple Crown recognizes:

- Best on-time performance
- Least complaints per customer
- Fewest lost bags per passenger

The company's focus on competitive superiority within a well-defined product-market has also led to extraordinary performance results. Using almost any industry performance benchmark (Figure 2.6), Southwest outperforms the industry as a whole, both financially and operationally.

Southwest Airlines, of course, is a niche player, succeeding in a tightly defined set of product-markets because of the discipline that a well-defined niche can make possible. Not all companies have that luxury. It remains to be seen whether Southwest will be able to maintain its tight product-market focus as it expands, adds more routes, and ultimately moves toward more of a market share orientation. Nevertheless, it's an impressive accomplishment and, to say the least, one that highlights the advantages of carefully defining, and then playing to win, in a targeted, well-selected group of product-markets.

Benchmark	Southwest Airlines	Industry Average
Annual revenue growth	28 %	12 %
Operating Profits (as a % of revenues)	12.7 %	3.1 %
Flights per aircraft	10-11 per day	6-8 per day
Passengers per employee	2,438	900
Employees per aircraft	72	125

Figure 2.6 Airline industry 1993 financial and operational benchmarks

Summary

A sound market coverage model – one that connects the right products with the right customers – is the cornerstone of an effective, high-growth channel strategy. Looking at channels doesn't make any sense until it is clear which products and customers need to be brought together.

To build a strong market coverage model – to select the best product-markets – a company must have a way to compare the relative merits of different product-markets and to focus decisively on the best ones. Revenue segmentation is one way to do this. The strength of this approach is that it provides a simple way to segment product-markets by the degree of ease with which profitable revenue growth can be achieved. This approach fits well with the simple, compelling goal in most organizations: to make more money, faster.

The purpose of product-market planning is to identify the product-markets that offer the best selling opportunities. Once those opportunities become clear, channel strategy jumps to centre stage as a critical management issue. After all, there is only one known way to connect a product with a market – through a sales channel. Now the question becomes: which sales channel, and why?

The next chapter, 'Aligning channels with how customers buy', gets the ball rolling on the question of which channels should be used to connect products with customers. In the opinion of many (including the authors), customer buying behavior is one of the most important factors that impact and influence the selection of sales channels. Aligning channels with how customers want to do business – and with how they *actually* make their purchases – is a central component of any successful channel selection effort.

Notes

[1] The name has been changed at the request of the client.
[2] Of course, market share driven companies, those that are willing to exchange some profitability for maximum market exposure, may choose to capture as much revenue as possible from new customer acquisition.
[3] This applies primarily to large, established companies in relatively mature industries. New companies, obviously, get 100 per cent of their revenue by selling new products. In technology-driven industries, growth is often fuelled primarily through new product innovation.
[4] And in fact has only recently been out of the red.
[5] *St. Petersburg Times*, 28 January 1996.

Chapter 3

Aligning channels with how customers buy

Your company decides to evaluate, say, the Internet as a viable channel. Weeks or months of research are conducted by armies of analysts to study the new channel. Mounds of paper pile up in executives' offices – ironically, given the channel. Countless full-day meetings are held. Whole new careers and titles are born, like 'e-commerce manager'. In short, a new bureaucracy has been created.

And what is the focus of all this energy? Typically, how much the new channel will cost, how incredible the savings will be once the new channel replaces an older one, and how much more revenue will be produced with the new channel. In other words, the focus is usually on the *economics* of the channel. This is precisely the wrong place to start. Ultimately all of this economic work is important, but there is something far more crucial to the success of *any* business initiative – *customers*. Unless and until a channel is aligned with how customers want to do business, the rest is a moot point. Here is the essential truth:

> Customers will buy more if you meet them where they want to do business. Otherwise, they will buy less.

This rule has been operative for thousands of years, and it applies just as well to new technologies as it did to life in the bazaar four thousand years ago. In the bazaar, those who set up their stalls a mile or two from the centre of the

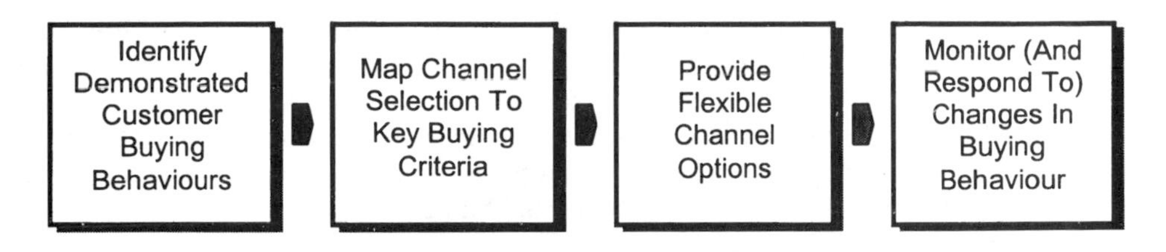

Figure 3.1 Aligning customer buying behaviour

action carried home a lot of heavy carpets at the end of the day. On the other hand, merchants who found themselves a central location at a good crossroads stood a chance of converting all those heavy carpets into cash (or goats perhaps).

It's the same situation with channels. Meet customers where they're ready to do business – whether it's in a retail store, on the Internet, or in their homes with mail order catalogues – and you'll probably make more sales. Try to force a channel onto customers who want something else, and it won't work. You can have a truly world-class, industry-leading, globally-integrated telesales operation, but if customers won't buy your products over the phone, all that effort is going to come to naught. In evaluating channel options, the acceptance and willingness of customers to use a new channel is more important, by several orders of magnitude, than any other single factor.

This chapter looks at concepts and tools for aligning channel selection with customer buying preferences and behavior. It is organized around four action steps, as shown in Figure 3.1.

1. Identify customers' channel preferences and buying behaviors

In *every* industry, customers have channel preferences as well as actual histories of buying behavior. These preferences and behaviors define the outer boundaries of what could possibly work in terms of new channels. As a result, there is just no substitute for building a clear fact-base about customer's preferences and proven buying patterns. In addition to defining the limits of the possible in channel selection, this fact-base will often pinpoint a specific, attractive channel opportunity that has been ignored or overlooked.

The first line of attack is an analysis of customer channel preferences. Which channels do they want, or at least *think* they want? A customer survey is the best way to get this information, and it can sometimes be performed with in-house staff rather quickly[1]. Customers will generally volunteer a wealth of information in a survey about their channel preferences. The best surveys get the input of a range of customers across different market segments, not just a handful of 'friendlies' – major, very satisfied key accounts. The survey should collect information on the following:

- **Key information about the customer** The following data must be collected so the survey can establish which kinds of customers use, and want to use, which kinds of channels. At a minimum, information should be collected on:
  - Customer size (e.g. last year's revenue)
  - Transaction volume ('How many widgets did you purchase last year?')
  - Market segment ('Which of the following products did you buy from us last year...')
- **Channel usage and preferences** The survey should ask customers which channels they use, which channels they think they want, and which channels they would at least be willing to consider. It is *essential* to ask these questions for specific products and services, so that channel preferences can be correlated with markets and types of sales. A comprehensive set of channels currently in use or soon to be available in the industry should be suggested. Figure 3.2 shows an example of this part of the survey.
- **Customer speculation** The survey should have some open-ended questions such as 'Which channels do you believe represent the future, in terms of how your company purchases goods and services?' Questions like these make customers think speculatively, and as a result often produce some valuable information on longer-term channel trends in the industry.

Please consider the Model T4600 and the ways in which you buy or would like to buy this product. Indicate your preferences with a check mark in the appropriate boxes.

Channel	I already buy through this channel	I'm not using it, but would like to	I might consider it if it was offered	I would never buy this way
Sales rep				
Distributor				
Retail store				
Mail order				
Web site				
Supermarket				
Over the phone				
Kiosk				

Figure 3.2 Channel preference survey – sample

Channel surveys often yield surprising results. Sometimes these results can have a substantial impact on channel selection and, ultimately, on business results. Last year, for example, a well-known computer server manufacturer commissioned a study to assess the willingness of its customers to buy through alternative channels. The conventional wisdom in the high-end server business is that sales require either field sales reps or experienced business partners, due to the size and complexity of the product. Among other enlightening results of the survey, four per cent of the vendor's customers indicated a willingness to buy mainframe computers, one of the most expensive capital expenditures ever made by the average company, over the Internet. That is an amazingly high percentage of customers willing to engage in such a complex transaction through such an impersonal, low-cost channel. This is no trivial matter. For the vendor, a shift of four per cent of sales to the Internet would take about $12 million out of the cost of sales and would increase net margins by almost 10 per cent. These kinds of findings are not atypical in a channel preference survey. There is often a lot to be gained by finding out how customers feel about different channel scenarios.

There's a huge caveat, though. Whether those customers would *actually* buy mainframe computers over the Internet is a more difficult question than whether they *think* they might. In a channel survey, customers tend to indicate a far greater willingness to use alternative channels than they really would utilize in a buying situation. When push comes to shove – when real money is involved – customers suddenly become aware of risks and issues that they failed to consider when casually filling out a survey. Managers are well advised not to rely too much on customers' 'willingness' to use new channels in the absence of a real commitment in a real purchasing situation.

Thus, there is more to building the fact-base than simply surveying a group of customers. That information is helpful but inconclusive and sometimes just incorrect. A far more accurate predictor of customers' channel preferences is their demonstrated, proven buying habits. How do they really buy? Which channels are they already using? Are they in fact already migrating to alternative channels, and if so, which ones and for which types of purchases? Customer buying behavior – real, proven purchasing patterns – is an essential element of channel selection because it provides the most certainty about what will work and what won't.

Analysis of demonstrated customer buying behavior should include at least three types of customers:

- **Existing customers** How are they already buying? In which channels is sales volume going up, and where is it going down? Have forays into various alternative channels met with stiff resistance or have they been readily accepted by the customer base?
- **Competitors' customers** These are the most important customers, because they're the ones you want to acquire. How are these customers buying? What chan-

nels are they being offered by competitors, and which ones are they using? Which channels offered by competitors have met with resistance? Which channels offered by competitors are experiencing the fastest sales growth?

- **Out-of-industry customers** Most companies sell products that look something like those offered in another industry. Companies that sell boats share common ground with those that sell cars, planes, and even in-ground summary pools ('big, luxury consumer goods'). There is almost always an out-of-industry near-equivalent for a product line. So what channel innovations are taking place in other, similar industries? Cars, for example, are being sold through alternative, low-cost channels; what can boat vendors learn from these out-of-industry developments? Channel usage in related industries can provide a vendor with a wealth of information about customers' channel preferences and migrations in channel buying activity.

Companies that fail to assess customer behavior and channel preferences put themselves at tremendous risk. New channels in an industry can fundamentally change or reset customers' purchasing behaviors and expectations, and the results can be ugly for those who don't stay on top of these developments. *Encyclopaedia Britannica*, for example, has suffered this fate. Everyone agrees that Britannica's encyclopaedias have sophisticated, excellent content. Selling that content in huge, expensive sets of books through door-to-door reps, though, just didn't cut it in a world of $50 CD-ROM-based encyclopaedias sold through retail stores, OEMs (the PC manufacturers, such as Compaq and IBM), mail-order houses, etc. *Encyclopaedia Britannica* had fallen behind the times. Its competitors had succeeded in moving the encyclopaedia-buying public to lower-cost channels, and they had a more channel-ready product for those channels too. As a result of these trends, Britannica suffered an eighty-three per cent reduction in sales between 1990 and 1996, and has since disbanded its entire 500-person sales force. It is now moving to lower-cost channel alternatives, but it has suffered irreparable damage to its brand by failing to keep up with changes in customer behavior.

A good survey of customer channel preferences, combined with an empirical fact-base on proven customer behavior, can go a long way toward identifying desirable new channels. These tools won't go all the way, though. Stated channel preferences, as noted, can be wrong. And customer behavior is about what customers are doing *today*, not necessarily what they will be doing tomorrow. Though good and necessary starting points, they do not represent a complete approach to customer analysis. To get even closer to the core of which channels will work best with a group of customers, you have to examine customers' buying criteria – *why* they buy what they buy.

2. Map channel selection to key buying criteria

Remember that first sales training course – years and years ago, perhaps? Most of it has probably been long forgotten, but there is always one compelling concept that everyone remembers. *Customers make purchases when products meet their specific needs and requirements.* A customer who values a low price above all else will buy a low-cost product and shun a higher-priced offering. A customer who values quality will often be willing to pay a premium to get it. Customers, in other words, have different buying criteria, or priorities against which they evaluate their purchasing opportunities. The skill of selling, for the most part, is about figuring out what those criteria are – and responding with products that satisfy them.

A channels is, in a sense, just another type of 'product.' It's a competitive offering, something a company hopes its customers will find better suited to their needs than an alternative solution from a competitor. Think back to Amazon.com, the Internet bookseller, for a moment. What is the 'product' it sells that gives the company a competitive advantage? Books? Not really; its competitors sell the same books. It's the channel; what they're selling is convenience and self-service. A channel, simply, is something offered to customers to induce them to do business. And just like products, channels must respond to customers' requirements and priorities – their buying criteria. To the extent that they do, sales will typically go up.

Thus, just as the key selling question '*What do our customers really want?*' should guide product development and sales positioning, so too should it guide channel selection. Are you selling your customers expensive computer equipment that will have a mission-critical role in their organization? If so, they are likely to value things such as training, 24x7 support, and customization. Alternatively, customers buying industrial capital goods tend to put a high premium on seller credentials, industry experience, reliability and safety. Small businesses purchasing commodity office supplies typically want fast service, low prices and reordering efficiency. Some large accounts may value a personal relationship and a partnership, while mid-sized accounts may just want efficient service and competitive pricing. In short, customers have different buying criteria, depending on who they are and what they're purchasing.

This is a key issue in channel selection, because *channels differ in their ability to satisfy various buying criteria.* A field sales force, for example, can provide extensive on-site support and user training, but it can never be the lowest-cost alternative. If customers have one main buying criteria, and it is price, a field sales force will simply not be the most competitive channel offering. As another example, catalogue sales offer the advantages of convenience, self-service and efficiency. But if *your* customers want direct contact and partnership, it isn't going to be an effective sales channel. Each channel has different strengths and weaknesses, and thus an ability to respond extremely well to certain customer buying criteria – but not to others.

Customers' buying criteria – their priorities – are often an even better basis for channel selection than customer behavior. Customer behavior, after all, is about what customers *are already doing*, in *existing* channels. When evaluating channel opportunities, though, the idea is to find an *innovative* and *new* way to meet customers in the market place. Did Dell Computer decide to sell computers over the Internet and telephone by observing existing customer buying behavior? No; there was no existing customer behavior in those channels. Dell's innovative approach was based on very clear thinking about how customers would be willing to buy, based on what's important to them in the PC sale: low price, exact configuration to customers' specifications, and ease of doing business, among other things. All of those needs could be met – and met better – by selling through direct channels such as the telephone and Internet. This is the origin of the success of most leading channel strategies: a tight linkage between channel selection and the underlying reasons why customers buy. Figure 3.3 shows ten common criteria of buyers in business-to-business sales[2], and maps them against the ability of different channels to satisfy them. It's a generic chart, of course; the onus is on the individual company to identify its customers' specific priorities and map these against the channel alternatives it is considering. This chart is a useful starting point and well worth customizing to a unique selling environment as part of the channel selection process. The key to this chart is that the issue is not 'which channels should we use?' but 'which channels can respond to our customer's top priorities?'

Incidentally, the usual response when managers work through and customize the matrix in Figure 3.3 is the following: "No one channel can satisfy all of our different customers' needs'. That's often the right response; only in very simple sales can one channel respond to the full range of customers' priorities.

Buying Criteria / Channel	Direct Sales Force	Distributors/ Partners	Retail Stores	Call Centres	Internet
Expert Advice	✓✓✓	✓✓	✓✓	✓	✓
Training	✓✓✓	✓✓✓	✓✓	✓	✓
Customization to Specs	✓✓✓	✓✓✓	✓	✓✓	✓
Delivery Flexibility	✓✓	✓✓✓	✓✓	✓✓✓	✓✓✓
On-site Installation	✓✓	✓✓✓	✓✓	✓	✓
Fast/Local Support	✓✓	✓✓✓	✓✓✓	✓	✓
Ordering Speed/Ease	✓	✓✓	✓✓	✓✓✓	✓✓✓
Self-service	✓	✓	✓✓	✓✓✓	✓✓✓
Lowest Price	✓	✓	✓✓	✓✓	✓✓✓
24x7 Support	✓	✓	✓	✓✓✓	✓✓

Figure 3.3 Alignment of channels with customers' buying criteria

Customers may want 24x7 support for some types of purchases, for example, but the lowest rock-bottom prices for others. No single channel can deliver both. One answer is to try to force customers into one channel and hope for the best. It rarely works; in most selling situations, different customers – or even the same customers at different times – have different needs, not all of which fit neatly into a single channel. The other answer is to provide flexible channel options that, collectively, meet customers' diverse purchasing needs. That's the better approach, and it delivers better results.

Provide flexible channel options

For many companies, different customers buy products in different ways. Even an individual customer can have different channel preferences, depending on what they're buying, when, and why. Customers, in other words, participate in different types of purchasing situations. More often than not, multiple channels will be needed to respond to these various purchasing situations in all of their glorious diversity

The lingerie business offers a simple example of how purchasing diversity pushes vendors in the direction of multiple channels. People buy lingerie in different ways for different reasons. One type of purchase, often made on impulse, is the addition of, say, a silk nightgown to a wardrobe. Another type of lingerie purchase, of course, has a more private and personal motivation. These two purchasing situations have very different channel implications. For customers adding innocuous items to a wardrobe, the appropriate channel is one that is in a convenient place where people are already shopping. For naughtier, more intimate purchases, the appropriate channel is one that offers privacy and discretion. Lingerie vendors have to respond to these two different purchasing situations with two different channels.

Thus, Victoria's Secret has retail stores in shopping malls but also offers shop-at-home catalogues. Shopping mall stores are ideal for impulse buyers and those who are buying underthings as part of a larger shopping trip. Catalogue shopping, on the other hand, is ideal for privacy and discretion. Even racier competitors such as Frederick's of Hollywood, whose products are more given to discrete purchasing behavior, understand the importance of meeting customers in the market place at different ways to satisfy different needs. Frederick's offers retail shops, mail order catalogues, and telephone-based channels. In the lingerie business, there's no single channel that, by itself, can respond optimally to every purchasing situation. You have to offer at least two, and perhaps three, different channels to be a growth player.

Managers should raise questions that will bring to the surface the wide variety of purchasing situations in which their customers participate. Failure to respond with appropriate channel diversity can mean writing off whole groups of customers or whole types of purchasing situations. Figure 3.4 pro-

1. Who are our *current* customers?
2. What kinds of different criteria do they use to make a purchase?
3. When/how do they do business – what are their 'purchasing situations'?
4. Do they (want to) buy some products one way, and perhaps other products another way?
5. Do they (want to) buy the same products in different ways at different times?
6. Do we have different types of customers – each with their own types of needs?
7. If so, how do those needs vary across different customer types?
8. Have we identified new customers, or a new type of customer, that we want?
9. How will those new, future customers' needs be different than our current customers'?
10. Which channels are needed to respond to the diversity of all of these buyer needs?

Figure 3.4 Becoming more channel flexible – 10 stretching exercises

vides some stretching exercises – some broad questions to ask about customers' purchasing situations – to make sure all the rocks are turned over when looking at alternative channel solutions.

Many companies are slow to pick up on the idea of multiple channels as a way to respond to the diversity of buyer behavior in their markets. They assume that their channel selection task is to target a product-market and identify a good choice of channel (one channel) for that product-market. This kind of thinking collides eventually with a stubborn fact about customer behavior: *customers do not like being 'owned' by a channel; they prefer to 'surf' across channels*. Many customers will not allow themselves to be forced into a channel by one vendor if another provides options that better map to their diverse purchasing behaviors. Put simply, they will purchase more items from a company that provides a variety of ways to do business. Channel offerings should be flexible enough to allow customers to migrate to their own preferred channels.

Monitor (and respond to) changes in buying behavior

Buying behavior changes over time; in fact, it rarely if ever stays in place. In most buying situations, customers begin by valuing high-touch service and lots of support. However, as these customers evolve into repeat buyers and become more comfortable with a product line or a type of service, they become more self-sufficient. Their priorities thus shift from criteria such as service, training and support toward efficient reordering, lower prices, and self-service. In response to these changing criteria, their channel preferences tend to migrate as well, from higher-cost channels such as field reps to lower-cost alternative channels. This is particularly true with savvy corporate customers who understand channels and channel costs.

As a result, it is often a losing battle to try to maintain the high margins that would justify the continued presence of a field sales force or value-added partners in existing large accounts. Over time, customers become less willing to pay for premium channels, such as these, that they feel they no longer need. Often, sales executives try to solve this dilemma by repositioning their product as a higher value-added sale that could justify the continued presence of expensive sales resources. This is the origin of a lot of the 'total integrated value-based solution' gobbledygook that vendors use to describe what, in essence, are usually pretty simple, straightforward products. A far better solution, most of the time, is to recognize that customer behavior migrates over time, and that some customers may just be ready for a shift to a more efficient channel with more streamlined services at lower prices. Meeting these customers wherever they are ready to buy is usually more productive than trying to convince them to meet you where you want to sell.

Declining margins in key accounts, in fact, can be a red flag suggesting that it is time to see whether customers might be ready for a lower-cost channel. Another red flag is lost sales. If customers are defecting to competitors, why are they doing it? Perhaps it's because a competitor has a better product, but perhaps it's because the competitor offers an easier, better way to do business – a new channel, which the customer is ready to use. Of course, both of these red flags pale in the shadow of the best indicator of all – getting out and talking to customers about their migrating channel preferences. Asking customers on an ongoing basis how they want to do business, and in particular which channels they feel ready to try, is about the best investment in channel strategy a company can ever make.

An example – the flower business

The flower business offers an excellent example of how customer behavior, buying criteria, and diverse types of purchasing situations all converge to drive channel selection in an industry. The flower business looks like a lot of fun; neighbourhood florists, unlike most burned-out corporate managers, get to work on things like the aromatic and visual aesthetics of floral arrangements. Don't be fooled about this business. It is one of the most competitive and hotly contested markets in the world. National distributors compete against each other for share of a market that exceeds $15 billion dollars annually[3]. Major players like 1-800-Flowers are some of the fastest-growing companies in the world, with growth in excess of twenty-five per cent per year[4].

There used to be a lot of players competing for space in this market. There aren't so many of them anymore. A handful of large, successful companies has destroyed much of the competition with clever marketing strategies and, primarily, better channels. Here is what all of the successful players have done:

- **They've aligned their channels with proven buying behavior** Customers in this industry already have dominant, demonstrated, proven buying behaviors. They are accustomed to using call centres, the Internet, and neighbourhood retail stores to make their purchases. Anyone wanting to be a player in this hotly contested market must thoroughly understand these existing channel biases of customers. As a flower vendor, you can thrive in any of the existing channels. But not necessarily in other channels. All of the surviving competitors in this business have exercised channel discipline, focusing their efforts on proven, successful channels that are demonstrated winners with the customer base.

- **They've aligned their channels with key buying criteria** People have *criteria* in mind when they buy flowers, and these criteria are largely known: price, fast delivery, expert advice, and so on. These criteria have, over time, shaped the channels through which flowers are offered. Today's global flower business, as noted, is generally operated through three channels: call centers, the Internet, and neighbourhood retail shops. The reason these channels are dominant is, simply, because they respond best to what customers think is important. Take a look at the top section of Figure 3.5. It shows the five main criteria in use by flower buyers and the relative responsiveness of the industry-standard channels in satisfying those criteria. It is, of course, critical in any industry to understand all of the different criteria that motivate customers' purchasing decisions, and to understand how well different channels can satisfy those criteria. If you were a player in the flower business, and wanted to consider a new channel to draw in new customers, where would you start? Existing customer channel biases only tell you where customers already are, not where they'd be willing to go. Buying criteria help take the next leap in the analysis. Any new channel in this business would have to make sense within the context of competing well (against other channels) on some or all of the known buying criteria of flower purchasers.

  One thing this figure does make clear is why some new channel initiatives are more readily accepted than others. The bottom line is that any new channel offering would have to:

  – satisfy the specific criteria of flower buyers, as shown in Figure 3.5;
  – exceed the performance of the existing industry channels on some, or all, of these dimensions.

Sometimes new channel initiatives are almost comical in their utter disregard for buying criteria or their inability to compete against existing channels on those criteria. The convenience store 7–11 is now selling a prepaid flower card for $36. Like a prepaid phone card, it lets customers prepay in advance, in this case for a flower purchase. A prepayment card is just another consumer channel like any other – a way to get your products into the hands of customers. Is this channel going to work? Here's the problem. Prepaid cards work when customers need emergency backup or out-of-town processing. Customers, in certain circumstances, will pay a small price premium to guarantee supply of a product when they need it, where they need it. That's why it works well with long-distance service; it's easier to carry around a phone card than to carry $5.00 in pocket change when you're out of

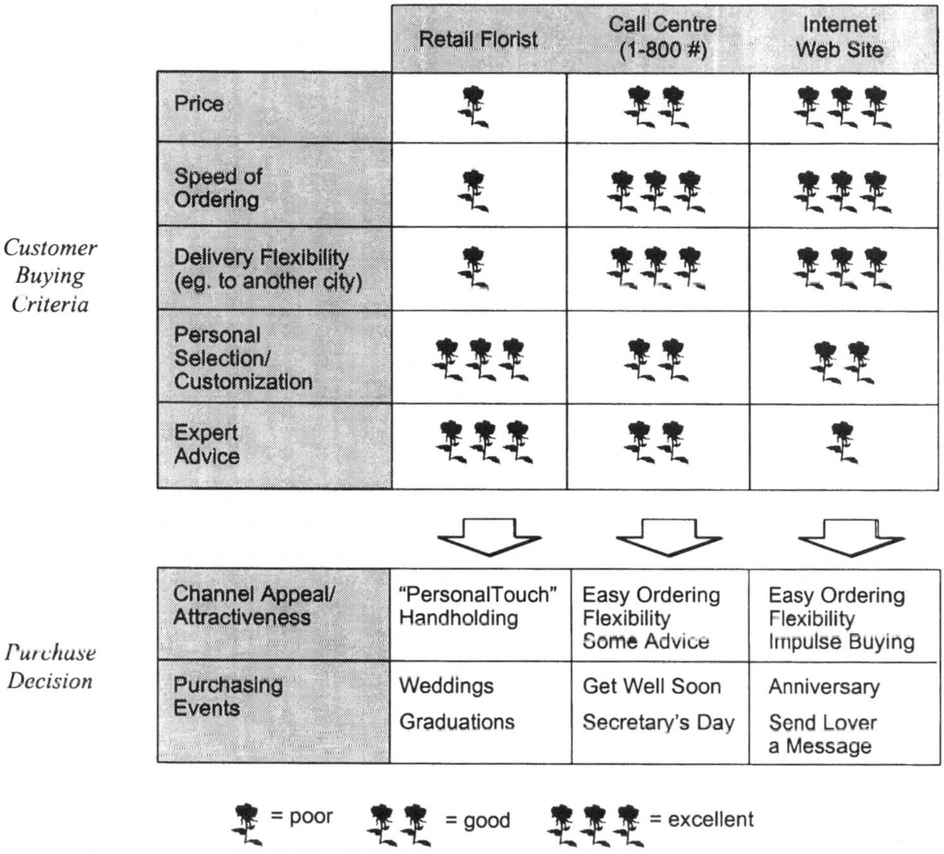

		Retail Florist	Call Centre (1-800 #)	Internet Web Site
Customer Buying Criteria	Price	🌹	🌹🌹	🌹🌹🌹
	Speed of Ordering	🌹	🌹🌹🌹	🌹🌹🌹
	Delivery Flexibility (eg. to another city)	🌹	🌹🌹🌹	🌹🌹🌹
	Personal Selection/ Customization	🌹🌹🌹	🌹🌹	🌹🌹
	Expert Advice	🌹🌹🌹	🌹🌹	🌹
Purchase Decision	Channel Appeal/ Attractiveness	"PersonalTouch" Handholding	Easy Ordering Flexibility Some Advice	Easy Ordering Flexibility Impulse Buying
	Purchasing Events	Weddings Graduations	Get Well Soon Secretary's Day	Anniversary Send Lover a Message

🌹 = poor 🌹🌹 = good 🌹🌹🌹 = excellent

Figure 3.5 Going to market in the flower business

town. Unfortunately, this advantage of prepaid cards doesn't seem to relate to any particular customer criteria in the flower purchase. A prepaid card cannot compete with any existing industry channel on price, speed of ordering, delivery flexibility, personal selection, or expert advice. We called the company marketing these cards and could not get anyone to talk about sales results. So we visited ten 7–11s in Virginia and Washington DC to ask how many people had purchased the cards. The answer – zero. No great surprise. It's not a harmful experiment, and a little experimentation on the side is a good thing. However, to be a player in this business, you better be knowledgeable about *why* customers buy what they buy – and exactly how a new alternative channel is going to satisfy their specific buying criteria better than an existing channel.

- **Channel diversity** As shown in the lower part of Figure 3.5, people buy flowers for lots of different reasons, from the whimsical (roses on a first date) to the very important (weddings), and everything in between. No single channel can hit every customer 'hot button'; each has its own strengths and weaknesses in satisfying customers' various needs. That's why flower vendors offer multiple channels. Retail florists, hitting on the 'hot buttons' of personal selection and expert advice, are going to be attractive for the 'personal touch' purchase, such as is made for a wedding or a child's graduation. Conversely, the Internet is much stronger on criteria such as price, speed, and delivery flexibility, and thus will appeal to purchasing events such as an impromptu show of affection to an out-of-town lover.

The diversity of purchasing events in the flower industry puts an onus on serious national or global competitors to meet customers in the market place with a variety of channels. As is common in many industries, flower vendors have the ability to tap into a lot of types of buying situations – if they can offer channels that are appealing for these different situations. Conversely, a flower vendor with a limited portfolio of channels will, as suggested in Figure 3.5, appeal only to a subset of the flower market and will have limited growth potential as a result.

In sum, the flower business has a lot of underlying structural similarity to other industries. To compete in this business, vendors must understand the existing, proven channel behavior of buyers in this market. To implement new channels for business growth, they must assess and understand the specific needs and requirements of customers. Finally, to achieve high growth and compete on a national or global level, they must appeal to customers in diverse buying circumstances – most likely, with multiple channels.

Summary

When channel initiatives fail – when Internet sites generate insignificant revenue, or when business partners deliver less revenue than they cost to maintain – most of the time it is because these channels didn't align correctly with customers' needs and buying behaviors. There is just no other way to think about it than this: *customer–channel alignment is the foundation of a successful channel strategy.*

Sometimes *demonstrated customer buying behavior* is all that is needed to make informed channel choices. If customers already have proven they will only buy through, say, a field sales rep, there is little point in investing in other channels. Thus, surveying customers and analysing their existing buying behaviors and preferences is an excellent investment.

However, buying behavior is only evidence of what already exists, not what is ultimately possible. To stay on the cutting edge, managers must look to the underlying *criteria* which customers use to make purchases in the first place. Do they value customization? low price? training? Understanding these criteria in relation to alternative channel solutions can help a company push the envelope out from what has already been done in the industry to something innovative and more attractive to customers.

Finally, managers must take a hard look at the *diversity* of buying situations in their markets. Are there a lot of types of customers? Do customers have a diverse set of ways in which they like to buy, each with different buying criteria? Do customers want extensive hand-holding and training for some purchases, but efficient, fast service for others? A 'yes' answer to these questions would suggest that multiple channels may be required to satisfy the needs of the customer base. Conversely, 'no' answers to those questions may imply that a company can get away with one lonely channel and save money, time and energy.

Needless to say, customer behavior is important but it is not the only factor to consider in channel selection. Other factors shape channel selection as well. For instance, not every product can be sold through every channel. Products, in fact, can place significant limitations on channel selection, regardless of what customers want. Thus, onward to the next chapter, 'The impact of products on channel selection'.

Notes

[1] Another approach is to outsource the survey. Several firms do this type of analysis. One advantage of outsourcing the survey is that a third party can perform it as a 'blind study,' thus not disclosing the name of the company sponsoring it. Invariably, this yields more objective, honest results.

[2] Incidentally, marketing to consumers can involve substantially different buyer criteria. For instance, in a new car purchase, criteria such as status, prestige, and image can come into play. These 'softer' buying criteria can be very difficult to map against alternative channels. Thus, Figure 3.3 is limited to the 'harder,' more substantive buying criteria typically involved in business-to-business transactions.

[3] As of March 1998.

[4] *Investor's Business Daily*, 4 May 1995.

Chapter 4

The impact of products on channel selection

Ever heard of jet aircraft being sold in supermarkets? Or funeral services sold over the Internet? How about euthanasia through local distributors? Or diamonds in vending machines? Each, of course, is a caricature of a bad product-channel fit. These are just a few extreme examples of one of the fundamental truths about channel selection: not every product can, or should, be sold through every channel. The penalty for a bad product-channel fit is easy enough to understand. If you try to sell airplanes in supermarkets, no one will buy them.

No one is really trying to sell airplanes in supermarkets, of course. Product-channel fit is usually a more subtle, difficult challenge. Take, for instance, an application software company trying to choose between value-added partners (such as Andersen Consulting) and retail stores (such as CompUSA). Is one of these two channel types more suited to the product than the other? What if the company chooses value-added partners, and it turns out – after the fact – that retail distribution would have resulted in fifty per cent higher sales at half the cost? That's the difference between dominating an industry and disappearing off the map. It's important to anticipate which channels offer the best fit with a product *before* committing to one of them. Product-channel fit is a central component of channel selection.

This chapter begins by looking at a good starting point for assessing product-channel fit: the relationship between *product complexity* and *channel touch*. Complex products that require a lot of service, training and support usually fit better with 'high-touch channels' that can provide for ample interaction between sellers and buyers. Conversely, simpler off-the-rack products can often be sold more effectively in low-touch (non-interactive) channels. As a starting point, the identification of a good fit between product complexity and channel touch is tough to beat. Occasionally, it's all that is needed to make a good product-channel marriage.

Next, the chapter goes a big step further. Most products must be assessed across a variety of dimensions – such as product maturity, customer risk, and customization – to determine channel appropriateness. These dimensions – the chapter looks at nine of them in all – have a significant impact on channel selection. To take just one example, some channels fit much better with mature products in mature markets, while other channels are better suited to new product introductions. Understanding how the different dimensions, or attributes, of a product affect the selection of a channel is the key to sound product-channel fit analysis.

Finally, the chapter looks at the issue of product 'channelization'. The challenge is not always to take a product and find an appropriate channel. Sometimes it's the reverse; many leading channel innovators start off with a compelling channel idea and then work their way back to their products to make sure these products are 'channel ready'. It's not always the channel that has to change to get a good product-channel fit. Sometimes it's the product itself.

The starting point: product complexity and channel touch

A useful starting point in the assessment of product-channel fit is the relationship between *product complexity* and *channel touch*. Channels differ in the amount of customer interaction, service and support they can provide or accommodate. A direct sales force, for example, can handle a wide range of interactions with customers, from pre-sale negotiation and configuration to post-sale service, training, and problem solving. Thus, a direct sales force is a very 'high-touch' channel – it can touch the customer frequently, intensely, and in lots of different ways. Conversely, the Internet and direct mail are low-touch channels; they offer virtually no interaction with the customer, and therefore practically no ability to provide service, support, negotiation or problem resolution. The amount of 'touch' typically provided by different channels exists on a continuum, as shown in Figure 4.1.

High-touch channels, such as sales forces, are more expensive to operate, but also provide more value. There are more things they can do, and more services they can provide throughout the sales process. Conversely, low-touch channels such as the Internet cost less to operate but also provide fewer services, such as configuration and support, in the sales process.

Product-channel fit assessment is sometimes as simple as identifying the right amount of channel touch required to accommodate the complexity of a product. A complex product such as a mainframe computer, for example, requires a significant amount of interaction, negotiation, support, training and

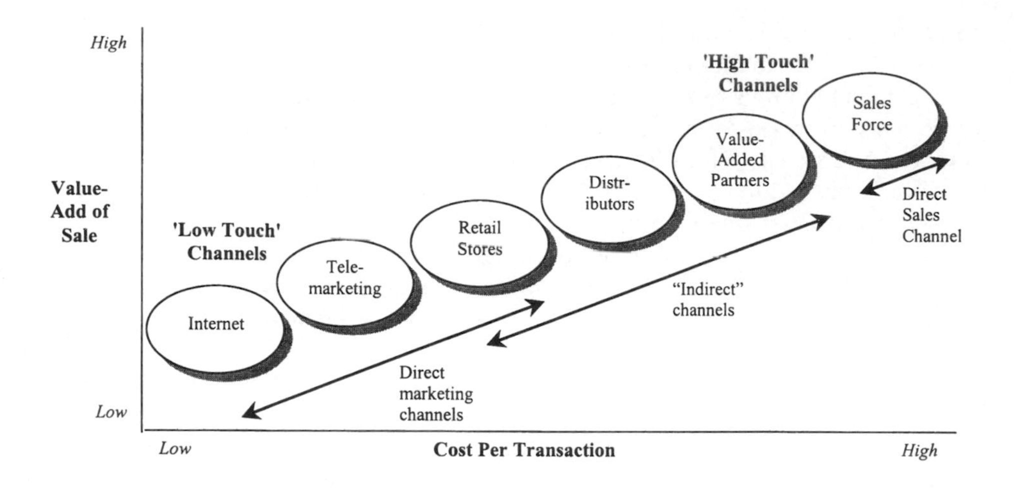

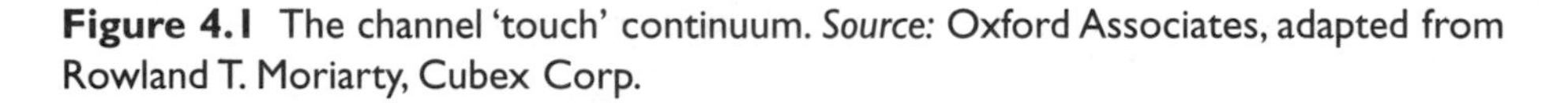
Figure 4.1 The channel 'touch' continuum. *Source:* Oxford Associates, adapted from Rowland T. Moriarty, Cubex Corp.

service before, during and after the sale. High-touch channels, such as field sales forces and value-added business partners, are often the only ones that can provide the intense levels of customer contact expected and required in this type of sale. Conversely, a simple, off-the-shelf product, such as a floppy disk or a mouse pad, requires little if any service or support and thus will be much better off in a cheaper, more efficient low-touch channel. There are exceptions and caveats, which are discussed later in this chapter, but in general, a good starting point is to make a sound intuitive judgment about the amount of channel touch required to accommodate the complexity of a product.

The channel touch continuum in Figure 4.1 also brings to light, visually, one of the key tenets of modern channel strategy:

> You always want to use lower-cost channels, because they cost less! So you should be dragged kicking and screaming up the channel touch continuum toward higher-value, more expensive channels. The goal is to 'push down' transactions into lower-cost channels. The question is whether those lower-cost channels can handle the product.

In other words, most companies should not be seeking out opportunities to involve their sales force more; they should be looking for opportunities to push transactions down the touch curve toward lower-cost, mass-distribution channels. That's how you make more profit, and often more sales too. Product-channel fit is frequently the basis for deciding if you can do it.

Figure 4.1 makes one other point worth mentioning. Products do not usually fit or not fit with an *individual* channel; they fit (or don't fit) with a *type* of channel. Channels come in one of three types:

- **Direct sales channel** The field sales force, consisting of sales representatives.
- **Indirect sales channels** Intermediaries, such as a value-added partner, distributor, or in some cases a retail store[1].
- **Direct marketing channels.** Channels that connect the manufacturer directly with a consumer, other than the sales force. There are many such channels, including telemarketing, direct mail, the Internet, and sometimes, retail stores.

Within one of these three channel types, a product that fits with one channel will often fit with another. Thus, although there are reasons why the Internet might be preferable to direct mail or a telechannel for a given product, any direct marketing channel will typically be as suitable as another for the product. The reasons one might be more desirable than another has more to do with how customers want to do business and how much each channel costs to operate. For the purpose of evaluating product-channel fit, it's usually effective to think in terms of whether the product belongs in the direct sales channel, the indirect sales channel, or a direct marketing channel.

The dimensions of product-channel fit

There are numerous product attributes that affect product-channel fit. This section discusses the nine most important ones. They are:

- Definition
- Customization
- Aggregation
- Exclusivity
- Customer education
- Substitution
- Maturity
- Customer risk
- Negotiation

Each is described below.

Definition

Definition consists of the extent to which a product or service:

- can be sold as a recognizable and easily-understood object

- has an evident usage and purpose
- has well-articulated benefits

Companies sell a wide variety of things at different levels of definition. Pencils, photocopiers, and drill bits are all highly-defined items. You know what they are, you know what they are used for, and you know what benefits you get from using them. Computer outsourcing management, self-help programs, and consulting services are all less well defined offerings. In all three cases, it's more difficult to identify (without some help) exactly what these things are, how they're supposed to be used, and what you get in return for purchasing them.

Products and *services* usually occupy opposite ends of a definition continuum. A product, such as a car, is often much better defined than the service, such as insurance, that exists along side it. A car is easily recognizable as a car. Its use is clear, as are the benefits of owning one. Car insurance is a little hazier. What, exactly, does an insurance policy consist of? What are the specific benefits offered? When can those benefits be used, and when can't they be used? Like cars and car insurance, most products and services differ substantially in their degrees of definition.

Definition is an important attribute in assessing product-channel fit. The less well defined a product (or service) is, the more the product, along with its purpose and benefits, will need to be explained and articulated to make a successful sale. Conversely, the more definition a product or service has, the less explanation it will require in the sales process. Thus:

- **A highly-defined product** that is easily recognizable, with evident usage and clear benefits, can typically be sold in any channel. These products, like pencils and drill bits, have enough clarity to sell themselves to the customers who want them. The goal for highly-defined products should be to move them to the lowest-cost channels possible, since there is no need to spend selling funds on expensive sales people to explain them. These products are usually suitable for direct marketing channels – the lowest-cost channels with the least 'touch'.
- **A mid-definition offering**, like some insurance services and numerous types of business software packages, is recognizable but lacks full clarity with respect either to its potential usage or the benefits of using it. These offerings require some selling by an actual human being. For this reason, mid-definition offerings generally are not appropriate in direct marketing channels; they require, depending on the degree of definition, distributors, value-added partners, or a direct sales force. Retail stores can be appropriate when the product is boxed, packaged and designed from the outset to be recognizable and relatively clear as to its use and the benefits of buying it.
- **A low-definition offering**, usually a professional service, is not recognizable without explanation, requires that the customer learn about its usage, *and* also cannot be sold without an explanation of its benefits. These offerings, of course,

require human contact in the sales process, and specifically, human contact by experienced, knowledgeable, and trained professionals. The field sales force is often the source of this level of professionalism, although value-added partners can sometimes perform the same function. Low-definition offerings rarely can be sold in mass-market distributor channels, and almost never can be sold successfully in direct marketing channels.

The rule of thumb in product definition is that the greater the definition of the product – the easier it is to recognize the product, its usage and its benefits – the more likely it will be that the product will survive and thrive in a lower-cost, lower-touch channel.

Customization

Products differ greatly in the amount of customization required in the sales process. Customization is usually what people have in mind when they talk about 'simple' versus 'complex' products. The simple–complex dichotomy is a false one, though. There are really three levels of customization that affect product-channel fit:

- Some products are **standard** or **off-the-rack** and are not configured at all for a customer. Light bulbs and napkins, for example, are sold 'as is'. Standard products do not offer choices, and therefore do not require a 'customizer' – a sales person, partner, or distributor – in the sales process. As a result, these products can be sold in any channel and should be pushed down to the lowest cost channels, particularly retail and direct marketing channels, that customers will find attractive.
- Many products are **mass customized**, meaning they are tailored to a customer's needs with a set of pre-configured, factory-set options. Cars, for instance, are customized to a buyer's specifications, but only according to a set list of manufacturer's options. Personal computers, as well, increasingly are sold with a structured set of options and add-ons. These products can sometimes be sold in a low-cost direct marketing channel, if all of the options and choices are very well-defined. The Internet is emerging as a particularly attractive medium for this type of product, since option selection is easy in this channel, and the channel has many advantages to both sellers (low costs) and buyers (independence, self-service).
- Some products require **unplanned customization**: the degree or type of customization required is not known until interaction with the buyer takes place. In unplanned customization the buyer is also typically unable to specify the exact configuration needed until provided with assistance by an expert. Custom home window treatments are an example; they require a seller and a buyer to configure the product together. Many custom business software applications, as well, require a seller and buyer to work together to co-design the product. In these cases, a high-

touch channel is required: either a direct sales force or a specialized value-added partner.

Aggregation

Aggregation is a special case that does not fall neatly onto the channel touch continuum. Aggregation refers to whether a product is a 'stand alone' offering or whether it is typically rolled up into a larger solution. A toaster is not an aggregated product; people buy it when they need a toaster, and the purchase is not often part of some larger 'kitchen appliance solution.' Conversely, database programs are almost always sold as an aggregated product; few companies buy them without also buying the applications that will run on them to extract meaningful information.

Aggregation affects whether a product will fit with a direct (direct sales or direct marketing) channel or an indirect (distributor) channel. For example, a vendor selling machine tools that are combined with its own lubrication products will have the option of using any kind of channel. But a vendor selling machine tools that are always combined with *another* company's lubrication products will not be able to sell the entire solution by itself. If customers only buy the overall solution, and not the individual products, the vendor will have to look to an intermediary – an indirect channel member – to build the total solution for the end customer.

So here's the big question. Does the product need to be combined with the offerings of another vendor? If so, the only option will be to place the product in an indirect (distributor/partner) channel[2].

Exclusivity

Some products are sold to as many buyers as possible. Other products are *exclusive* products, positioned as having higher prestige and a more limited (and usually wealthier) set of buyers. Many companies, such as Honda/Acura, offer an upscale version of a product or have an exclusive brand within their overall product mix. Some companies, such as Gucci, offer only exclusive products.

Product exclusivity has two implications for channel selection: higher-touch channels, and channel uniqueness.

- **Higher channel touch** The premium, high-status nature of exclusive products mandates the selection of a channel that will be deemed 'worthy' by customers. Customers will want better service and a channel that reflects the value and status of the product. In part, this explains both Gucci's fall from grace in the late 1980s as well as its resurrection a few years later. By the late 1980s Gucci, in a push toward faster growth, had taken its high-status product line into a mass-market channel consisting of thousands of retailers. The company's image was hurt; sales plummeted and the brand lost much of its traditional luster with consumers. Was it a premium product line, or just another brand you could buy in any store? People couldn't tell. Gucci's decisive response was to slash its distribution channel, replacing thousands of stores at various ends of the quality spectrum with 500 high-quality stores offering premium service. That is what people want when they buy an exclusive good. Gucci's performance has rebounded sharply as a result; a year after making this move, its profits were up forty-six per cent. Exclusive products must be sold through exclusive channels – and that usually means higher-touch channels with more expensive sales resources.

- **Channel uniqueness** People don't just want better service when they buy an exclusive product; often they want a tangible sign that they are buying a product of higher status. This was the driver behind Honda's decision in 1987, for example, to market the new Acura brand through a new Acura dealer network instead of through Honda's established dealer channel. It cost many millions of dollars to launch an entirely new dealer channel, but Honda had its finger on the pulse of the luxury car market. People buying a luxury car want to know they're buying something better and different than the everyday consumer. And they want other people to know it too. The way to do it is by giving them a unique channel that carries only the exclusive product line. Exclusive products don't just mean higher-touch channels; they can also imply the need for a *unique* channel serving only those customers buying the exclusive product.

Customer education

Products differ both in terms of how much customer education is required to use the product, and in terms of how much of this education the customer can do by himself (or can get elsewhere). Cellular phones, for example, require very little customer education, and most of it can be gleaned from reading a manual. Voice mail systems, another telecommunications product, require extensive training, little of which can be obtained except from the product vendor.

Products, such as cellular phones, that involve minimal training require very little face-to-face interaction in the sales process and as a result can frequently be sold in any channel. A lot of cellular phones are in fact sold through retail stores, mass market distributors, and direct marketing channels (such as direct-from-manufacturer television advertisements).

Products, such as voice mail systems, that require a lot of training and hand holding – either during or after the sale – are generally not suitable in direct marketing channels or other low-touch, mass-distribution channels. These products usually imply the use either of a direct sales force, a value-added partner, or at a minimum, a distributor who is trained to provide the required customer education.

Despite all the hoopla about newer computer-based training technologies making everyone smarter and making products easier to use, products with a very high training requirement still usually require a channel with a live human being to provide the customer education. The only way around this is to enlist a training specialist partner or internal division who can support the customer education requirement after the sale. It's a smart strategy, because it often enables a product to be moved into a low-touch, low-cost channel once the training issue is off the table.

Substitution

Product substitution is the ease with which a product can be substituted with a similar competitive offering. Ball-point pens are highly substitutable products; customers can easily switch over to another brand. At the other end of the spectrum, original pieces of art are completely non-substitutable – if you want a specific piece of artwork, you have to buy it; you can't get it anywhere else.

Substitution primarily affects the choice between a direct or indirect channel. The traditional principle is that *the more substitutable a product is, the more control you need to have over its distribution*. The theory goes as follows. Distributors, left to their own devices, will tend to substitute in competitive products based on minor price fluctuations or other unpleasant (and often uncontrollable) factors. As a result, highly substitutable products are often better kept in a direct channel – either a direct sales force or a direct marketing channel. Conversely, non-substitutable products can be sold through indirect channels, since distributors and partners won't be able to sell a competitive offering in place of the product.

It must be noted that, in many cases, substitution is used as an excuse for holding on to a direct sales force presence which could easily be replaced with a less expensive indirect channel. Fearing distributors' lack of loyalty to a product line and likelihood of substituting in competitive products, some manufacturers shun indirect channels. As a result, they incur a higher cost of sales than their competitors, who are more distributor-friendly. These higher costs can do much more damage than can a few lost sales through a distributor. Sometimes there is good reason to fear distributors' brand independence, and sometimes there isn't. It is often better to give the product to indirect partners, and monitor lost sales carefully in that channel, than it is to shun the often more cost-effective indirect channel option in favor of an expensive sales force.

Maturity

Product maturity is a familiar marketing concept; few marketing concepts, in fact, have had more impact on how companies launch and support products in the market place. Maturity is also a very helpful concept in evaluating product-channel fit. The product maturity curve, also called the product life cycle, is shown in Figure 4.2.

As Figure 4.2 suggests, products go through four distinct phases in their life cycle: introduction, growth, maturity, and decline. Figuring out where a product is in its life cycle can have a substantial impact on channel selection:

- **Introduction** New products are usually ill-defined, customer education-intensive, and in many cases highly customized to the needs and requirements of the first few buyers. These products typically meet few if any of the requirements for a low-touch, low-cost channel. In fact, new products usually require a high-touch channel to learn how to sell the product and position it effectively with customers. A direct sales force, or, in some cases, a value-added partner, is required.

  The exception is when a company has an established lower-cost channel that is already successfully selling a similar product. If Sony comes out with a new type of Walkman, it obviously doesn't need to hit the street with sales reps. It can market the product in its existing retail channels by providing a new product announcement to store owners.
- **Growth** In the growth phase, the goal is maximum market share. The most effective way to get market share is usually to use as many channels as possible. In this phase companies should be looking at every available channel and determining whether the product could possibly work in that channel. This is also the time to be looking at the full range of potential channel partners, and to be enlisting as many of them as possible to achieve reach into new market segments. Many companies with products that are still deeply ensconced in their growth phase use this approach.
- **Maturity** In this phase, the product becomes subject to increasing competition, market pressure, and substitutability. Indirect channel partners will become dissatisfied, and margins will begin to come down, affecting the ability to support the product in high-cost channels. One key in this phase is to reduce the number of indirect channel members and focus on motivating the partners who will continue

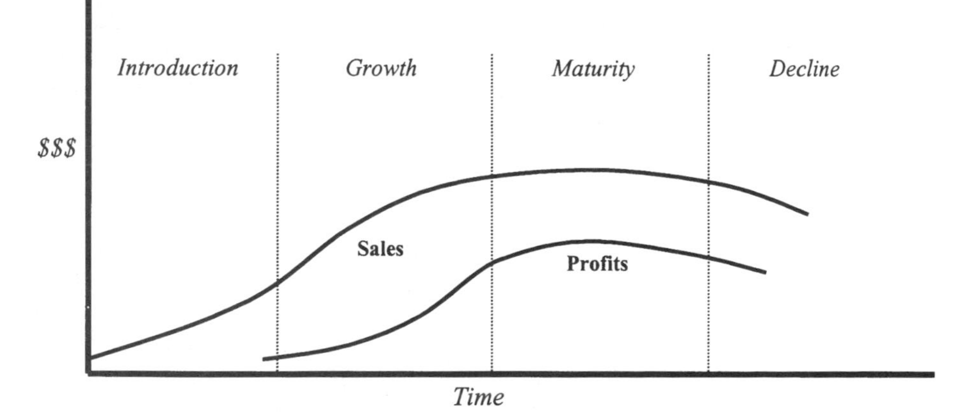

Figure 4.2 The product life cycle

to sell the product. Another is to continue to sell the product in multiple channels – the goal is still growth – but to be starting to focus on opportunities to migrate sales to lower-cost – often direct marketing – channels.

- **Decline** In the decline phase, margins come down, along with sales volume, and the product becomes increasingly unattractive to indirect channel members who are still selling it. As a result, products will not be pushed hard in an indirect channel, and may be outright discontinued. A product in decline is also probably not making enough profit to justify a direct sales force effort. Thus, the best play with a product in decline is to seek out opportunities in low-cost, manufacturer-owned channels. However, without ongoing support and funding, a product in decline, relegated to a direct marketing channel, can simply disappear off the radar screen of both sellers and buyers. Marketing support is crucial to this strategy – if the product is not simply to be discontinued.

Customer risk

Products pose different levels of risk to customers. Product risk comes in several varieties: business risk, personal risk, health risk, and so on. The most important one, from a channel selection perspective, is purchasing risk – the risk to the customer of making the wrong decision in buying the product. Some products have no purchasing risk, such as typing paper and ice cube trays. Other products pose a lot of risk to customers: an auditing service, a new office building, or a mail-order bride. Purchasing risk is higher when:

- The product is expensive
- The sales transaction cannot easily be reversed or cancelled
- The buyer will be stuck with the product for a very long time
- The performance of the product can drastically affect business results or, in the case of consumer products, the personal well-being of the consumer

Low-risk products (to the customer) can generally be sold in any channel. These products require little, if any, selling with regard to product performance, reliability or suitability. Customers buying low-risk products generally prefer to buy them as efficiently as possible, without a lot of assistance or interference. With these products, the goal should be to move them into low-cost direct marketing channels or, failing that, into retail stores and lower-cost distributors.

Higher-risk products, on the other hand, must be *sold*. A knowledgeable, trained person must be involved in the sales process to explain the risks and help the customer understand how the vendor and the product are able to overcome any risk issues and concerns. High-risk products belong in high-touch channels: a direct sales force, value-added partners, or a small, trusted group of distributors.

Negotiation

Some products involve negotiation; others don't. Negotiation is not always about price; it can also be about configuration, post-sale support, or even assumption of part of the risk by the seller. Real estate is a negotiated offering, as are public companies traded on a stock market. Those are both price-focused negotiations, however. The sale of a telephony–computer integration project involves negotiation of price, support, service and numerous other contract terms.

Products that require a lot of negotiation in the sales process require interaction between seller and buyer, often in a face-to-face setting. Negotiated products are thus not suitable in low-touch direct marketing channels, or in most cases even low-end distributor or retail channels. Direct sales force or value-added partner participation is usually required in this type of sale.

Products requiring little or no negotiation over price or contract terms – those that have a fixed price, standard return/exchange privileges, and standard service agreements – can often be sold in any channel. Non-negotiated products fare particularly well in direct marketing channels, because of their lower costs. Lower channel costs mean lower prices. Fixed-priced products that are also *lower* in price can be very hard to beat.

The nine product dimensions need to be examined *collectively* to identify an optimal product-channel fit. They may sometimes pull and tug in different directions. For instance, what about a big, expensive new product that has a fixed price (i.e. non-negotiated) and a high degree of definition? Big new products often require expensive, high-touch channels, but fixed prices and well-defined products often belong in lower-cost channels. So what is the most important attribute of the product? Its new-product-ness is probably the right attribute. It's nice to save money in a low-cost channel, but a big new product requires face-to-face interaction between sellers (who are learning how to sell the thing) and customers (who are trying to figure out what it is). When product attributes come into conflict, some judgment is called for, and specifically, a sound prioritization of what is really important in making the sale. Fortunately, in most cases, product attributes tend to point in the same general direction.

The conventional wisdom works ... most of the time

'High touch' channels, such as sales forces, have been the traditional channels of choice for complex products and services. Historically, simpler, less customized products have been pushed into lower-cost, lower-touch channels (e.g. retailers and distributors). And at the bottom of the food chain, off-the-shelf commodity products were relegated to the lowest-cost, lowest-touch direct marketing channels. This methodical alignment of product complexity with channel touch is often sensible, and it's a good starting point. No one has ever been fired for selecting channels that were already proven capable of handling a product. But does this yield the best channel solution?

It is important to recognize that the conventional wisdom about which channels are required to support which products has been breaking down. In large part, this has been driven by the increasing customer acceptance of direct marketing channels, spearheaded to some extent by the Internet. What would have seemed improbable a few years ago – customers buying expensive, complex products through impersonal, direct marketing channels – is looking very familiar and commonplace nowadays. The Internet and other technologies have given direct marketing channels a higher status, and customers increasingly have come to accept these channels – even for complex products.

In fact, companies that have experimented with the sale of very complex products through low-cost channels are finding customers willing to make large tradeoffs in hand-holding and support in exchange for flexibility, self-service (or, put another way, buyer independence) and cost-savings. IBM, for example, already gets fifteen per cent of its revenue – $11 billion – over the phone. That revenue includes large, complex systems such as RS6000 servers in addition to peripheral equipment and services. The company has also captured and qualified mainframe computer leads (System 390s, the biggest ones out there) on the Internet – though it has not yet fully closed a mainframe deal through that channel.

There are few products today that someone hasn't sold successfully through an alternative, low-cost channel. More and more products, from computers to automobiles to financial services, are showing up in low-cost direct marketing channels every day. This is a key channel trend for the beginning of the next millennium, and it will only continue to proliferate across more industries as customers become more comfortable with, and enthusiastic about, doing business through low-cost, self-service channels. Companies looking at channel opportunities need to stay on top of this trend and benefit from it. They need to push the envelope a little on product-channel fit and see what happens. It is becoming increasingly difficult to predict which channels are able or unable to handle certain types of products. Erring on the side of experimentation with new low-cost channels, even for complex products, is often a good idea. These days, you don't really know which channels will work for complex products until you try them out.

'Channelizing' a product

Product-channel fit is not just about finding an appropriate channel for a given product. On the contrary, as soon as a new channel is being evaluated, companies discover that product-channel fit works the other way around too. New channels almost invariably require at least some redesign or reconfiguration of the product. To succeed in a new channel, a product usually must first be made 'channel ready'.

The classic example is Hanes. Back in the 1960s, Hanes was just another player in the competitive apparel market, specializing in pantyhose and other, similar products. Both Hanes and its competitors fought for growth and market share in the traditional apparel channels: department stores and women's clothing stores. Growth was slow, and market share was difficult to increase in a finite market. Something new and radical was needed. Hanes came up with that new and radical idea in 1970 – supermarkets! Today, it seems sensible – but hardly radical – to use a supermarket channel for consumer items, what with supermarkets selling cameras and film processing, cash machine transactions, lottery tickets, and insurance policies. At the time, however, supermarkets were where you bought *food*.

It was clever thinking. Supermarkets reach tens of millions more customers than could ever be reached by the traditional apparel channels. The product is a simple one that can easily be added to a consumer's supermarket list. So far, so good – the company had an innovative channel idea, maybe even a stroke of genius. The problem, however, was that supermarkets require specialized packaging to facilitate high-volume distribution. Lots of units have to fit snugly in efficient boxes for this mass consumer channel to work. Hanes was thus forced to redesign its packaging for high-volume distribution and, as a result of a unique new design (for L'eggs) was able to build a presence and a strong brand in the supermarket channel. The strategy was a stunning success and has been written about extensively elsewhere. Basically, within a few years Hanes had built the leading market share in the industry, and had paved the way for a generation of channel strategists to update their thinking about the use of high-volume consumer channels. Today, Hanes is the largest brand of apparel in the world.

So what made it all possible? Very simply, Hanes willingness to revise its products to suit the needs of a new channel. Without the new packaging design, the product could never have been sold in the new channel. This is the flip side of product-channel fit. Sure, a company must evaluate its channel alternatives in light of the products it's selling. Just as importantly, though, it must evaluate its products against its desired channels, and often must modify those products to make them 'channel ready'.

The issue is particularly acute when lower-cost channels are being considered for an existing product that has traditionally been sold in higher-cost channels. Low-cost channels offer less 'touch' – less hand-holding throughout the sales process, less training, and less customization. As a result, products that were originally designed for higher-touch channels – that require a lot of assistance, support and training, in other words – often meet stiff resistance in lower-cost channels. As long as these products require high touch, they will likely to be unattractive to buyers in lower-cost channels. Low-cost channels often require low-touch product configurations.

The personal computer industry is an excellent example. This industry has gone through numerous channel migrations as it has struggled to adapt to downward pricing pressure and intense product competition over the past two decades. The burden has always been high to push the PC product into lower-cost, more efficient channels that could also reach more customers. In the 1970s, PCs were complex, fickle items that were sold in high-cost speciality shops. To achieve volume distribution, manufacturers had to migrate toward a distributor model, selling through stores such as CompUSA. However, to make that channel a success, computer manufacturers had to dispense with the notion of the personal computer as a totally-customized, unique purchase and had to make it into a product with relatively standardized models in fewer configurations.

More recently, to get from volume retail to cheaper direct marketing channels such as call centres and the Internet, these manufacturers have had to go a step further. Low-touch direct marketing channels work with simple products. PC manufacturers pursuing this route thus have had to standardize their products further, package CD-ROM training disks in with the computers, and developing clearer price points and feature levels. Standardization, feature reduction, and pricing simplification all reduce the need for interaction in the sales process, and are necessary elements of a product redesign when the goal is to migrate to lower-cost, lower-touch channels.

In fact, some, or all, of the product redesign approaches shown in Figure 4.3 are likely to be required when selecting a new channel. These will be particularly important when the goal is to migrate an existing product to a new, lower-cost channel.

Making The Product Channel-Ready: Six Tools of the Trade

❶ **Product simplification**	Reduction in the number of features.
❷ **Product standardization**	Elimination of unnecessary model variations and customizable options.
❸ **Channel pricing**	Identification of realistic target prices that can be supported in the alternative channel.
❹ **User self-sufficiency**	Inclusion of training, procedures, and post-sales support instructions as part of the basic product.
❺ **Purchase streamlining**	Elimination of confusing purchasing requirements, and simplification of contractual and financing terms.
❻ **Support integration**	A secondary support channel to provide any necessary services or post-sale support that cannot be provided well in the alternative channel.

Figure 4.3 Making the product channel-ready – six tools of the trade

Summary

Products are a key factor in the selection of sales channels. Some products can only be sold through one specific channel. Many others allow a little flexibility but still are only suitable in a handful of thoughtfully-chosen channels. A good rule of thumb in product-channel fit is to match the complexity of the product with the 'touch' of the channel. Very complex products, such as mainframe computers, typically require high-touch channels such as direct sales forces. Conversely, simple, off-the-rack products can often be sold more efficiently and effectively in lower-cost direct marketing channels. The goal should be to push products down into the lowest-cost channel that can deal with them. That's the way to make more profit and, often, more sales.

The mapping of product complexity to channel touch is only a starting point, and it doesn't frequently represent a complete analysis. In fact, most products are a little ambiguous, having numerous attributes that, only when analysed in detail and assessed collectively, can point toward a suitable channel solution. Analysis of the different dimensions of a product will be required to establish the tradeoffs and subtle issues that will affect its fit with a channel.

Product-channel fit is not always about finding a new channel for a fixed, defined product. Frequently, it works the other way around. In many cases, products must be redesigned or reconfigured to fit well into a new channel. This is especially true when existing products are being migrated to lower-cost channels. Lower-cost channels are lower-touch channels, and they require simpler, more standardized, more complete products to work effectively.

Finally, product-channel fit analysis tends to result in a channel *type* bias, such as 'direct marketing will work', but rarely do products themselves conclusively point to a *specific* channel, such as 'use the Internet' or 'stick with a catalogue'. So how do you drive the channel selection decision down to a specific channel? There are two answers.

One answer is that a product's characteristics tend to define a feasible range of channel solutions, but that within that range, channel selection should be based primarily on customers' preferences and buying behaviors. The compact disk may fit in general with direct marketing channels – which is a very valuable piece of information to have – but the *specific* direct marketing channel selected should be based on what customers want and where they are willing to do business. We know they will buy compact disks in volume through mail order houses; how about the Internet? This question can't be answered solely by looking at the product; you have to ask the customers who'll be buying it. In short, customer behavior must be taken into account in tandem with product–channel fit analysis to arrive at an optimal, specific channel.

The second answer is an economic one. Individual channels have their own economics: their own costs; returns on investment; and potential sales volume.

Within a range of possible channels, the relative economic performance of alternative channel solutions is often the final arbiter in the channel selection decision. That is the subject of the next chapter, 'The bottom line: the economics of channel selection'.

Notes

[1] The exact status of a retail store can be a little fuzzy. For simplicity, we have included retail stores as indirect channels because most of the time retail stores are intermediaries between a manufacturer and a consumer. When a retail store is owned by the manufacturer, however, it can be considered a direct channel. Not everyone agrees with these definitions.

[2] Another option, of course, is to buy the partner – or the other vendor. That's outside the scope of this book, however.

Chapter 5

The bottom line: the economics of channel selection

Ever wonder why most US retail banks are open for business Monday to Saturday – except on Wednesday afternoons, or Saturdays after 1:00 pm, or every day between 2:00 and 3:00 pm, or for just about any holiday anyone has conjured up over the last 220 years? One reason is shown in Figure 5.1.

Annoying as it may be to consumers, the fact is that a bank makes far more money if it can force its customers to use alternative channels such as online banking, phone-based account services and automated teller machines. Each of those channels costs less than half as much per transaction as does a face-to-

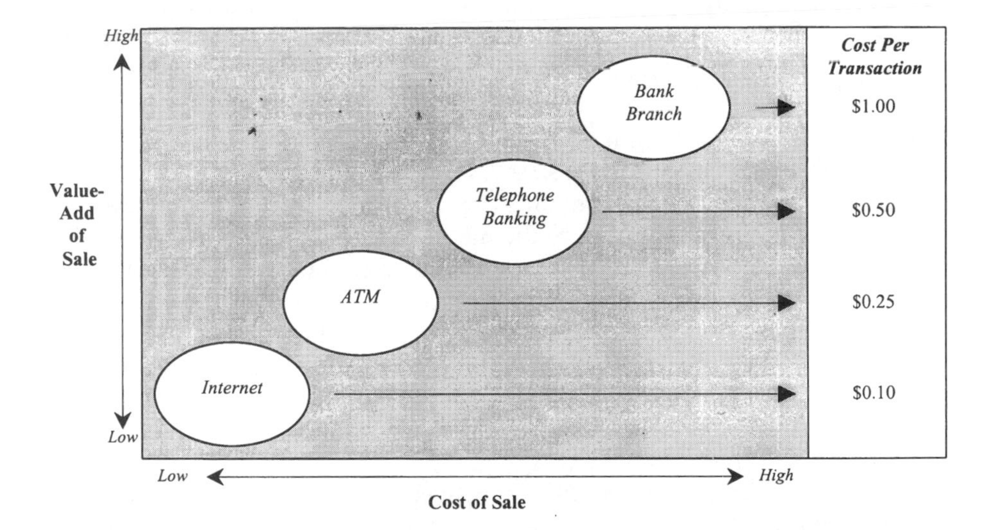

Figure 5.1 Transaction cost by channel retail banking industry (estimated 1996 data)
Source: Oxford Associates

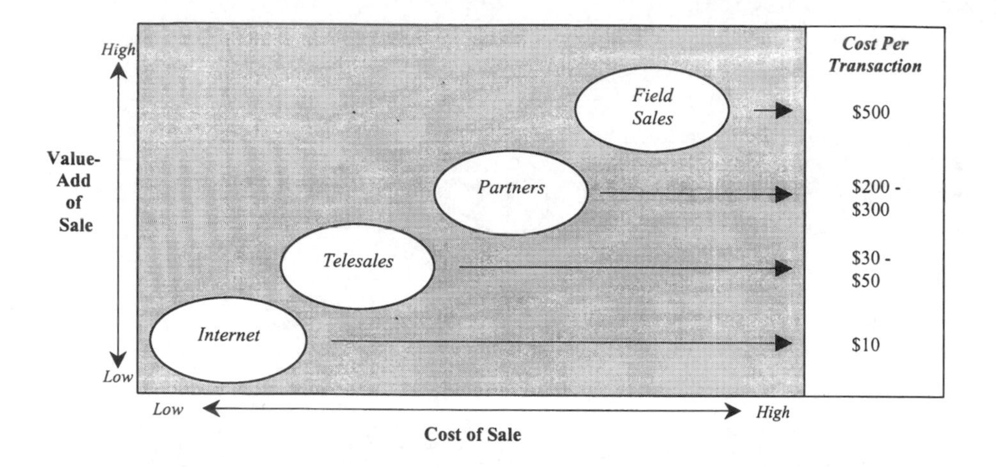

Figure 5.2 Transaction cost by channel – industrial products: $2000–$5000 sale (aggregated from industry data – manufacturing, chemicals, paper, 1996) *Source:* Oxford Associates

face retail branch. To achieve high profitability, retail banks must get their customers out of expensive branch offices and into channels that will deliver lower-cost transactions.

Retail banks are hardly alone in recognizing the huge differences in transaction costs across channels – and in doing everything possible to get customers into lower-cost alternatives. In many industries, transaction costs across channels can differ *by orders of magnitude*. Figure 5.2, for instance, shows the average cost of four different channels in a typical $2,000–$5,000 transaction in the manufacturing, paper, and chemicals industries[1].

As Figure 5.2 shows, in small industrial sales, a distributor-based transaction can cost less than half as much as one made by a field sales rep, and a phone transaction can cost as little as a sixth as much as one made by a distributor. Needless to say, this is why many industrial companies are moving like gangbusters to get their products out of the hands of sales reps and into alternative channels. Like banks, industrial companies have come to realize that they can make more money, faster, by *migrating transactions toward lower-cost channels*. Lower-cost channels generate *higher profits* per sale, and also enable a company to pursue more sales per investment dollar, leading to *faster growth*. Indeed, figuring out which channels can most profitably capture the available business in a market is the key to a financially successful channel strategy – and is the subject of this chapter.

Channel economic analysis has a deserved reputation for being an arcane and mysterious discipline rarely understood by mortals. Companies frequently put together large teams of people with doctorates in finance and economics, who, armed with the latest methods in statistical research and the best computer equipment in the company, spend months and months crunching numbers to come up with something like 'we could make more money if we sell over the telephone'. The recommendations are often sensible, so no one asks – or wants to know – what strange analytical processes took place to reach those conclusions. This chapter does not attempt to describe the painful levels of economic analysis often involved in channel selection. The chapter takes a simpler approach: there are some basic tools of economic analysis that managers need to be able to use to make informed judgments about channel selection. Specifically, the chapter looks at:

- **Pre-defining the realistic channel range** As a starting point, it's helpful to keep in mind that channel economics is not the sole issue in channel selection. As discussed in the last two chapters, customer behavior and product-channel fit are also significant factors that each bring shape to a channel selection initiative. Analysing customers and products *first* can help in the definition of a realistic group of channels, thus minimizing wasted effort spent in economic analysis. The chapter begins with a very brief look at this topic.
- **Channel profitability** Next, the chapter looks at channel profitability. Channel profitability plays a central role in channel selection. A channel that consumes only five per cent of sales revenue per transaction, for example, is better than one that consumes fifteen per cent, all other things being equal. Assessing a channel's profitability can be a bit tricky, and the section looks at a number of issues involved in establishing an accurate picture of channel costs and profit levels. The section also makes some recommendations about how to use profitability data to make sound channel selection decisions.
- **Channel capacity** Channel profitability is concerned only with the *cost* side of channel selection. It is also important to look at the *revenue* side of the equation: the capacity of different channels to achieve a target sales level. A channel that costs little but cannot generate a sufficient level of sales can be far worse than a more expensive channel solution that can deliver a higher level of revenue. Channel capacity, like profitability, is thus an important yardstick in the channel selection process.

Pre-defining the realistic channel range

'Triple your sales for almost nothing!' read a brochure received at our offices in Virginia. It continued:

> Our data base of over 50,000 companies and 4,000,000 names is a who's-who of American business. Our email distribution services can get you in touch with every single one of those companies, and can literally bring thousands of new customers

> to your doorstep! We have affordable programs to meet every budget, and can help you make sales for half of what you are spending today!

The brochure was wrong on two counts. This company's programs would do more than reduce selling costs by half – much more. An e-mail campaign that brought in a new client to *any* consulting firm would represent an infinitesimally small amount of investment compared to the huge cost associated with putting skilled, knowledgeable consultants in touch with prospective clients.

Unfortunately, the other error was assuming that it would *work*. Companies do not usually hire marketing consultants through mass e-mail; impersonal electronic communication is a poor medium for a transaction that is based, in large part, on trust and word of mouth. In addition, mass e-mail is a poor choice of medium for the product – a professional service – that is developed collaboratively with the client. It's quite an accomplishment to reduce selling costs by 90 per cent or more – if it can be done. The problem is that it can't be done.

The lesson is a simple one. Alternative channels can be compelling in their dramatic implications for growth in sales and profits, but they aren't always suitable. Specifically, they may be poorly tuned to the buying behaviors and needs of customers within a market, and they may also be poorly tuned to the nature of the products they are supposed to be selling. A low-cost channel may indeed be low cost – but it may also be unable to do any business.

Managers are thus well advised to think of channel economics as an activity that comes *after* some thoughtful analysis has been done on both customer behavior and product-channel fit. It often makes sense to look at customer behavior first to establish a general range of channel alternatives, and then to look at these channels in terms of their ability to carry the intended product line. Only then does it make much sense to get involved with economic analysis. This approach – the sequencing of channel selection activities – is shown in Figure 5.3.

As shown in the figure, a disciplined approach of evaluating customers, then products, and finally economics, can help in whittling down a universe of channel opportunities into a focused set of realistic, market-ready alternatives. Unfortunately, few channel selection initiatives follow such a well-organized and sequential path. More often, numerous channels are evaluated concurrently, across different customer, product and economic factors. As a general approach, however, Figure 5.3 communicates a sound principle of channel design. Management teams are notorious for spending most of their strategy development time searching for the lowest-possible-cost channels – channels that aren't always suitable and that don't always work. Determining right up front which channels are the most suitable for a set of customers and products can result in a more efficient and, in the end, successful channel selection effort.

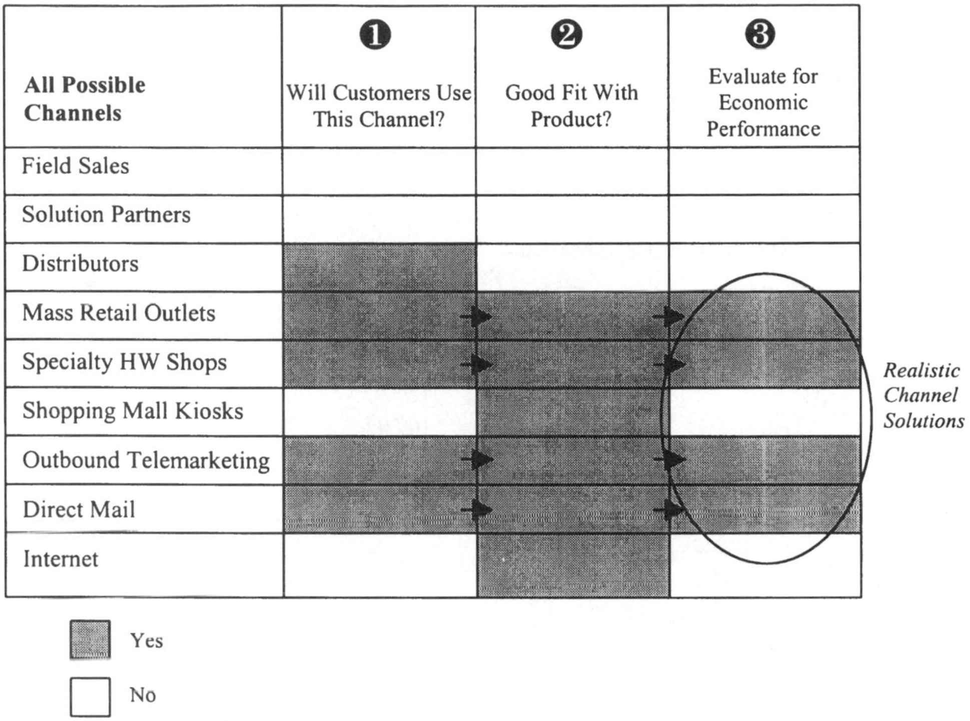

All Possible Channels	❶ Will Customers Use This Channel?	❷ Good Fit With Product?	❸ Evaluate for Economic Performance
Field Sales			
Solution Partners			
Distributors			
Mass Retail Outlets			
Specialty HW Shops			
Shopping Mall Kiosks			
Outbound Telemarketing			
Direct Mail			
Internet			

Realistic Channel Solutions

Yes

No

Figure 5.3 Sequencing the channel selection process. Sample – Turbo-R Home Lawn Mower

Channel profitability

Like customer behavior and product-channel fit, *channel profitability* is a key factor in channel selection. The reason is simple: the cost of going to market (the combined cost of sales and marketing across all channels) is often a company's single largest expense. This cost is usually larger than the R&D budget, and is sometimes larger than the total cost of making all products combined. It can consume over forty per cent of total revenues, and rarely consumes less than fifteen to twenty per cent. The prominent position of selling costs in a company's financial performance is shown in the sample income statement in Figure 5.4.

Because of the size and prominence of selling costs in a corporate budget, even modest reductions can make a big difference in overall profitability. For instance, in Figure 5.4, a reduction of even ten per cent in selling costs – $30,000 – would increase operating (pre-tax) profits by twelve per cent, from $250,000 to $280,000. That's a significant increase, and it explains much of the enthusiasm that now exists for alternative, low-cost channels – particularly since

Sales:		1,000,000	
	Cost of Goods Sold	300,000	
	Gross Profit	*700,000*	
Operating Expenses			
	Selling, General & Administrative	300,000	Sales and Marketing / Administrative Overhead
	R&D	100,000	
	Non-recurring expenses	50,000	
	Operating Profit	*250,000*	
Taxes		110,000	
Net Profit		*140,000*	

Figure 5.4 Selling expenses in context – typical income statement

alternative channels often can achieve selling cost reductions far in excess of ten per cent.

As noted earlier in Figure 5.2, for example, a sales transaction that costs $500 when made by a field sales rep can cost as little as $30 when made over the phone. For a $2,000 sale, that would mean a reduction in selling expense from twenty-five per cent of revenues to two per cent. The $470 saved – on every single transaction – represents pure profit. For many companies, there are few, if any, other sources of such dramatic improvement in bottom-line performance.

In practical terms, what this means for channel selection is that a sound and accurate assessment of which channels can deliver the most profitable business is an essential component of the selection process. This is the time to move beyond anecdotes and assumptions – 'The Internet costs practically nothing!' or 'The sales force is too expensive!' – and to perform a rigorous analysis of the profitability that different channels can really deliver, in specific markets. This section looks at the two main components of a profitability analysis:

- Establishing the channel 'cost-per-transaction'
- Using the cost-per-transaction as a basis for comparing channel profitability

Establishing the channel cost-per-transaction

A channel's profitability is often expressed in terms of its expense-to-revenue ratio, or *E*/*R*. A channel's *E/R* in any particular market is equal to its average transaction cost divided by the average order size.

As an example, consider the market of photocopying machines sold to SOHO (small office–home office) customers. Copiers in this market – typically around $400 – might be sold by a distributor at a transaction cost of $40 – in which case the distributor would have an *E/R* ratio of ten per cent (i.e. $40/$400). Alternatively, the same $400 sale might be made by a telemarketing rep for $20, which would give the telechannel an *E/R* of five per cent ($20/$400).

The important point is that a lower *E/R* indicates that less money is being spent on selling costs for every dollar of revenue. Thus, the lower a channel's *E/R*, the more profit will be realized on each and every selling transaction.

As suggested, two pieces of information are required to calculate a channel's *E/R* – the *average order size* in the market, and the channel's *cost-per-transaction*. Of the two, the average order size (or average revenue per sale) is much easier to determine. It is equal to the total revenue achieved in a market divided by the number of sales transactions. A company selling 1,000 copiers and making $400,000 in sales, for example, would have an average order size of $400. Most companies have no difficulty calculating the average order size within and across markets.

The average cost-per-transaction of a channel, on the other hand, can be far more difficult to determine. Sometimes, the information already exists within an industry, as shown earlier in the chapter for the retail banking industry (see Figure 5.1). Sometimes, this information can also be gleaned by analysing competitors' channel usage as well as the performance of out-of-industry companies selling similar products through similar channels. In many cases, however, the average cost-per-transaction of a channel must be calculated. The formula for making this calculation is shown in Figure 5.5.

Channel Cost-Per-Transaction

$$\text{Cost-Per-Transaction} = \frac{\text{Total Channel Expense}}{\text{\# of Transactions}}$$

Example:

Field sales force costing $10 million, doing 5,000 transactions.

$$\text{Cost-Per-Transaction} = \frac{\$10{,}000{,}000}{\$5000} = \$2{,}000$$

Figure 5.5 Channel cost-per-transaction

As shown in Figure 5.5, a channel's average cost-per-transaction is equal to its total selling expense divided by the number of transactions in which it participates. Thus, a sales force that costs $10 million, and which participates in 5,000 sales transactions, has a cost-per-transaction of $2,000.

The tricky part, of course, involves estimating a channel's total expense: where, for example, did the $10 million figure come from? The answer is that the only way to determine the probable cost of a channel, in the absence of published industry data, is to build and populate a *channel cost model*. A cost model defines the different categories of selling expenses that will be incurred by any channel. Its purpose is to help managers identify and account for the wide variety of costs that typically are associated with a channel. A basic framework for building a channel cost model is shown in Figure 5.6.

By covering all the bases in Figure 5.6 and making a few assumptions along the way, a company can make a reasonable estimate of a channel's total expense. It should be noted, however, that channel expense modeling is one of

1. Direct Selling	Sales rep salaries and commissions Indirect field expenses (travel, site demos, etc.) Sales management allocation
2. Distributor Costs	Distributor or partner margins Indirect channel program costs Indirect channel marketing and promotion costs
3. Telemarketing / Telesales	Telerep salaries and commissions Phone costs Computer and systems costs Sales management allocation
4. Electronic Commerce / Internet	E-commerce start-up (design/build) E-commerce operating (maintenance) costs Fulfillment system linkage costs
5. Marketing and Advertising	Channel-support marketing and promotions Advertising and media support Corporate marketing allocation
6. Fulfillment	Shipping Order processing Inventory carrying costs Financing / Risk assumption
7. Overhead Allocation	G&A corporate overhead allocation Other allocated expenses

Figure 5.6 Basic framework for establishing channel expenses

the fuzzier areas of channel analysis. At one extreme, a channel's cost can include just the direct expenses involved in making sales transactions – literally, the salaries of field reps and their travel costs plus a few other odds and ends. At the other extreme, a channel's cost can include an allocation of many different types of corporate expenses, such as administrative overhead, officer salaries, corporate advertising, inventory carrying costs, and so on.

There is a lot of debate about whether or not a channel's cost should be 'fully loaded' with indirect expense allocations. For the purpose of comparing channel profitability, however, the only important point is that whichever expenses are included in a cost estimate should be the same ones used for *every* channel, consistently. If the sales force is 'paying' a portion of a company's air conditioning bill, then a new Internet site should be allocated a part of this overhead cost as well. Failure to establish an 'apples to apples' basis for comparing channel costs can lead to inaccurate and harmful conclusions. Existing channels with their many indirect expense allocations will tend to appear more expensive than they really are. Conversely, new channels without any indirect expense baggage will appear more profitable than they would ever really be once loaded up with corporate overhead and other indirect costs. In short, whether or not indirect selling expenses are included in the cost model, each channel being evaluated for profitability should be allocated the same set of cost factors.

The purpose of all this work – of building a channel cost model – is to determine an overall channel expense figure that can then be divided by the number of transactions in which the channel is expected to participate – to yield an average cost per transaction. For example, a new partner channel estimated to cost $10 million, and expected to participate in 25,000 sales transactions, would have a cost per transaction of $400. When this analysis has been done for every channel under consideration, the result should look like the one shown in Figure 5.7.

This chart can be developed the easy way, sometimes by finding it in an industry journal, and more often by paying a consultant or industry expert to create it. The chart can also be developed the hard way, by building a complicated cost model in-house from the ground up. Either way, it is the basis for a profitability comparison across channels. A company must understand, and quantify, the cost per transaction of different channels before it can figure out how profitable each of those channels will be in a sales transaction.

Using cost per transaction as a basis for comparing channel profitability

Once the cost-per-transaction of each channel has been established, the profitability of each channel in a market can easily be calculated. Channel profitability, as described earlier, equals the cost per transaction divided by the average order size. Figure 5.8 shows how this plays out.

Channel Cost-Per-Transaction Summary
Office Security Products Firm

Channel	Cost-Per-Transaction
Field Sales Force	$600
Installer/Distributors	$350
Retail Store	$275
Telesales	$70

Figure 5.7 Channel cost-per-transaction summary – office security products firm

As Figure 5.8 shows, different channel transaction costs result in different channel E/R ratios. For example, the field sales force, at $600 per transaction, is shown as having a relatively high E/R of twenty-four per cent in a $2,500 sale: in other words, the sales force will consume twenty-four cents on every revenue dollar. On the other hand, a telemarketing transaction, costing only $70 per transaction, will consume only three per cent of a $2,500 sale.

So which is the right channel to use? There are two different answers to this important question.

- **Use the lowest-cost channel** In general, the lowest-cost channel that will be accepted by customers and that also represents a good fit with a product line is

Market: Small business alarm and anti-theft systems.
Average order size: $2,500.

Channel	Cost-Per-Transaction	Channel E/R
Field Sales Force	$600	24 %
Installer/Distributors	$350	14 %
Retail Store	$275	11 %
Telesales	$70	3 %

Figure 5.8 Channel profitability analysis – office security products firm

the best choice, because it will yield the highest profits. For example, assuming that customers will buy $2,500 security products over the phone, a telechannel certainly would offer a much higher profit per transaction than any other channel. It is always worth testing and re-testing whether a lowest-cost channel will work in a product-market. The impact on selling profitability, as shown in Figure 5.8, can be dramatic.

- **Take a more balanced approach** It is important to keep in mind that channel profitability ultimately reflects the level of service being provided to customers. Lower-cost channels generally cost less because they provide fewer services in the sales process. In some circumstances – for example, when high service levels are a key differentiator for a business – it may make sense to select a channel that can deliver an *acceptable level of profitability* rather than the *highest possible level*. For instance, the security products firm in Figure 5.8 might decide that a fourteen per cent channel E/R is acceptable, and that the high-quality installers who can sell at this cost level are a better solution for building strong customer relationships than a telesales rep.

  Companies, in short, are sometimes better off using some good judgment, and making a few compromises, rather than pushing as many sales as possible into lower-cost channels. A company with an existing E/R of sixteen per cent, for example, would improve its overall profitability by shifting sales to *any* channel with an E/R below sixteen per cent – not just the lowest cost channel. Figure 5.9 shows how this approach can allow for a little more flexibility in the channel selection process.

  One key advantage of the flexible approach is that it tends to yield a *group* of channels – specifically, those channels that can each do business more profitably than a company's current channel – rather than an individual lowest-cost channel. There is

Market: Small business alarm and anti-theft systems.
Average order size: $2,500.

Channel	Cost-Per-Transaction	Channel E/R
Field Sales Force	$600	24 %
Installer/Distributors	$350	14 %
Retail Store	$275	11 %
Telesales	$70	3 %

Existing Overall Corporate E/R: 16 percent

= *Acceptable (profit-enhancing) channels*

Figure 5.9 Channel 'acceptability' – the flexible approach

often no benefit in stuffing every conceivable sale into the lowest cost channel. At a slightly higher overall *E/R*, a company may be able to offer a *suite* of channels that will give customers greater flexibility and pull in more sales transactions[2].

Finally, a cautionary note about profitability analysis is that it focuses exclusively on the *cost* side of channel selection. As discussed in the next section, there is another perspective that needs to be taken into account: a channel's ability to generate an acceptable level of sales volume.

Channel capacity – the revenue side of channel selection

Channel *E/R* is an excellent measure for comparing channel economic performance. It is not always a complete answer, however. It looks only at the ability of different channels to perform at relatively lower transaction costs. Another question concerns *revenue*: whether a new channel has the capacity to achieve the desired level of sales in a market. Channel capacity is important for two reasons:

- A new low-cost channel won't do much good if it is incapable of achieving a target level of sales revenue.
- A new low-cost channel won't necessarily be so 'low cost' by the time a company is finished investing in it properly to achieve an actual revenue target.

Ignoring the capacity of a channel to achieve a target level of revenue can have serious consequences in a channel selection initiative. Take as an example Vista Networks, a $30 million computer networking firm with, in 1994, with a revenue target of $50 million by 1998[3]. Early in 1994, the company made the decision to migrate from a field sales force model to a large network of value-added partners and systems integrators, in order to grow as well as to reduce selling costs. Vista's plan – at least in theory – was a good one. There are over 500 firms that potentially could have served as Vista's partners, many doing at least $10 million in annual business. Even one per cent of that $5 billion plus market, it was reasoned, would deliver Vista's sales target of $50 million.

After investing heavily in partner recruitment, however, Vista learned its first important channel lesson: 500 *available* partners is not the same thing as 500 *committed* partners. In fact, out of all the available firms, only ninety-four formally joined Vista's Network Solutions Partner Program, and of those, only fifty-two became 'active' partners generating any sales for Vista[4].

The second lesson Vista learned was the more painful one. The company had made a rough-cut estimate that each active partner would deliver upwards of $1 million in new revenue. This figure turned out to be highly optimistic – and inaccurate. Figure 5.10 provides the breakdown of revenue at Vista's active partnerships[5].

Number of Partners:	**52**	
Per Partner (Averages)		
Total revenues	$17 million	
Network products revenue:	$7.4 million	(44 % of sales)
Passed through to product vendors:	$2.4 million	(32 % of network revenue)
# of product vendors (e.g. Vista):	6	
Pass-through per product vendor:	$400,000	
Total partner channel capacity:	$20,800,000	(= 52 x $400,000)
Revenue Target:	$50,000,000	
Channel Revenue Shortfall:	**($29,200,000)**	

Figure 5.10 Vista's channel capacity problem

As the figure shows, Vista's partner channel was capable of generating far less than the $1 million per partner than was initially planned – in fact, at $400,000, less than half of plan. The reason was that only $7.4 million of the partners' average $17 million in revenues came from network-related services, and of that, only $2.4 million was paid out to Vista and its many competitors. This $2.4 million was divided on average among six product vendors, leaving about $400,000 per vendor for Vista and its many competitors to fight over. Assuming that every single one of Vista's new, untested partnerships would deliver this amount of revenue – a very optimistic assumption – the total revenue available through this new channel of fifty-two partners was $20,800,000.

Vista, in short, had a *channel capacity* problem. Its intended new channel lacked the ability to deliver even half of its $50 million revenue target. Where were the additional revenues going to come from? The company had two choices:

- **More partners** Using the $400,000 per-partner sales benchmark, an additional seventy-three partners would have been required to achieve $50 million in sales (125 active partners total).

  Required: Massive increase in partner recruitment spending, and a revamping of partner marketing materials to attract a larger, more diverse set of partners.
  Outcome: Much higher channel E/R.

- **More sales per partner** Relying solely on the existing fifty-two partners, the $50 million sales target could also be achieved – at least in theory – by increasing per-partner revenue from $400,000 to $961,500.

Required: Massive increases in per-partner marketing funds, co-branded solutions development, joint selling activities, and some divine intervention.
Outcome: Much higher channel E/R.

Either solution to the problem would have entailed significantly higher channel expenses. A third option would have been to add another channel – which is what Vista did, adding a telemarketing channel as well as maintaining a small field sales force. No matter what solution the company used to solve the problem, however, its initial investment expectations were highly unrealistic – because it had not accounted for the heavy marketing and sales investments required to get a $20.8 million channel to perform at a $50 million level.

In short, in evaluating channels, managers must take account not only of channel costs, but also of the capacity of those channels to capture the desired revenue. An analysis of a channel's revenue capacity will highlight whether cost estimates are realistic or whether these estimates will need to be revised upward to account for increased channel-building investments. The analysis will also help determine if the channel under consideration is a sound option in the first place. A channel that will never, ever yield more than $20.8 million in sales may be a poor choice for a company needing $50 million in sales through that channel to hit its revenue targets.

A simple formula for assessing channel capacity is shown in Figure 5.11. Although simple, the formula shown in Figure 5.11 can be challenging to calculate. It requires:

- **Realistic estimates of channel productivity** Like Vista Networks, many companies assume a much higher level of productivity per selling resource than actually will occur in the market place. Productivity can fail to meet expectations in almost any channel:
  - Business partners or distributors, for any number of reasons, may sell far less than initially anticipated. Per-partner productivity will depend on factors such as the degree of competition for those partners as well as the partners' own revenue and growth levels. The portion of a partner's revenue that is realistically achievable may be a small fraction of what is initially assumed.
  - Telemarketing reps may be unable to close large deals and may thus achieve an average telesales order size that falls far short of a company's overall average order size. For example, a company might estimate per-telerep productivity at $500,000 per year, based on fifty sales of $10,000 – its standard order size across all channels. However, if its telereps are only able to close orders at around $5,000, the channel's per-unit productivity will be $250,000 – half the amount initially anticipated.
  - Even with a direct sales force, often the most predictable of channels[6], additional

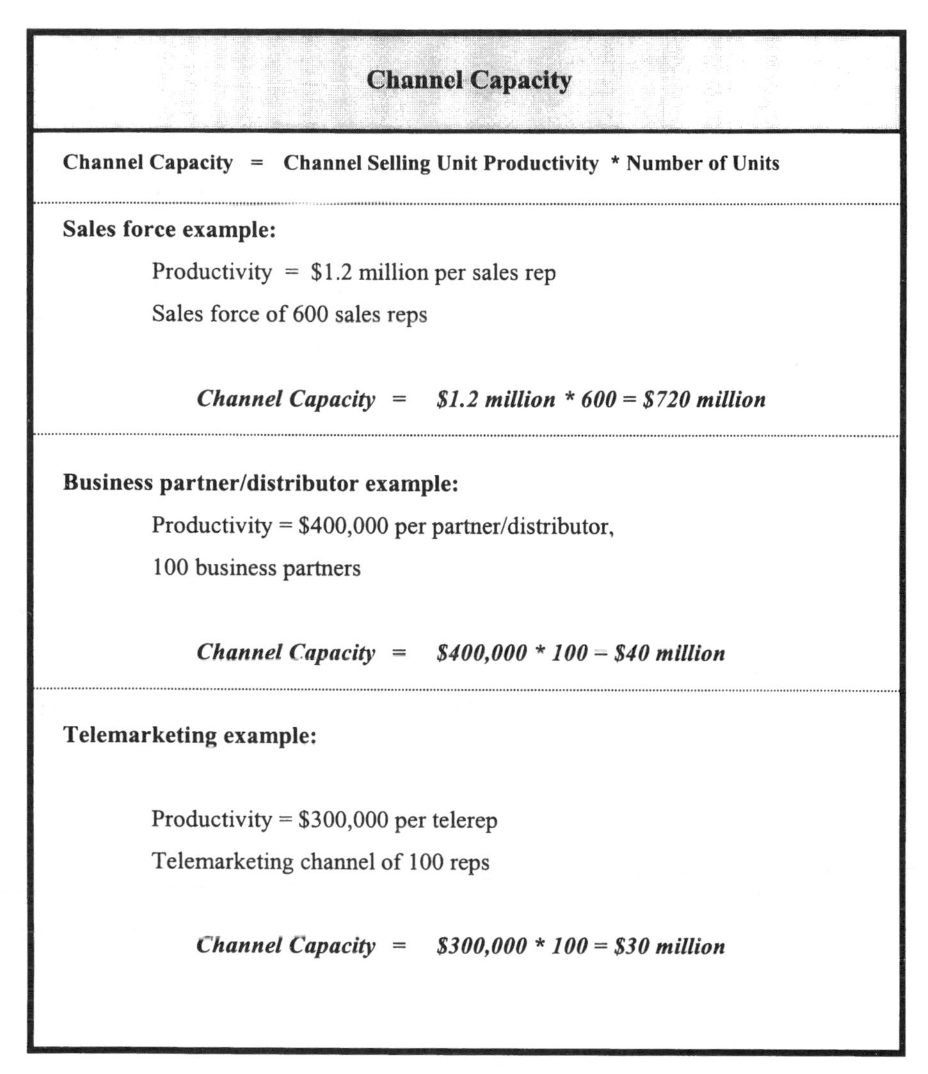

Figure 5.11 Channel capacity

new sales reps may require a long training and familiarization process before delivering historical sales averages. As a result, per-rep productivity will likely decline during a sales force expansion – sometimes significantly, depending on the complexity of the product.

- **Realistic estimates of channel size** Channel capacity is also a factor of the overall size of the channel: the number of field sales reps, business partners, telemarketing reps, etc. Particularly with indirect channels, companies tend to be far too optimistic in estimating the number of channel members that will actually participate in sales. A business partner network of 1000 partners may only yield fifty to 100 active partners and certainly far less than 1000. Even with direct channels, companies tend to overestimate channel size. A direct sales force of 500, for example, may only contain 300 actual deal-closing sales reps, after management, inside sales, sales support, administrative support, and technical support personnel are factored out. No matter which channel is being considered, an accurate assessment of channel capacity requires a realistic picture of how many channel members will actively be involved in generating revenue.

In sum, an assessment of channel capacity, based on sound assumptions about channel size and per-unit productivity, is crucial in the channel selection process. Channel capacity analysis can highlight whether a channel will realistically be able to support a revenue target. This analysis can also indicate whether or not channel cost assumptions are realistic for a specific target level of revenue production. Both are critical components of an effective economic comparison of channels.

Summary

Channel selection ultimately boils down to three factors:

- identifying channels that are well suited to customers' buying behaviors and needs
- ensuring that there is a good fit between those channels and a set of products and services
- determining which of those channels offer the most favourable economics

Although not a rigid sequence, there is some merit in making sure that a channel will be suitable for customers and products *before* investing a lot of time in evaluating its economic benefits. This simple idea can save some effort, as well as prevent disappointments when low-cost channels which are fundamentally unsuitable for a given product-market don't pan out.

Once it's clear which channels are worth the effort of economic analysis, channel evaluation is rooted in the concept of channel efficiency, expressed as channel E/R (expense-to-revenue). Channel E/R describes the percentage of sales revenue spent by a channel in performing a business transaction. Channel E/R can vary wildly across a range of channels, opening up both a risk of failing to identify the most profitable channel opportunities, as well as an opportunity to drive transactions into lower-cost channels and significantly improve selling profitability. The onus falls onto a management team to calculate E/R across different channels – not always an easy task – and to use this tool as a basis for making sound, profitable channel choices.

Importantly, while E/R may be the key metric of channel efficiency, the goal should not necessarily be the lowest-possible E/R. Channel expenses ultimately reflect the level and degree of services being provided to customers;

more services cost more money. It is often wise to think in terms of a threshold level of profitability, such as a company's existing overall *E/R*, and to seek out channels that can deliver transaction profitability at that level or better.

Channel *E/R* focuses on the cost side of the equation, which is important but not the whole story. It is also important to look at the growth side – a channel's capacity to deliver sales revenue. The role of channel capacity planning is to make sure that a channel under consideration can realistically do the volume of business desired in a market. If not, the channel may either require substantial new investments – leading to lower profitability – or may just not be the best channel choice. Channel capacity is rarely a show-stopper in the selection process, but on the other hand, it is almost always a good safeguard against the unbridled optimism for low-cost channels that can result from focusing too much on the cost side of the equation. A low-cost channel won't do much good if it can't handle the volume of business necessary to achieve sales and growth targets.

Channel economic analysis is the last piece of the puzzle in terms of evaluating individual channels against each other. Customer behavior will often point toward a group of acceptable channels, and product-channel fit analysis can help in narrowing down that group to a more manageable set of alternatives. It is only when channels are compared in terms of economic performance, however, that an optimal choice can be made. Economic analysis will, in fact, usually point in the direction of a channel or two that can best deliver high growth and profitability within the context of a particular product-market. Then the issue becomes how to build that channel, or those channels. That is the subject of the next four chapters.

Notes

[1] At this small order size, most transactions are not new sales; they are resupply orders or automatic repurchase transactions.

[2] The use of a mix of channels to balance channel profitability with sales volume is discussed more fully in Chapter 10, 'The art of channel mix and integration'.

[3] The name has been changed.

[4] Many technology companies fare far worse, with less than ten per cent of their partners generating any significant revenue.

[5] Based on a sample of seventeen of the fifty-two partners.

[6] In many companies, the field sales force is the channel with the most complete historical data that can be used in a capacity analysis.

Part Two

... And Building Them

Chapter 6

The 'leveraged' sales force

It may seem strange to include a chapter on the direct sales force in a book on channel strategy. In some peoples' minds, the sales force is the anti-channel – the last vestige of traditional 'pound the pavement' thinking in an exciting new world of Internet commerce, customer databases and technology-driven direct marketing channels.

The truth is that sales forces are alive and well. They perform a critical function in most organizations – a function that no other channel can perform as well or even adequately. A sales force is *still* the only channel that can sell complex products and solutions into large, key accounts with a high degree of control over the sales process. Not everyone makes those kinds of sales, but for companies that do, a sales force is an indispensable part of the channel mix.

While sales forces are just as important as they've always been, there is no question that they are undergoing fundamental change. Today's sales force is generally a smaller, more focused and more specialized organization than its 'do everything and be everything' forebears. Likewise, today's sales rep is more likely to have a targeted list of important, key accounts than a territory of hundreds or thousands of prospects. Further, many companies have developed new rules to constrain the activities of their sales reps, such as 'No selling in accounts under $200,000'. This is all a real departure from the traditional *do it all!* role of the field sales force.

The reason for this change is the increasing acceptance and use of alternative channels. In a multiple-channel system, sales reps are generally the most expensive types of selling resources. Other channels can almost always make sales at a lower cost, though they usually cannot handle the most complex deals for which a field sales rep is uniquely trained and qualified. This is why many companies are starting to limit the participation of their sales forces to the kinds of complex transactions that really do require the high-end capabilities of field reps, while sending other transactions into other channels. This approach gives the sales force *leverage*: it frees up the time and energy of sales

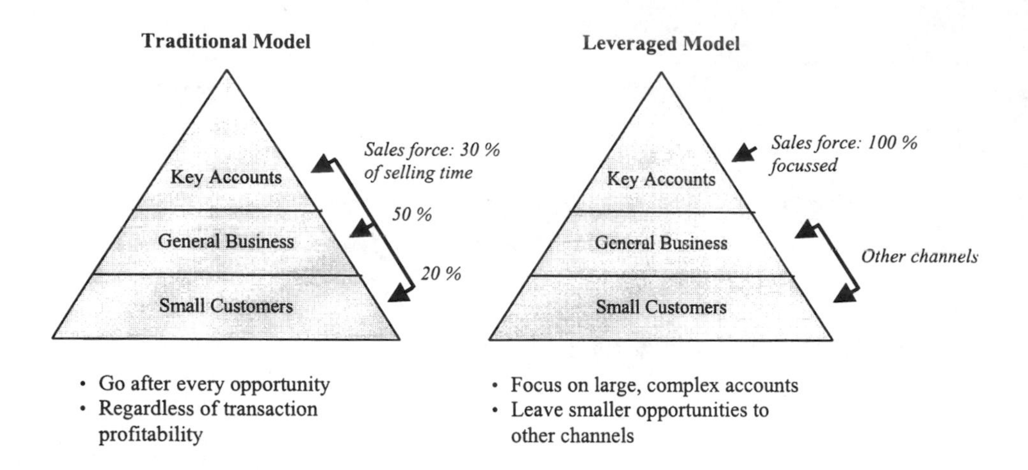

Figure 6.1 Traditional versus leveraged sales force model

reps to focus on the largest and most important market opportunities. The basic idea of sales force leverage is illustrated in Figure 6.1.

Companies with multiple channels invariably migrate toward leveraged sales force models. They have to! The alternative is to send the sales force out to compete against all other channels in every selling opportunity. That doesn't work – and it's a waste of valuable field sales resources. The better strategy is to use field reps where they really count. In many organizations, this has led to a new sales force 'look and feel,' as suggested in Figure 6.2.

Collectively, the items in Figure 6.2 suggest that a leveraged sales force – a sales force redesigned for optimal use in a multiple channel environment – is one that is oriented toward:

- Narrower participation in the market place
- Greater emphasis on acquiring and building key account relationships
- Integration with other channels to increase selling productivity

This chapter discusses how to migrate a sales force from its old role as 'owner' of all sales activity toward a new role as a specialized and high-impact participant in the sales process. The goal here is not to reinvent the wheel. Many, many books have been written about sales force design and management; the world can easily make do without another one. The focus is on reconfiguring an existing sales force to make it successful within the context of a multiple-channel system. We will look at five key principles for doing just that. To get started, the chapter begins with a closer look at where and when a sales force's participation makes sense within a broader go-to-market mix.

The Leveraged Sales Force: What It Looks Like	
❶ **Large Account Focus**	Increased emphasis on getting field reps out of small accounts and into the right selling opportunities.
❷ **Complex Product Focus**	Increased emphasis on transferring simpler products to other channels so the sales force can focus on selling complex, customized solutions.
❸ **Fewer Accounts**	Reduction in the number of accounts assigned to each rep, with higher expectations per account.
❹ **Effectiveness Focus**	More emphasis on making the right calls and winning the right deals, rather than just generating activity.
❺ **'Inside' Sales**	Increased use of 'inside sales' organizations to leverage the time and energy of outbound field reps.
❻ **Integration w/ Other Channels**	Increased focus on integrating field sales with other channels (e.g. call centres) throughout the sales process.
❼ **Enhanced SalesTraining**	More emphasis on giving field reps the specific skills they need to grow large, complex accounts.
❽ **Emphasis On Partnering**	More emphasis on building long-term, mutually beneficial relationships with key customers
❾ **New Compensation Systems**	Realignment of sales rep compensation plans to reward key account success and discourage low-end (small sale, simple product) selling.

Figure 6.2 The leveraged sales force – what it looks like

The 'sweet spot' of a field sales force

When a sales force coexists with other channels in a go-to-market system, the first and most important question is: When do you really need to use a sales rep? Put another way, what is the sales force's 'sweet spot' – that place in the market where it can make its biggest contribution and where its cost is most justified?

A sales force is not always required or even appropriate. For example, a company that sells simple products such as books or flowers may not need a sales force at all. These products, and lots of others like them, can be sold through alternative channels at a lower cost. Likewise, a company that sells only to small businesses and consumers may not need or want a sales force. Smaller, dispersed customers are usually hard to reach with a direct sales force, and can be served much more profitably with other channels.

Where sales reps *are* needed – and where they make sense economically – is in the sale of complex, customized solutions to large accounts. Complex solutions and large accounts require technical expertise, professional account management and a high degree of selling skill – exactly what a sales force is usually good at. Figure 6.3 illustrates how this typically influences the design of sales force coverage in a multiple-channel system.

As Figure 6.3 suggests, a sales force is generally best deployed against the most complex sales opportunities: highly customized solutions, large customers, and complex products. Conversely, in the broad middle market and small-customer market, where transactions are generally simpler, other channels can do a more cost-effective job – and can often reach more customers.

There are a couple of caveats, though. Two important issues should be taken into account when scaling back the participation of a sales force in the broader market:

- **Account control** Account control – and the loss of it that goes along with narrowing the role of the sales force – can be a serious issue. A computer systems client of ours, for example, discovered back in 1993 that almost half of the leads it had provided to its new distributor network had indeed resulted in sales – of competitors' equipment. The client, at the time, was struggling to build its brand and win market recognition. The company could ill-afford to give its best leads to partners, most of whom had strong loyalties to other, established manufacturers. Eventually – after the company's single largest customer defected to a competitor on a distributor's recommendation – the decision was made to bring sales back

Customers / Products	Supplies and peripherals	Standard product	Customized solutions
Key accounts	Indirect channels (Distributors/Business partners)	Indirect channels (Distributors/Business partners)	Field sales force
Mid-sized corporate	Indirect channels (Distributors/Business partners)	Indirect channels (Distributors/Business partners)	Field sales force
Small corporate/ individual	Direct marketing (eg internet, call centres)	Indirect channels (Distributors/Business partners)	(No sales)

Figure 6.3 Sales force coverage in a multiple-channel system

in-house. The sales force was resurrected and most distributors were sent packing. The moral of the story is that sometimes control over accounts is more important than expanded coverage through distributors. Managers must think carefully about which of these two goals – control or coverage – is more important in a particular business context, because these goals tend to pull against each other. Only a sales force can guarantee the highest level of control over the sales process.

- **Customers expectations** In some industries, customers demand a high level of personal attention and relationship-building as a precondition for doing business. There are examples across all sorts of industries: semiconductor fabrication equipment, strategy consulting services, auditing services, architectural design, and so on. Generally, when risk is perceived as high, and intense expertise is required in the sale, customers will want a vendor to provide a real, live representative of the company[1]. This is a huge caveat to the basic principle of off-loading simple sales onto alternative channels. Migration of sales toward lower-cost channels only works if customers are willing to accept it.

In sum, a sales force should generally be used where it will do the most good and where it will add the most value: in complex, large accounts. In other types of sales, alternative channels can often do the job just as, or more, effectively, and at a lower cost. Before making any changes to a sales force's coverage model, however, it's important to determine just how much control is needed or desired over the sales process. Even more importantly, customers must be given the channels they want to use. In some industries, a field rep is still the de-facto standard and the expectation of customers. It is worth confirming what customers want and expect before narrowing sales force participation to a smaller segment of the market place.

Five principles for building a leveraged sales force

Redirecting a sales force toward its sweet spot – complex, large accounts – is a smart approach in a multiple-channel system. It is not always an easy task, however. Most sales forces have in place long-standing systems and processes that reflect a bias toward broad, undifferentiated coverage of the market place. This bias can get in the way of an effort to increase leverage and productivity through a narrower focus on key accounts. For example:

- Traditional sales training programs teach reps to close accounts aggressively and fast, and often in a manipulative manner. This approach might make sense when a sales force's goal is to sell as much product as possible into as many accounts as possible. Key account selling is different, however. It requires superior problem-solving skills, a 'partnership' orientation to customers, and the ability to work collaboratively with other channels and other vendors over a long sales cycle. In emphasizing quick deal closure and aggressive – and sometimes manipulative – selling techniques, traditional training programs often teach field reps to do the opposite of what is required to build key account relationships.

- Traditional compensation systems tend to reward sales reps for short-term revenue production of any sort. This makes sense when the sales force is responsible for selling into any and all accounts. However, in encouraging field reps to go all over the map in search of revenue – and to pursue deals that can be closed quickly – these systems contradict efforts to concentrate sales force activity on a smaller set of long-term key account opportunities.
- Traditional sales processes tend to involve field reps in every step of the sales process, from lead generation all the way to post-sale support. As new channels are added, sales forces often continue to perform this 'do everything' role, fighting for share in every account and dominating every step in the sales process. As a result, many companies find their newer channels bumping up, and competing, against the field sales force throughout the selling process – leading to margin-reducing and brand-damaging channel conflict.

The list could go on and on. The point, though, is a simple one. To build a more effective and well-leveraged sales force, sales force processes, systems and skill development programs must be re-evaluated and in many cases redesigned. This section describes five well-tested principles for moving toward a more leveraged sales force, as shown in Figure 6.4.

1. Focus sales force activity on large account acquisition

The big issue in most sales forces today is that field reps spend too much time with existing customers and small transactions. The reason is that most reps find it easier to court small opportunities with familiar customers than to get out there and acquire major, new accounts. Unfortunately, small transactions in existing accounts represent a supreme waste of time for highly-skilled, highly-compensated sales reps. The first step in a sales force redesign should

1. Focus sales force activity on large account acquisition.
2. Use other channels to offload 'low value' selling tasks.
3. Provide more extensive technology support to field reps.
4. Redesign sales force skill development programs.
5. Align performance measurement and compensation with large account focus.

Figure 6.4 Five principles for building a leveraged sales force

Old Model: Spend majority of time in existing accounts.

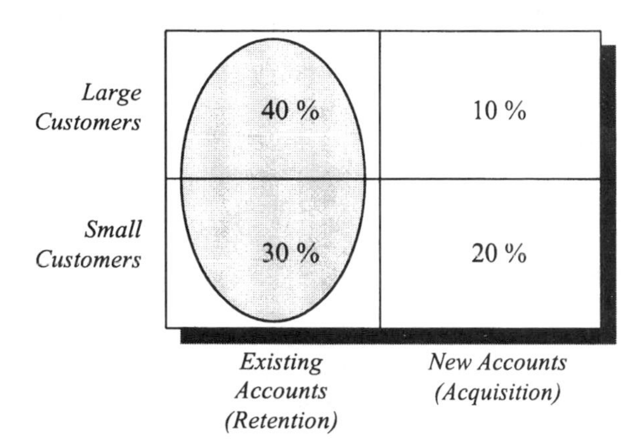

New Model: Focus on the acquisition of large, new customers

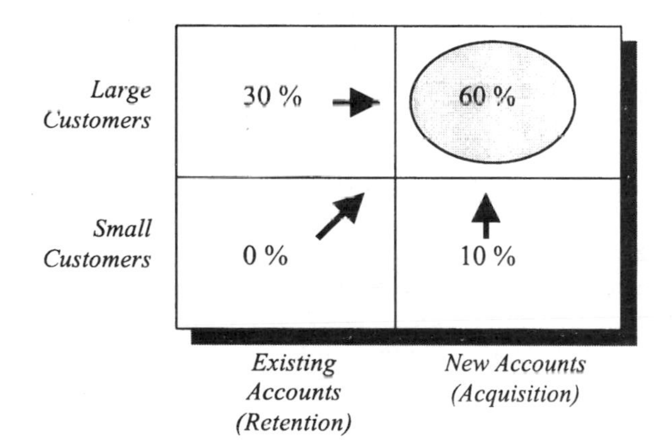

Figure 6.5 Shifting the account mix of the sales force

be to help the sales force get out of unprofitable, under-leveraged situations and into the right types of sales opportunities. Figure 6.5 illustrates the basic challenge here.

As Figure 6.5 suggests, most companies should be thinking in terms of getting their sales reps out of small transactions and focused on large account acquisition and penetration. So how do you do that? Four useful approaches are described below.

Redefine sales force 'territories'

The traditional sales force territory is geographically organized, and this is Problem Number One when trying to achieve a large account focus. The reason is simple. A typical geography (e.g. 'Western Europe') will consist of large customers and small customers, easy sales and complex sales, new high-growth accounts and old, slowly dying ones. By assigning a rep to a geographic territory, you're telling that rep to go after *everything* – all the good business, and all the bad business too. The fact is that there is often no particular reason – other than tradition – why the *location* of an account should be the dominant factor in its assignment to a sales rep. There are other factors, such as *account size, sale complexity* and *growth potential,* that are far more important in terms of sales force assignment.

Of course, geographical territories serve a purpose. A field rep stationed in Argentina cannot usually sell efficiently to customers in Moscow. Within reason, though, segmentation by accounts makes more sense than segmentation by geography. If you want reps to focus on $500 million plus opportunities, why not segment accounts into 'greater than $500 million' and 'less than $500 million' – and assign field reps only to the former?

Many companies, in fact, are beginning to discard the traditional 'go sell anything within this specific region' approach. They are pushing sales reps to sell only into certain types of accounts, sometimes across much more expansive physical territories. They've realized that close proximity of accounts is less important than whether the accounts are the right ones in the first place. Geographic territories are fine – and often necessary – but even within a territory, an account's location is a less useful basis for assignment to a sales rep than its size, complexity and potential value.

Define the 'right' opportunities with precision

To help sales reps focus on the right types of accounts, you have to define what those types of accounts look like! Many companies miss this seemingly obvious point. One client, for example, lamented to us that his reps were wasting their time selling peripheral equipment into slow-growth existing accounts; they needed, he explained, to apply their skills to the right types of opportunities. 'So what are the right types of opportunities?' we asked. His answer: 'You know, big sales. The big game'. Unfortunately, his four hundred reps had four hundred different interpretations of what 'big sales' meant.

In short, it's important to identify the criteria that constitute the 'right' accounts for sales force attention. Is the 'right account' defined by a certain customer size (e.g. in sales)? How about potential purchase volume? Or accounts with a certain type of business need? Whatever the criteria are, they should be made clear to the sales force. Two or three articulate criteria that bring precision to the notion of a 'big, important account' can do a lot more good than a general exhortation to target large, new customers.

Reduce the number of accounts per rep

Many companies are reducing the number of accounts in which their sales reps can participate, and it's an effective tool for increasing sales force leverage. Dell

Computer, for example, allows its field reps to 'own' only ten accounts for life[2]; all others accounts must be turned over to other channels. This encourages reps to think hard and carefully about whether they want to commit to a continued presence in an account after an initial sale to a new customer. The result is less emphasis on selling to existing customers, and more time spent finding new high-potential business.

Reduce/eliminate the sales force's role in fulfillment and post-sale support

If you *really* want to help a sales force pull out of existing accounts and focus on new customer acquisition, a powerful approach is to limit its role in post-sale fulfillment and customer support – either partially or completely. Nothing can get a sales force back onto the street and over to new customer sites faster than a rule prohibiting participation in accounts after a sale has been closed. However, this approach does raise a question: if the sales force isn't going to support customers after sales have been completed, who will? This is where other channels can play a powerful role, as described in the next section.

2. Use other channels to offload 'low value' selling tasks

In a multiple-channel system, sales force time should be spent primarily – or perhaps exclusively – on high-value selling tasks. These tasks include *account planning, customer negotiation* (face-to-face selling) and *sale closure*. These are high-value tasks because they result directly in closed sales and require the highest levels of skill. Other selling tasks are important, but generally have a less direct relationship to actual revenue production. These include lead generation and qualification, proposal writing, fulfillment, and post-sale support. These all take up an inordinate amount of sales rep time – often over fifty per cent of total sales rep working hours[3]. Getting some or all of these tasks off the plate of the sales force – by giving them to other channels – is a key source of leverage and improvement in sales force productivity.

Lead generation and qualification

Most field reps spend a large amount of their time prospecting for sales leads. They have no choice; prospecting is where new business comes from. The problem is that prospecting is a consuming activity. It eats into the time which a sales rep could be spending with major account customers – exploring their needs, developing solutions and closing deals. Finding and qualifying leads is something that can often be performed just as well, and much less expensively, by an alternative channel such as a telemarketing group.

Two issues tend to limit the success of companies who give lead-generation responsibility to another channel. First, this approach only works if the lead-generating channel comes up with good opportunities for the sales force. Alternative channels are usually better at generating leads for small transactions and small customers than they are at generating leads for high-end business opportunities. It's important to assess whether the people in a telemarketing centre or other lead-generating channel have the skills and business acumen to call into large accounts, uncover opportunities, and make contact with senior buyers. If not, it may be necessary to upgrade the level of personnel as well as the types of training they receive. An alternative channel's ability to generate good major account leads should always be tested in a controlled, small market segment before taking this task out of the hands of the sales force.

Second, and perhaps more importantly, a lead-generating channel must deliver *well-qualified* leads to the sales force. Poorly qualified leads waste the time of sales reps and discourage them from following up on future ones. As a result, important potential business begins to falls through the cracks. Thus, it's crucial to define exactly what a 'well-qualified' lead really is. Is it a buyer with a certain level of budget, a specific business need, and a firm date for making a purchase – or is it something else? Whatever the exact criteria are for judging a lead as 'qualified', they should be articulated clearly, and managers should ensure that *all* leads given to the sales force meet these criteria.

Proposal writing/pre-sale preparation

Another task that can often be offloaded from the field sales force is proposal writing and preparation. In some sales forces, reps spend upwards of fifteen to thirty per cent of their time preparing documentation, writing proposals, and fussing with pre-sale paperwork, all of which is a huge distraction from the core business of meeting with customers and selling. Imagine what a sales force with fifteen to thirty per cent more *selling* time could achieve in terms of new sales! Pre-sales documentation, proposals and paperwork should be transferred to another channel or pre-sale processing team whenever possible[4]. This is a substantial source of leverage for just about any sales force.

Fulfillment

A company seeking to focus its sales force on major account acquisition *must* take a look at the amount of time its reps spend in post-sale fulfillment. In complex sales, it isn't unusual for field reps to spend over twenty to twenty-five per cent of their time processing orders, overseeing delivery, managing installations, and providing hands-on training. In many cases, these tasks can be performed by less expensive fulfillment resources, such as customer satisfaction teams, installation groups, and training personnel. The transfer of these tasks to a lower-cost fulfillment channel can yield a substantial increase in selling profitability and improved sales rep productivity.

Post-sale support

Ongoing customer support is the real quagmire for most sales forces. In some companies, sales reps spend over *half* of their time following up on completed sales and solving routine problems. Indeed, this is what many sales reps like to do with their time and believe they have been hired to do. Of course, mingling with customers and protecting existing accounts is a big part of the sales functions; the key is to determine how much time reps are actually *selling* in existing accounts versus *supporting existing sales*. There are other channels that can handle basic problem resolution and ongoing post-sale support at a fraction of the cost. For instance, a telecentre can usually handle a post-sale support inquiry at a cost of fifty to ninety per cent less than a field rep. Here again, the offloading of a basic sales process task to another channel can free up substantial field rep selling time.

In sum, many companies task their sales forces with too many different things, leaving their field reps with very little time to sell. Getting sales reps out of non-value-added tasks can have a dramatic impact on field rep productivity.

3. Provide more extensive technology support to field reps

Technology support is a key source of sales productivity enhancement, and one that is becoming increasingly important. A few sales forces have taken advantage of the tremendous potential of new technologies to improve productivity, but most still rely on some combination of back-of-the-napkin account planning, rolodex-like software programs, and the occasional newspaper clipping service. Collectively, these traditional tools represent a completely inadequate response to the technology challenge. As a result, most sales organizations need to invest substantially in a technology upgrade. Figure 6.6 suggests a few key principles for rethinking the role of technology in a sales force.

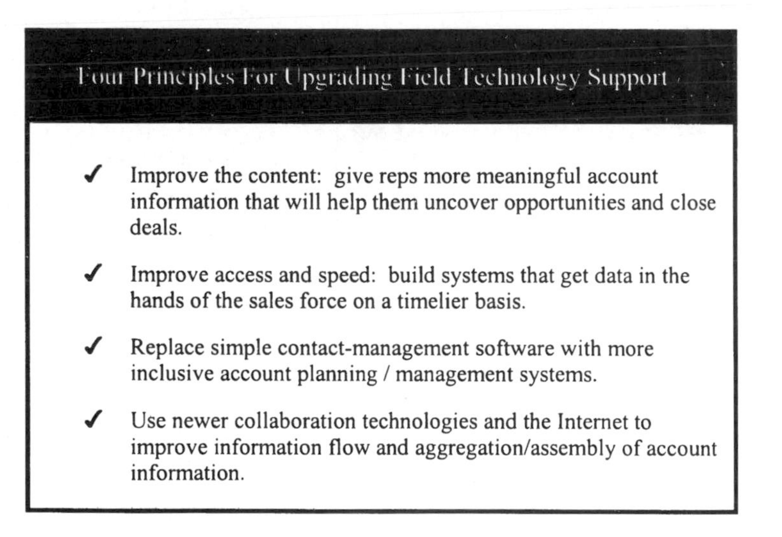

Figure 6.6 Supporting the sales force with technology

Technology design and implementation, of course, is a complex, expensive matter. A complete discussion of technology support is well beyond the scope of this book. This section provides just a brief look at two main initiatives that managers should consider when evaluating the kinds of technological support to provide to a sales force.

Improve the content

In general, the account information provided to – and collected from – sales reps tends to consist of low-value contact and transaction data, such as: How many calls? What is the customer's address and telephone number? What is their payment history? When was the last call made? All of this information is important, but it's only a starting point.

To get *big* gains in productivity, sales reps must be provided with a different kind of data that will contribute directly to new business development. Figure 6.7 provides an overview of this type of data.

It is easy to see how enhanced business development data, as suggested in Figure 6.7, can make a big difference. Imagine a sales rep armed with up-to-the-minute breaking news in his ten largest accounts. Now add to that a just-released report on key trends in his customers' industries, a weekly report on

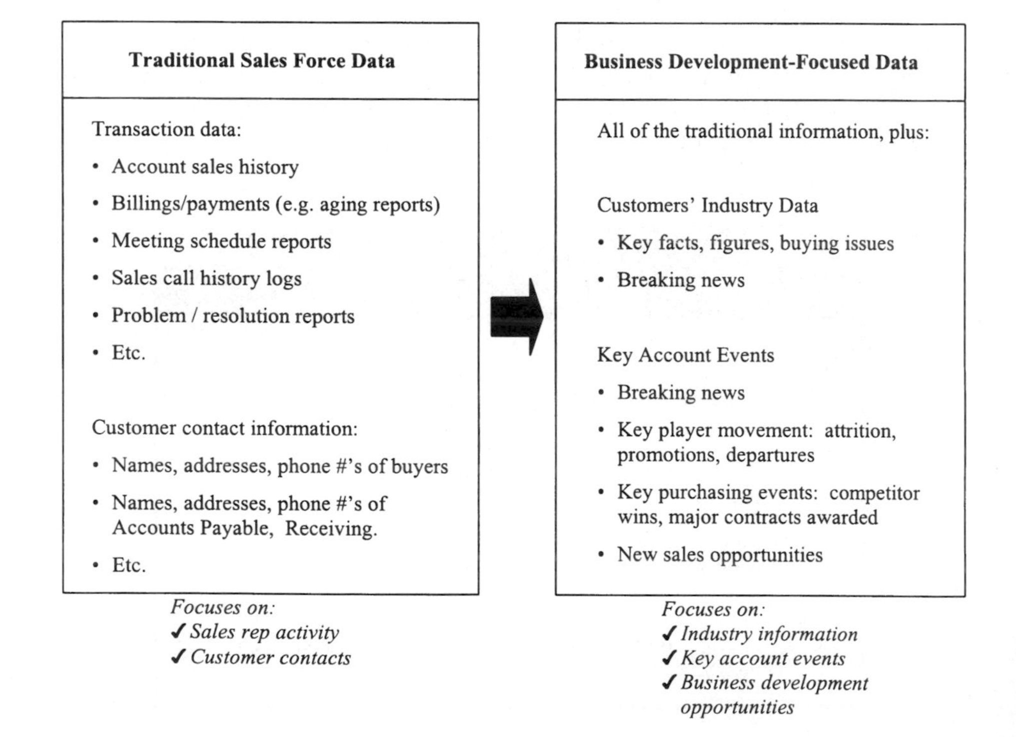

Figure 6.7 Enhancing the *content* of sales force information

the movement of personnel into and out of key accounts, and a monthly report on major contract awards in key accounts. Though this level of information may sound impossible to acquire, most of it is readily available through a variety of traditional media as well as newer online subscription services. It is well worth the effort to look into the extent and quality of data that can be gathered by the various corporate research/intelligence firms who provide this information.

Improve delivery of the content

For all the talk about the Internet and other communication technologies, few sales forces are actually taking advantage of their potential. Many still do not even have computers; those that do tend to use them for simple tasks like creating form letters, sending e-mail, and managing appointments. These kinds of activities do not even begin to tap into the ability of new technologies to aggregate and deliver information. When a sales force really gets down to the business of exploiting new technologies, the results speak for themselves. Take this example, from the Vice President Sales at a plastic components manufacturer in New York[5]:

> This year, we bought laptop computers for every SE [sales executive] and invested in a new sales force automation package. Each time an SE wins a new account, this information is relayed back to CIS [the corporate information system] through e-mail. The system immediately pulls down customer data from Hoover's and several other online information services, and then integrates all of it into a comprehensive report for the sales rep. This report details the customer's industry, history, business operation, executive team, and anything else the system can find in the news. SEs usually receive this report within two days of starting a new customer relationship.
>
> Going forward, the SE receives an e-mail automatically, any time an event takes place in the customer's organization, whether that event concerns people, contract awards, earnings results, or something else that appears in the various services we subscribe to. All of this information is kept together in files, along with the SE's call logs and contact information. Sales managers can review these files and monitor SE account progress, not just in terms of sales activity but also in terms of overall progress against the total business opportunity in major accounts.

Though this client was exceptionally ambitious on the technology front, many other companies can likewise benefit by using new communication technologies, such as the Internet, to collect, aggregate and deliver value-added selling information to sales reps in the field.

In sum, it's important to take a fresh look at the technology support systems that can help make a sales force more effective and successful. A technology review should look at the kinds of information sales reps receive, as well as they ways in which that information can be aggregated and delivered to the field. These are both significant sources of enhanced sales rep productivity.

3. Redesign sales force training programs

In most companies, sales force training programs are outdated. Often, these programs are hopelessly out of sync with the requirements of large, complex account selling. And in very few companies does sales training even *begin* to account for the unique skill and knowledge requirements of selling alongside (and with) alternative channels.

The current state of sales training is not encouraging. In many organizations, training manuals with vaguely manipulative titles such as 'Sure-Fire Closing Techniques' exist alongside new programs with bizarre titles like 'The Strategic Customer-Focused Value Selling Process'. Each year, more programs are rolled out by managers in search of 'the next big thing'. And each year, field reps sit through these programs, shaking their heads and trying to figure out how this year's Concept Du Jour might relate, if at all, to their actual jobs. As Gene McCluskey of Oracle Corporation put it, 'Executives just do not want to think about this issue. There are too many other things going on now in terms of market expansion and channel conflict. Basically, they figure that good reps will be able to sell, and that the bad ones will eventually leave.'[6]

The bottom line is that companies need to revisit the whole issue of sales force skills development in light of the shift toward multiple-channel systems. The reason is straightforward and compelling. As alternative channels take over the simpler transactions, what is left for the sales force? Answer: complex sales opportunities with demanding customers in the most important accounts. These high-end customers are notorious in their distaste for tricky closing techniques and sales scripts. They expect to be serviced by professionals with a deep knowledge of their businesses and industries, and they demand an exceptionally high level of sales rep integrity and professionalism. At the same time, sales reps also face a new burden: the navigation of accounts alongside other, alternative channels. Reps have to know how and when other channels should be included, excluded, managed and integrated in the completion and support of a sale. Put simply, in many organizations the complexity and difficulty of the sales rep's job has increased exponentially, and training needs to reflect this fact.

This section describes a process for getting started on the path toward upgraded and up-to-date sales training. The process is shown in Figure 6.8.

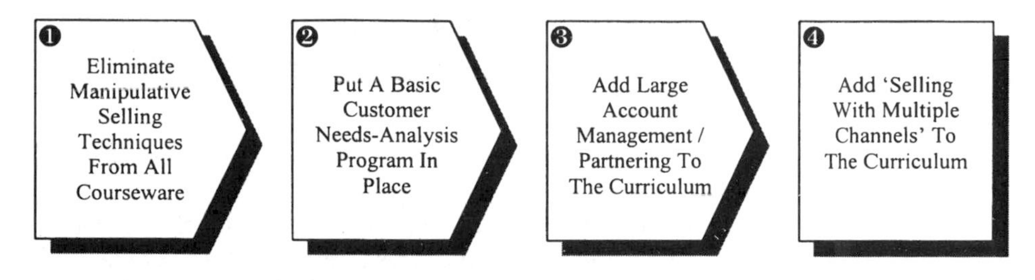

Figure 6.8 Getting serious about sales training – a simple process

Eliminate manipulative selling techniques from all courseware

Customers in key accounts expect to be treated professionally and honestly. So first and foremost, all training programs should be reviewed with an eye toward making them 'key account ready'. Pushy sales scripts should be eliminated or, at a minimum, toned down. Quick-close techniques should be re-evaluated in light of the longer sales cycles that are typical of large account selling. Closing techniques should be redesigned away from the 'what would I have to do to get your business today?' approach toward something more win–win and collaborative in nature. Sales manipulation isn't always easy to define, but you know it when you see it, and so do customers. It has no valid role in high-end key account development, and it should be exorcised from a sales training curriculum.

Put a basic needs-analysis program in place

The single largest responsibility of a sales rep in a key account is the exploration, development and articulation of customers' needs. It is what field reps get paid to do, and it is the skill that customers most value. A needs-analysis training program should, at a minimum, help field reps to:

- Ask questions to explore, define and extend customers' needs
- Practice the application of questioning techniques to specific customer business problems
- Try out this 'interrogative' process as a foundation for identifying solutions to customers' problems

In recent years, interrogative (questioning) skills programs have come under pressure. New vendors have attempted to build markets for themselves by replacing these programs with catchy-sounding seminars on various five-step processes and value-added this-and-that programs. Much of this new coursework is a waste of time. The bottom line is that sales reps must be able to explore, understand and develop customers' needs to sell effectively in key accounts. A well-organized program that can help them do that can be of great value to a sales force.

Add large account management/partnering to the curriculum

Sales into complex, large accounts require a wider range of skills and knowledge than sales into simpler accounts. Account navigation can be more time consuming and confusing, decision makers can be harder to find, and customers' expectations for 'partner'-oriented vendors can come into conflict with sales reps' instincts to close deals quickly. As a result, it is wise to think in terms of adding curriculum content that introduces field reps to the subtle challenges of large account management and customer partnering – both of which often go together in a complex sale. At a minimum, the curriculum should include the following topics:

- Gaining access to, and penetrating, complex accounts
- Finding the right buyers, and navigating to decision makers
- Mapping sales activities and expectations to the customer's buying cycle
- Building alternative solutions to satisfy multiple buyers/business units
- Working with customers as 'partners'
- Managing post-sale fulfillment and support resources
- Balancing post-sale account maintenance with account development goals

Add 'selling with multiple channels' to the curriculum

In a recent survey of fifteen companies with multiple channels, the following number were providing training for their field reps on how to use, work with, and manage alternative channels in their accounts: two[7]. That should sound an alarm, because rarely does a sales force work independently of other sales channels. Alternative channels are often responsible for creating leads, managing fulfillment, providing training, handling post-sale support, or perform other critical selling tasks. In each of these cases, they interact with field reps in the sale and with customers. Yet sales reps are generally left to their own devices to determine how and when to make the best use of these channels in the selling process. This is a recipe for disaster, and it shouldn't be allowed to happen. If you use multiple channels in the sales process, you *must* have some curriculum content to instruct reps how to use and manage those channels before, during, and after the sale. A sample curriculum for a 'selling with multiple channels' program is shown in Figure 6.9.

In sum, sales force training is an essential part of the retooling process to get a sales force ready for a world of focused selling in key accounts alongside other channels. This is an important source of sales force leverage and productivity, and one that deserves more sustained attention than it typically receives.

5. Align performance measurement and compensation with large account focus

As in any organizational initiative – but particularly with field sales forces –

Day One	Day Two
• Business/economic case for multiple channels • Overview: ♦ Corporate market coverage model ♦ Role of the field rep in the sales process ♦ Role of other channels in the sales process • Pre-sale use and integration of other channels: ♦ Lead development/qualification ♦ Proposal development / other pre-sale activities • Post-sale use and integration of other channels: ♦ Role of the sales rep, other channels in fulfillment ♦ Role of the sales rep, other channels in post-sale support • How to build a multiple-channel account plan • Case studies: ambiguous selling situations	• Dealing with channel coordination -- and chaos ♦ Channel hand-offs within accounts ♦ Dealing with distributors in accounts ♦ How to handle channel conflict ♦ Managing customer 'channel queaziness' • Dealing with the gray areas ♦ Which channel management options are within the discretion of the field rep -- and which aren't ♦ When to call in other channels -- and when not to • Who 'owns' the account in a multiple-channel sale? ♦ What is the account owner responsible for doing? ♦ How should in-account problems be resolved? • Case studies: successful multiple-channel sales ♦ What made them successful? ♦ What was the role of the field rep in making them work? ♦ Lessons learned for effective multiple-channel selling

Figure 6.9 'Selling with multiple channels' seminar – core curriculum

performance measurement and compensation are powerful tools for aligning behavior with corporate objectives. Three behaviors in particular should be emphasized:

- Aggressive pursuit of new, large accounts – and avoidance of small, unprofitable transactions
- Effective, professional 'high end' selling in key accounts
- Self-managed avoidance of unnecessary conflict with other channels

Each is discussed below.

Aggressive pursuit of new, large accounts – and avoidance of small, unprofitable transactions

This is the key behavior that must be encouraged and rewarded. The most effective way to encourage it is very straightforward and intuitive. Reward sales reps for bringing in the big deals, don't reward them for the small ones, and – to add one little increment of subtlety – make it worth their while to hand smaller opportunities and transactions over to other channels. This approach is simple, and it works.

Hewlett-Packard provides a good example. In 1995, its enterprise field sales force was spending fifty per cent of its time in 'strategic opportunities' and the other fifty per cent in small transactions, customer service, and a variety of account maintenance activities. That is not a disastrous or even unusual allocation of field rep time, but it is hardly optimal for a company seeking aggressive penetration of large, strategic accounts. As a result, HP rolled out a new selling model called the Field Collaboration Program (FCP). In the FCP, most transactions under $300,000 are handed directly over to Certified Solution Institute (CSI) reseller partners, who team with HP to close sales and then take primary or sole responsibility for product installation and support.

Here's the interesting part. In the FCP, an HP rep receives a commission on sales made through the company's CSI partners; in addition, the rep gets to count part of the reseller's sales toward his or her own sales quota. On the other hand, HP reps who choose to close a sale under $300,000 receive *nothing*: no commission, and no credit toward sales quota.

The FCP is a classic example of the use of reward systems to encourage large account selling – and to discourage participation in smaller transactions that can be served better by other channels. The net result of this program is as follows. Between 1995 and 1997, field rep time spent in strategic sales opportunities increased from fifty per cent to eighty-five per cent, while time spent in account maintenance and small transactions decreased from fifty per cent to fifteen per cent. That's a thirty-five per cent shift in sales rep time away from smaller transactions and toward large business opportunities (over $300,000).

The important point here is that field reps do what they get paid to do. Pay them to bring in large deals and offload smaller transactions to other channels, and that's exactly what they will do. As in HP's case, this can be accomplished by establishing a transaction size 'floor' – a deal size below which field reps will be compensated less, or perhaps not at all. This is the easiest and most effective way to encourage field reps to focus on the right types of sales opportunities.

Effective, professional selling in key accounts

As noted earlier, large account selling requires a different set of behaviors and skills than transactional, small account selling. In small transaction selling, the emphasis is on *activity* with lots of sales calls per week and lots of deals closed quickly. In large account selling, the emphasis is on the effective longer-term strategic penetration of key accounts and the acquisition of new large customers. This shift in emphasis requires new performance measures to encourage the right sales force behaviors. A short-list of performance metrics, each of which says something useful and important about sales effectiveness in key accounts, is shown in Figure 6.10.

Although the figure suggests seven different measures of performance, it usually makes sense to choose three or four selectively, based on unique circumstances. For instance, a company seeking a massive increase in new account acquisition might want to focus exclusively on the new business ratio. Alternatively, a company that's more interested in improving effectiveness in large account sales calls might focus on the number of face hours

Metric	What It Is / Why It's Useful
✓ Average revenue per account	An excellent overall indicator of the extent to which a sales rep is focusing on large, strategic accounts.
✓ Average transaction size	Always a useful metric, it suggests the kinds of transactions in which field reps are participating (i.e. large vs. small transactions).
✓ Key account revenue growth	Year-over-year sales growth within an account. An important indicator of long-term account penetration and success in selling effectively to large customers.
✓ Key account share-of-wallet	Percentage of total account spending going to you. A useful indicator of effectiveness in establishing a dominant competitive position in key accounts.
✓ New business ratio	Sales to new customers divided by sales to existing customers. A good measure of the the extent to which a sales force – or sales rep – is focused on new account acquisition.
✓ # of face hours	Total time spent in face-to-face sales calls (e.g. hours per month). An excellent barometer of how well sales reps are focusing on high-value-added selling activities.
✓ $$$ per face hour	Revenue generated per face-to-face selling hour. A fundamental and important measure of sales effectiveness.

Figure 6.10 Measuring key account sales effectiveness – a short list of key performance metrics

and the revenue generated per face hour. Most organizations measure and monitor their field reps along too many different dimensions; the selective choosing of a few key metrics can bring focus and clarity to a field sales force's efforts.

Self-managed avoidance of unnecessary conflict with other channels

Conflict between a field sales force and other channels is inevitable in a multiple-channel system; it cannot be prevented or entirely eliminated. The only question is whether the conflict will be managed *reactively* from corporate headquarters – after it has become a problem – or avoided *proactively* by field reps themselves. The goal should be to push most of the responsibility for channel conflict down to a local, field rep level, where it can be an issue of avoidance rather than one of post-conflict management.

The simplest way to encourage field reps to avoid channel conflict is to restructure the assignment of revenue credit. At issue here is the following: who gets the credit (and thus the commission) for a sale? If channels are competing for revenue credit, it can only be expected that each channel will struggle vigorously to 'own' every possible account and take credit for as many sales as possible. The behavior that comes out of this inter-channel competition is, predictably, a refusal to involve other channels in the sales process. The behavior you *want*, on the other hand, is *channel cooperation* – within accounts and across sales opportunities. Revenue credit redesign is an effective way to get this type of cooperation.

Here's a simple example. Let's say a company sells $5,000 photocopiers as well as $500,000 office automation solutions. Its sales force spends fifty per cent of its time selling photocopiers, which can be sold more efficiently and in higher volume by the company's distributors. The goal, therefore, is to get the sales force out of small photocopier transactions and into more $500,000 opportunities. The problem is that there is only one sales commission to be made – $100 – by either a field rep or a distributor when a photocopier is sold. Field reps, obviously, will want to capture and get credit for as much sales volume as they can, leading them to spend most of their time chasing easy photocopier transactions. What's the solution?

One good solution is to reward *both* channels when a distributor sells a photocopier. Give the sales rep some or all of the $100 – and give the distributor most or all of the $100 too. Then increase the quota of the field sales force – which is fair, because now sales reps have distributors to help them close more deals. In this manner, the sales rep earns a commission – and perhaps the exact same commission – no matter which channel completes the transaction. This is called 'dual revenue credit', and it's a powerful tool for minimizing channel conflict. It encourages sales reps not to compete with other channels, and in fact, it encourages them to leverage other channels wherever possible so they can get onto the business of making bigger sales to meet their new, higher sales goals. This is, in fact, what Hewlett-Packard did (see above), in that it pays its reps for sales made through its reseller partners.

Dual revenue credit, in most circumstances, is a smarter way to pay channels than a system in which channels compete for the same commissions. It always improves a sales force's willingness to work with other channels, and thus helps in the avoidance of inter-channel conflict on a local level. This is not an area for uninformed experimentation, however. If you dual-pay channels, sales volume has to go up substantially for the system to work; otherwise you end up with higher transaction costs and lower profits. In this area, it is best to seek expert advice or, at a minimum, to take a careful look at how leading competitors compensate their channels.

Summary

Multiple-channel systems offer companies the chance to free up the time of their sales reps to concentrate on the best and most important accounts and selling opportunities. The challenge is to get sales reps out of small, unprofitable transactions, which can be served more efficiently and effectively by other channels, and to focus their time and energy on large accounts and big, profitable deals. When done right, it's a powerful approach that gives a sales force *leverage* and increases its selling productivity. However, there's a price to pay to get these kinds of benefits. To achieve leverage and enhanced productivity, most sales forces require substantial rethinking in terms of systems, processes, and training programs.

The chapter began by looking at one element of this rethinking: the building of a new coverage model that more narrowly defines the participation of the sales force in the market place. In a nutshell, the idea is to define a market segment of large, key accounts that are buying complex products and customized solutions. These are the opportunities that really do require the participation of a sales rep. Most other opportunities can be offloaded to other, lower-cost channels.

The chapter then looked at five techniques for helping a sales force to transition toward a focus on large, complex customers and new account acquisition:

- **Focus sales force activity on large account acquisition** The most essential issue is to take concrete steps to help the sales force identify and focus on the most important and complex selling opportunities.
- **Use other channels to offload 'low value' selling tasks** Here, low-value-added selling tasks are offloaded to alternative channels – to free up sales rep time. This is the key source of sales force leverage in a multiple-channel system. (It is discussed in greater depth in Chapter 10).
- **Provide more extensive technology support** There is no mistaking the role of technology in helping sales reps to be more effective in large accounts. Most companies need to take a close look at how well and how extensively they are taking advantage of sales force support technologies.
- **Redesign sales force training programs** In many companies, sales training is in a state of disarray or, at a minimum, is just unsuited to the demands of key account selling. A thorough re-evaluation of skills development programs should go along with any initiative to refocus the sales force on large account acquisition and penetration.
- **Align performance measurement and compensation with large account focus** Performance measurement and compensation each play a critical role in realigning sales force behavior toward a new objective of key account development. In particular, compensation systems should be redesigned to reward reps for focusing on larger accounts, selling more effectively into those accounts, and working cooperatively with other channels.

In any sales force redesign initiative, it is crucial to keep in mind a central fact about sales forces: they consist of *people*. We have seen numerous companies get carried away in the redesign of compensation systems, the reconfiguration of sales territories, the inclusion of new channels in the sales force's traditional turf, and so on – all without a sufficient communication to the field as to what was happening and why. The simple truth is that well-intentioned corporate initiatives fail when people don't support them in the field. As a result, sales force redesign should never consist of an endless and haphazard series of ongoing, chaotic experiments. It is extremely important to execute a sales force redesign in an orderly manner, and to get the buy-in of a sales force before, during, and after, a process or system redesign. A strong and committed sales force is a company's most important asset and should always be treated as such – especially when big changes are taking place.

Notes

[1] In some cases, distributor partners can play this role in local markets, and are more trusted and accepted than a manufacturer's own sales reps.
[2] 'Life' meaning for the duration of their employment with Dell.
[3] *Source*: Oxford Associates, aggregated from a variety of industry sales force productivity studies.
[4] Of course, it is not always possible. In some types of complex sales, proposal writing *is* the key selling activity.
[5] The client has requested not to be named.
[6] Interview with the authors, 20 July 1998.
[7] Conducted by the authors.

Chapter 7

Business partner (indirect) channels

A business partner might be a giant multinational company with three thousand sales reps on the payroll, or a housewife who's signed up to sell an asparagus steamer to her friends and neighbours. Partners come in many shapes and sizes, with labels such as manufacturer's agents, brokers, wholesalers, retailers, distributors, aggregators, resellers, value-added dealers and so on[1]. They are the *intermediaries* that sell, support, or sometimes even build a manufacturer's products for its customers, in return for a commission or other form of payment. A few examples, showing the diversity of this type of channel arrangement, include the following:

- **Snap-On Incorporated**, the $1.7 billion manufacturer of power and hand tools[2], uses an independent distributor model. The company's 4000+ distributors drive around in specially-equipped vans that have elaborate equipment displays as well as computer systems for running the mobile business. These 'showrooms on wheels' are driven right up to the doors of the customer base: professional technicians, automotive repair shops and industrial buyers.
- **Lotus Development Corporation** has over 19,000 partners worldwide who develop applications, provide training, and do other types of computer consulting work to support its software products. In addition to providing marketing support to its partners, Lotus actively facilitates alliances *between* its partners so they can go to market in teams to win complex projects. In fact, fully twenty per cent of its partners' revenues comes from deal making between the partners themselves[3].
- **Avon** takes the idea of a mass distribution channel to a higher level. This $4.8 billion manufacturer of cosmetics, fragrances, and toiletries has *two million* independent sales reps in 131 countries selling its wide range of products[4].
- Not every partner channel consists of thousands of distributors working at arm's length from the manufacturer. It can be just the opposite. **Caterpillar**, the $19

billion manufacturer of engines, agricultural equipment and other machines, relies on a network of just 197 dealers. These are big players – their average revenue exceeds $100 million – and their relationship with Caterpillar gives substance to the abused word 'partner.' The average dealer has been on board with Caterpillar for over fifty years[5].

From just this small set of examples, it may appear that companies who go 'indirect' – who do business through intermediaries – have little in common with each other. However, leading companies tend to use similar design principles when building a partner channel, and many are moving in the same direction in terms of overall channel trends. Some of the more dominant trends are shown in Figure 7.1.

This chapter looks at these trends, but more importantly, it looks at them in the context of seven core principles of sound partner channel design. It begins, though, with a brief look at when – and when not – to use business partners.

When to use business partners – and when not to

Almost all business partner channels have the same purpose: to help a company penetrate more deeply into dispersed markets and reach more customers – thereby growing revenues and market share. This basis purpose is shown in Figure 7.2.

❶ **Quality Vs. Quantity**	In many industries, more emphasis on getting better performance from a smaller, more productive group of partners.
❷ **Performance Management**	Increased emphasis on channel performance measurement, monitoring and management.
❸ **Go-To-Market Integration**	Increased attention on the integration of partners with other channels in the sales process.
❹ **Technology Support**	Increased use of technology – particularly the Internet – to support partners in the field.
❺ **Market Targeting**	Decreased use of partners in simple, off-the-rack sales: migration of low-end market segments to direct marketing channels.
❻ **Channel Feedback**	Increased use of formal, structured mechanisms for getting market information back from the channel.

Figure 7.1 Trends in indirect (partner) channel design

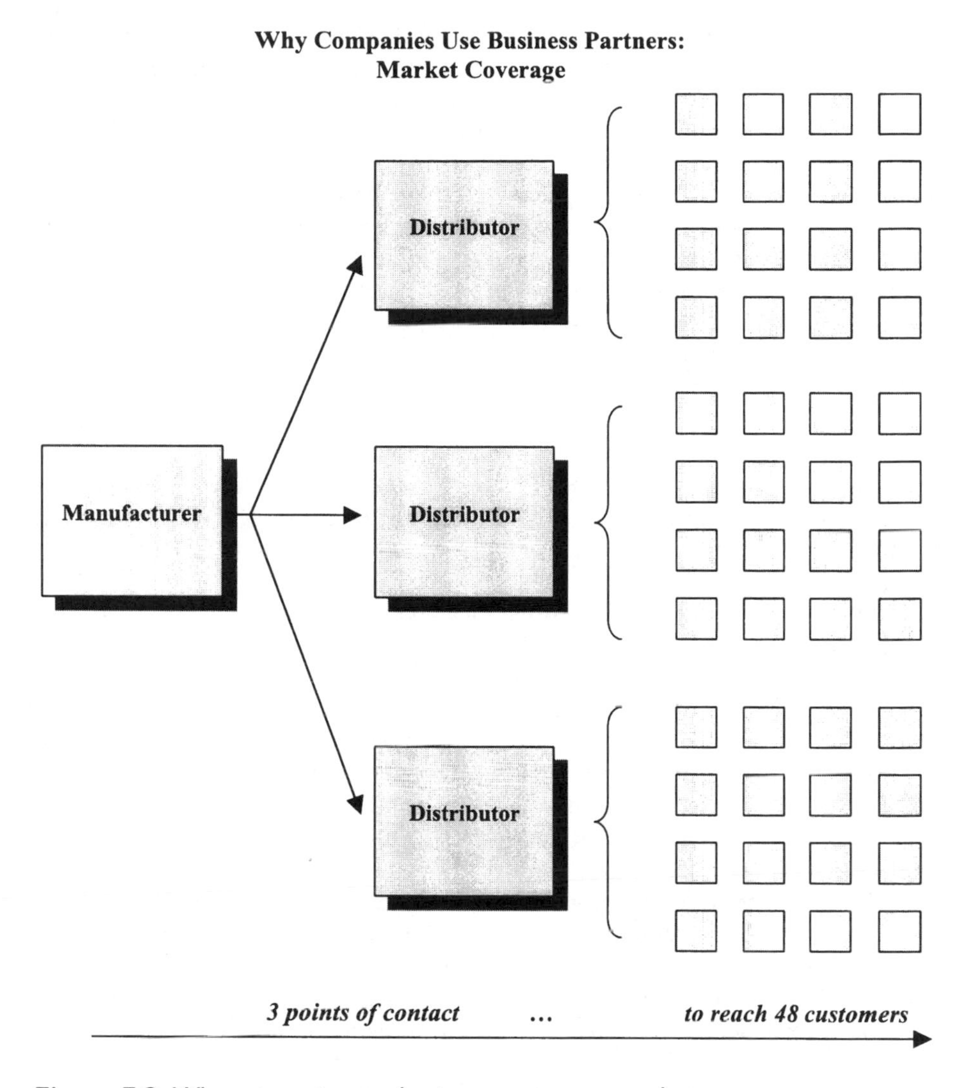

Figure 7.2 Why companies use business partners – market coverage

As Figure 7.2 suggests, partners' special contribution is their ability to increase sales and market share by accessing a broad customer base. Companies that are market share-driven – that measure success primarily or solely in terms of customer and revenue growth – are therefore prime candidates for business partner channels. Other factors that influence the decision to build a partner channel include the following:

- **Selling costs** Partners usually cost somewhere between fifteen and forty per cent less to maintain than a field sales force[6]. Yet, while requiring less investment, they are often still able to provide a level of personal selling and customer relationship management similar to that of a sales rep. They are thus a good solution when the goal is to reduce selling costs – particularly when other lower-cost channels, such as call centres or the Internet, are deemed too impersonal or too limited for the types of transactions involved.

- **Local support** Imagine if every Sony television set had to be serviced by a Sony technician at a Sony service centre, in every corner of the world in which television sets are sold. It would never work. Its business partners – retail distributors – perform an essential role in the sales process: namely, *post-sale support and service*. Any manufacturer selling in high volume across a broad territory is likely to require partners to perform this function.
- **Aggregation** Some products must be combined with the offerings of another vendor to build a total solution for an end-customer. Oracle's database software, for example, has little utility until it is combined with a business application such as a customer information system or a financial accounting package. Manufacturers such as Oracle *must* have business partners who can aggregate their products into complete offerings for end-customers[7].

Alternatively, there are some circumstances where a business partner channel is not a good solution.

- **Cost – the other view** Partners may be cheaper to maintain than direct field reps, but they are also considerably more expensive than direct marketing channels such as call centres, catalogue/mail order operations, and the Internet. Simple, low-cost products can often be sold in these channels at a lower cost and with even broader market coverage. Using partners for these types of transactions can be a waste of money.
- **Control** Partner channels always involve some loss of selling control. Partners are rarely as loyal or as committed to a product or a manufacturer as the manufacturer's own sales force. As a result, products that are easily replaced by competitors' offerings, or that have an exclusive brand image that requires protection and nurturing, may be better off in a channel owned by the manufacturer.

On occasion, a partner channel will be a manufacturer's only route to market. For example, companies that make retail products often sell them only through distributors (e.g. Philip Morris). OEM (original equipment manufacturer) suppliers such as Intel, who make products that are incorporated into another vendor's finished goods, also tend to sell exclusively through partners. In addition, a few companies such as Microsoft have made the strategic decision for one reason or another to sell exclusively or primarily through business partners.

More often, though, companies use partners in markets where they are needed for a specific purpose – e.g. wider market coverage or local product support – and use other channels where these can do a better job. Partners are often utilized in the middle-market: the large base of business which cannot be covered

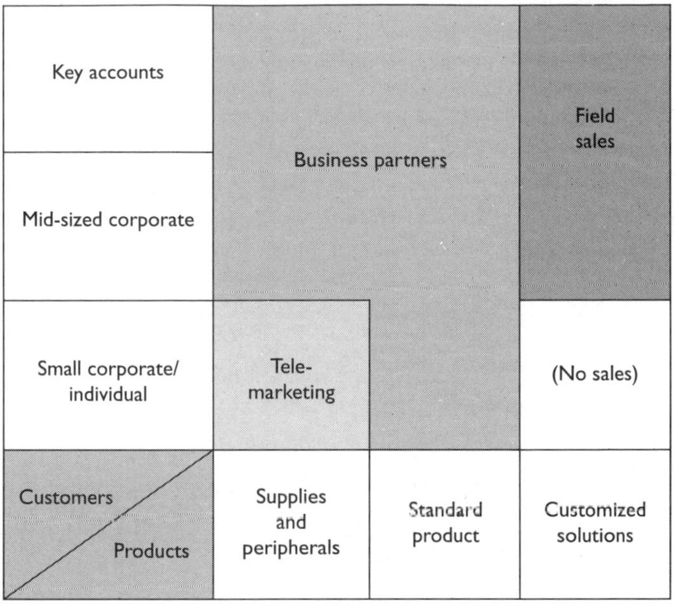

Key accounts
Business partners
Field sales
Mid-sized corporate
Small corporate/ individual
Tele-marketing
(No sales)
Customers
Products
Supplies and peripherals
Standard product
Customized solutions

Figure 7.3 Typical business partner coverage map

adequately or served economically by a field sales force, and yet which involve products that are too complex for a low-cost direct marketing channel. For many companies, this yields a partner coverage model that looks like Figure 7.3.

Finally, as with all channels, the decision about whether to use business partners should ultimately reflect customer behaviour. There is no sense trying to sell products through distributors if customers will only buy these products from a direct field rep. Conversely, there is no point in continuing to sell a product through a field sales force if customers are ready and willing to buy from a lower-cost distributor. It is always important to get back to basics – evaluating what customers want, and giving them the channels that best respond to their needs.

Seven best practices of partner channel design

This section describes seven best practices for building a partner channel, most of which are in use at just about every leading partner-oriented company. The seven are shown in Figure 7.4.

1. Define the scope of the channel

You can't build a strong channel if you don't know how many partners are needed and toward what end. As a result, the first order of business is to define

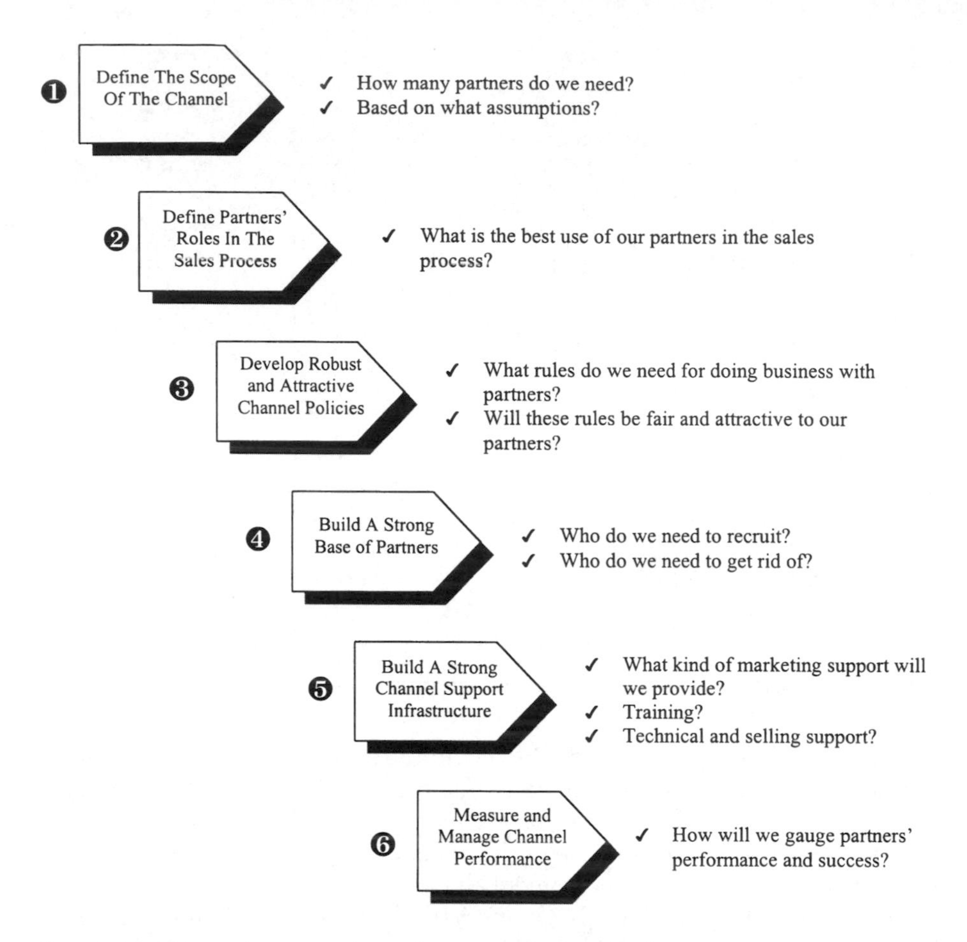

Figure 7.4 Seven best practices of partner channel design

the overall scope of the channel: the markets in which it will participate, the amount of revenue available in those markets, and the size of channel required to capture (or service) that revenue. Without this basic information, channel performance results can get very ugly, very fast.

One company, for example, a high-tech firm, made the decision in 1991 to double the size of its distributor channel in Europe from 800 to 1600 partners[8]. Its reasoning sounded plausible enough. The company had made $450 million in sales in Europe from its 800 partners during the previous year. So if it doubled its number of partners, then revenues would increase to around $900 million. Recruitment of 800 partners in Europe thus became one of the company's key initiatives.

In 1994, three years later, the company found itself with 800 partners – a net channel growth of zero – and revenues had actually *decreased* from $450 million to $340 million. Partners had come and gone, and along the way were now selling a quarter less product than they had been in 1991. The company's brand image had been severely damaged, and it was now consistently rated by the channel community as the single worst vendor with whom to do business.

There are some complex reasons why all this happened, but the bottom line was that there was only enough revenue in the market for 800 partners to share. Newly-recruited channel members competed strenuously against existing ones for this revenue, leading to a downward spiraling of prices and partner margins, and finally to a mass defection of the company's best partners. New partners were found to replace some of the ones who left, but lacking in experience, they produced less revenue. All told, this mess cost the company $110 million in lost sales as well as its reputation with both its partners and its customers.

The company could just as easily have had the opposite problem, by the way: 800 partners in a market that really did need 1600 of them, thus leaving half of the available money on the table. That is certainly a more common problem, and the one the company thought it had. Either way – whether partners are too few or too many – the negative impact on sales can be severe. Too many partners for a given market size can result in bone-crunching channel conflict, lower sales volume, and a damaged brand. Too few partners will result in a major lost selling opportunity. Channel size, in short, needs to be based on the size of the market in which partners will do business. A good (though admittedly simplistic) way to align channel size with market size involves three steps:

- Size the markets in which partners will participate: what is the total revenue opportunity?
- Determine a realistic per-partner sales (or service) benchmark
- Calculate the number of partners needed in the channel

First, sizing the partner market involves adding up the revenue opportunity in all of the product-markets in which the channel will participate. Figure 7.5 shows how this approach can work[9].

As suggested in the figure, a partner channel may operate in a number of different product-markets. By adding together the forecasted revenues in each product-market, it is possible to create an *overall revenue forecast for the partner channel*.

The second step is to determine the average productivity of a channel partner. This number will greatly influence the size of the channel. For example, in terms of *selling* partners, a revenue target of $100 million can be achieved by just twenty-five partners if they're each contributing $4 million. However, if an individual partner can only do $1 million in sales, it'll take 100 partners to hit the target. Similarly, in terms of *post-sale support* partners, a $100 million revenue target can be supported by twenty-five partners if they are each capable of providing support and service to $4 million worth of sales.

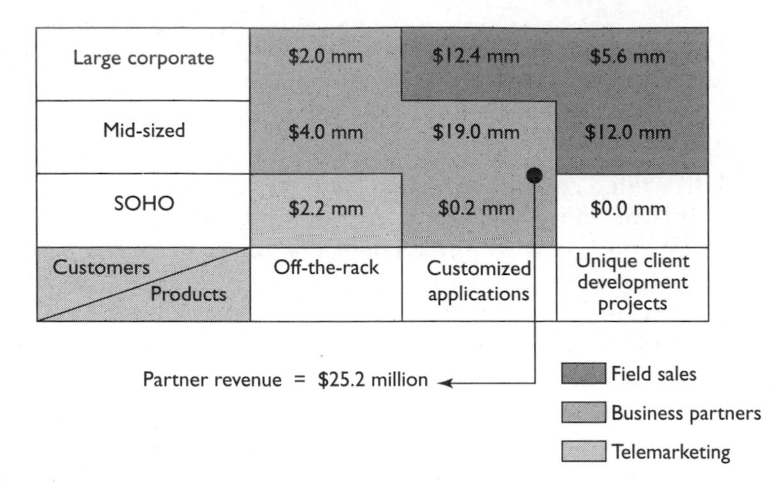

Figure 7.5 Meridian solutions business partner revenue forecast 1998.

However, if a partner can realistically support only $1 million in sales, then a hundred support partners will be needed.

In short, what's needed is a benchmark of partner productivity, a gauge of the average expected revenue (or support) contribution per partner. This information may already exist in-house, or, alternatively, it can come from an analysis of competitors' partner channels. The risk in looking at competitors is that they may have well-established channels that are producing per-partner sales or support figures vastly in excess of what could be expected from a new, inexperienced channel. Whether the data comes from internal or external sources, though, the goal is the same: to establish a benchmark of the average sales volume that can be produced or supported by a business partner.

The final step is to estimate the required channel size. This calculation is straightforward once channel revenue and partner productivity levels have been determined. The formula is shown in Figure 7.6.

So much for the easy part. Unfortunately, most companies that need business partners already have business partners, and the luxury of sizing a partner channel from scratch rarely exists. More commonly, the issue is how to *adjust* a partner channel to support an increasing revenue target. Take as an example Snap-On Tools, with its 4,000 distributors and $1.7 billion in revenues, and thus per-partner productivity of $425,000[10]. What if the company decided its revenue goal for the year 2002 was going to be $3 billion? That would give Snap-On three years to increase the sales of its channel by $1.3 billion, or seventy-six per cent! How would it accomplish this?

Like any company selling through distributors, Snap-On would have two choices – neither of which would be easy:

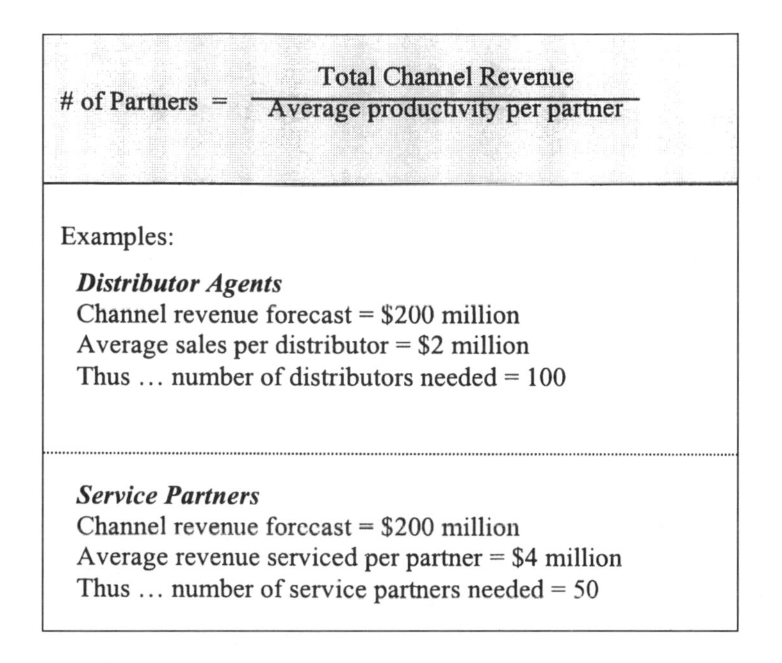

Figure 7.6 Channel size calculation ('how many partners do we need?')

- **Increase the number of partners** At its current sales productivity of $425,000 per partner, Snap-On would need a total of 7,059 partners – 3,059 new ones – to achieve $3 billion in sales. Snap-On could, at least in theory, recruit this many new partners. However, the company would have to find new territories or market segments for them. Throwing new partners into markets that are already crowded with distributors leads to intra-channel competition. This would result in all the assorted unpleasantries of channel conflict, such as flat sales, partner defections, and eroding margins.
- **Increase partner productivity** Alternatively, Snap-On could seek to increase per-partner sales productivity from $425,000 to $750,000 (which would generate the $3 billion, since they have 4,000 distributors). The company could try to do this by introducing new products, improving partner training and incentives, and creating more demand through increased marketing and promotion. This usually works to an extent, though it is unlikely that partners would be able to increase their average sales by seventy-six per cent through such tactics. Ten to fifteen per cent is usually a more reasonable figure.

One suggestion is that Snap-On, like most companies, would benefit by starting off with partner productivity, not channel size, as the initial focal point. It is at least worth seeing if average per-distributor sales could be bumped up by ten to fifteen per cent by giving them new and more products, more marketing support, and better training. Even a ten per cent increase in per-partner productivity would significantly reduce the number of new distributors needed to hit the $3 billion mark. However, at some point the company would hit a plateau; partners cannot infinitely improve their productivity to keep up with a company's growth targets.

More importantly, everything would depend on whether the $3 billion revenue target for 2002 was realistic in the first place. There may simply not be $3 billion worth of business for Snap-On, based on its current product offerings and customer base. An unrealistic growth target can lead to an overstuffing of the channel with new partners, along with unrealistic demands for per-partner sales performance. The end results are always the same: angry partners and increased channel conflict. Put simply, a sound and *realistic* revenue forecast is the starting point of an effective channel sizing and planning effort.

2. Define partners' roles in the sales process

Part of a good channel design involves figuring out what roles partners should play in the sales process. There are basically three choices, though they are not mutually exclusive: *lead generation*, *selling*, and *support/service*. Figure 7.7 depicts how these roles are often integrated with other channels in the broader go-to-market system.

Each of these ways of using partners is described below.

Lead generation partners

A good example of this kind of partner channel is Amazon.com's Associates program. The company pays a sales commission of five to fifteen per cent to anyone whose routes a customer from their own web site to www.amazon.com for a book or compact disk purchase. Since the cost of setting up a little web site is negligible, thousands of individuals have set up sites that recommend and review books – and then send readers over to Amazon.com for the sales transaction. These Associates are *lead generators*. They aren't involved in the actual sales transaction, nor do they play any role in shipping, billing or customer support. Their function is solely to create sales leads[11].

Lead generation is generally a good task to give a partner channel when you are perfectly capable of performing all of the tasks in the sales process – and yet want to build a larger lead stream than can be generated with in-house resources. That is exactly the situation with Amazon.

From a design perspective, the key to the design of a successful lead-generating partner channel is the *centralized management* of incoming leads from the partners. Leads that are routed from a partner channel directly to selling channels – telemarketers or field reps, in most cases – tend to disappear into a black hole. Partners' leads are often deemed unworthy or poor in quality, at a local level, by people whose responsibilities should not include lead adjudication[12], but rather, just plain follow-up and closing. In fact, upwards of fifty per cent of

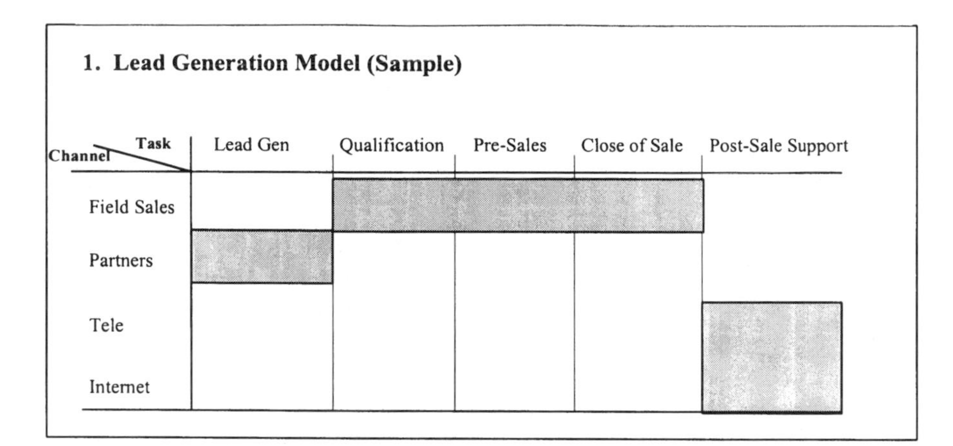

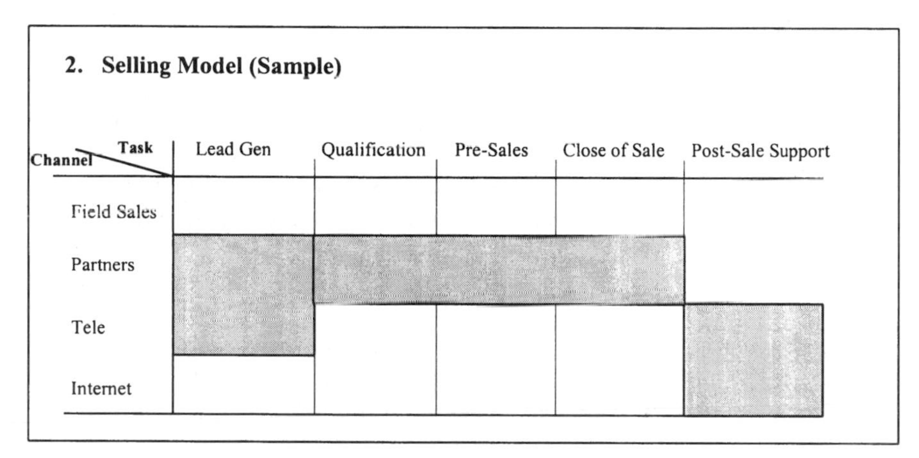

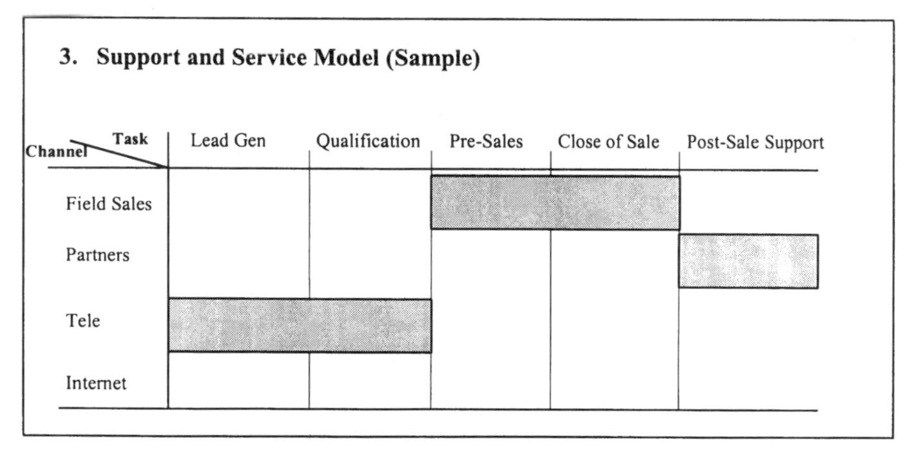

Figure 7.7 Three different models for using partners in the sales process

all leads can disappear when partners' leads are transmitted directly to field personnel. As a result, a lead-generating partner channel should report all leads to a central management system for routing to an appropriate sales resource.

Selling partners

Selling partners are the various agents, brokers, distributors, etc., who sell products on behalf of a manufacturer or vendor. Avon reps and Wal-Mart stores, for instance, are examples of manufacturers' selling partners, since, from a manufacturer's point of view, their main function is to make sales in return for a payment. Selling partners are, by far, the most common types of partners. In general:

> Selling partners are an appropriate type of channel for a manufacturer who cannot afford a large enough sales force, or cannot reach enough customers in dispersed markets, to capture the available sales opportunity on its own.

Selling partners must be carefully integrated into the go-to-market system. On the front end of the sales process, if they are going to create their own leads, then data on their lead generation activity must be reported back as a key indicator of their selling performance. If they will be provided with leads by another channel (such as a telemarketing channel), these leads must be tracked and monitored from the beginning to the end of the sales process, to ensure that partners are following up on sales opportunities and achieving reasonable lead-to-close ratios[13].

On the back end of the sales process, the line between sales and post-sale support can get a little fuzzy and contentious with selling partners. In selling a home security system for example, is installation of the system considered part of the *sale* or part of the *post-sale support*? Partners who consider themselves selling agents – and who are paid on raw revenue production – often don't want to be bothered with any post-sale support activities. That makes sense – but someone still has to install the alarm system! In fact, the installation may need to be defined formally by the manufacturer as part of the sale itself. As a rule, it is very unwise to leave the transition point between deal-closing and post-sale support up to the individual discretion of channel partners. This transition point should be clearly defined, documented, and communicated to the partner channel.

Support and service partners

A third type of partner services and supports an existing customer base. Authorized service centres, which exist in many industries, perform this type of function.

Post-sale support and service is generally a good role for the channel when customers are too spread out or too many in number to have their post-sale needs met directly by the manufacturer.

There is one dominant issue with any post-sale support partner channel: ensuring that customer inquiries and problems are indeed resolved by the channel on a timely, professional and satisfactory basis. One way to do this is to make the certification process stringent and comprehensive for authorized support partners, so that the bad apples in the support and service community don't end up with your logo on their front doors in the first place.

However, even with certified, high-quality channel partners, it is essential to follow up with customers to ensure that they are getting the care and feeding they require. Thus, a service and support channel requires an accompanying set of systems for monitoring which customers have been serviced by which partners, contacting those customers, and ensuring that partners' service levels are meeting the needs and expectations of the customer base.

Lead generation, selling, and post-sale support are certainly not mutually exclusive roles, and many channels and channel partners combine all three. Best Buy, for example, a retail distributor for many manufacturers of media, technology and publishing products, generates its own sales leads (through advertising), closes its own sales, and provides technical support to its own customers. At the other extreme, some companies set up separate business partner channels for every conceivable selling task. They might have 'master distributors' handling country or regional distribution, local partners working through the master distributors to move products within those regions, aggregators to combine these products into solutions, and authorized service centres to support customers after final sales have been completed. There is an infinite variety of designs when it comes to partner role assignment. The key is to make sure that each type of partner has a role which makes sense in the broader context of the sales process – and that the whole system of multiple channels works together seamlessly to create loyal, repeat customers.

3. Develop robust and attractive channel policies

A partner channel must have a set of robust policies, or as they are commonly known, *terms and conditions*. 'Robust' means that the policies must be complete enough, thorough enough, and flexible enough to provide clear guidance on the range of circumstances in which partners may find themselves. Channel policies include things such as whether partners can sell competitors' products, whether they can return unsold goods, and when and how they get paid. The importance of clarifying these types of issues speaks for itself.

Policies can be written down in a contract, but in many cases they exist more informally as a set of understandings between a manufacturer and its partners regarding mutual obligations. The degree of formality is not usually the central issue. Much more important is the extent to which the policies will hold up in the diverse range of circumstances in which partners become involved. As a

General Issues	Questions To Address
Brand and Trademarks	What restrictions are there on using a brand name, logo, or other trademarks?
Contract Renewal	What is the term of the distributor agreement; what are the conditions for renewal?
Termination	What are the specific ground for partner termination? Will warnings be provided?
Management Reporting	What information is the partner required to provide? How often?
Auditing	What kinds of visits, inspections, etc., will be made? When/how often?
Ownership	Who takes title to the product?
Sales and Compensation	
Sales Resources	Is the partner required to commit a specific level of sales (or support) resources?
Compensation	On what basis are partners paid? What is the commission or discount schedule?
Bonus/Incentives	What incentives exist separately from the standard commission/discount schedule?
Pricing	Are partners allowed to discount prices? If so, by how much, and when?
Sales Credit	Do partners get credit for all sales in their territories, or just the ones they initiate?
Customer Collections	Who is responsible for customer billing and debt collection?
Terms of Payment	When is payment due from customers? From the partner?
Inventory / Facilities	
Inventory Maintenance	Are partners required to stock a specified level of inventory?
Return Privileges	Can partners return unsold inventory? Under what circumstances? Any limitations?
Facilities Design	Are partners required to use specific interior or exterior layouts?
Inventory Displays	Are partners responsible for maintaining specified types of in-store displays?
Restrictions	
Territorial Integrity	Are partners confined to specific territories or markets?
Full-Line Enforcement	Are partners required to carry the complete product line?
Resale Restrictions	Can partners sell to other distributors (e.g. unauthorized, out-of-territory)?
Customer Restrictions	Are there certain types of accounts that partners are not allowed to pursue?
Exclusivity	Can partners sell competitors' products? If so, are there any limitations?

Figure 7.8 Framework for establishing business partner policies

result, the key design task with channel policies is to ensure that all the potentially relevant issues are being addressed and considered. Figure 7.8 provides a fairly comprehensive list of twenty-two different policy design issues. The relevant ones (for a particular channel) should be analysed, documented, and baked into a standard channel policy memorandum or contract.

Just as important as having a robust set of policies is ensuring that they are *attractive* to partners. Stating that partners cannot work outside narrow territories, cannot reduce prices, cannot call on the manufacturer's key accounts, cannot sell competitors' products and cannot return unsold inventory may be *complete*, but is hardly *compelling*. The simple fact is that high-quality distributors – the most desirable ones – aren't going to put up with a manufacturer that thinks it can manipulate every aspect of channel behavior to its own advantage. Competition for good partners is fierce in most industries, and partners know they have lots of choices in terms of which brands and products they carry. They will go elsewhere if asked to comply with harsh or unfair policies.

In short, channel policies should be developed toward a goal of *high channel acceptance*. If partners will be asked to sell new, complex products into tough, competitive markets, they must be provided with some pricing flexibility and liberal return privileges. If they will be selling products with six-month sales cycles, they shouldn't be asked to report sales data on a daily or weekly basis. Channel members should be consulted in the development of the policies, and their acceptance or lack of acceptance should be weighed as a significant factor in the setting of any channel rule.

4. Build a strong base of partners

A partner channel is only as good as the partners who inhabit it. Good recruiting is an essential component of a channel design, and so is the periodic pruning of underperforming partners.

The first step in partner recruitment is to develop an *Ideal Partner Profile*. This profile should establish a clear picture of what a perfect partner would look like, by asking (and answering) questions such as:

- How big would the perfect partner organization be?
- What kinds of experience and expertise would it have?
- Which markets would it play in?
- What kinds of customers would it have?
- How many sales reps would it have?
- What kinds of support personnel and service infrastructure would it have?

Even a one-page description of the ideal partner can serve as a valuable focusing mechanism for recruitment efforts. Since local partner recruitment is often delegated way, way down the food chain of a corporation, an ideal partner profile can serve as a good tool for ensuring that everyone is on board with the basic expectations for new partners – *before* they recruit those partners.

A more rigorous and systematic way to control the recruitment process is to develop a partner evaluation checklist. Figure 7.9 provides a sample partner checklist, using common and effective selection criteria.

Some judgment is called for when using evaluation checklists. Few if any partners will be perfect in all areas, which raises the question: which criteria are really the most important? For example, in complex technology sales, a partner's inability to provide post-sale support and service may be a deal buster. In simple consumer products, however, the size of a distributor's sales force may be the only thing that counts. Deciding which criteria really count – and which don't – can lead to a much more efficient recruiting effort.

Finally, a key method for controlling partner quality in the recruiting process

		Excellent	Good	Average	Poor
General Management	Overall management quality / stability				
	Years in business				
	Previous success/failure as a partner				
	Extent of competitor relationships				
	Reputation in the market place				
Financial Strength	Revenue growth				
	Profitability				
	Financial stability				
	Net worth				
	Payment / credit history				
Capacity / Resources	Size, quality of sales force				
	Service/support capabilities and systems				
	Advertising and marketing budget				
	Inventory				
Market Performance	Customer retention / stability				
	Key account development				
	Market share / penetration				
	Experience in our product-markets				
	Customer satisfaction				
	Pricing stability (vs. discounting)				

Figure 7.9 Partner evaluation checklist

– and one which can open the door to marginal partners who might later emerge into good ones – is to offer new partners a level of probationary membership. Although the word 'probation' is not advised, the idea is to have an entry-level tier of channel membership that involves little commitment and investment until, for example, a specified level of revenue has been achieved. Probationary channel tiers have all the benefits of probationary employee hiring or, for that matter, a lengthy engagement to a lover: you get to see what develops before making a real commitment.

Just as important as recruiting good partners is getting rid of the bad ones. In most partner channels, a handful of the partners produce a vast majority of the profitable, desirable business. In a study conducted by sales research firm Huthwaite, Inc., for example, eighty-four per cent of the channel revenue produced across a range of high-tech firms was contributed by just ten per cent of the partners[14]. The other ninety per cent were producing very little in sales. Yet they represented an inordinate expense, in partner administration, programs and maintenance.

Low-productivity partners may not be 'bad'; they are most likely committed to another company's products or focused elsewhere in the market place. Regardless, a company must have the guts to pull the plug on under-performing partners[15]. A good rule of thumb is to prune the five to ten per cent of channel partners each year who are generating the lowest sales. If this sounds too unpleasant, a softer version is to drop these partners into a lower tier of channel membership with fewer benefits. Most will get the idea and move on; the ones who stay won't continue to drain as much in the way of resources or funds.

In sum, the performance of a partner channel is highly dependent on the quality of its partners. Good recruiting, combined with ongoing channel pruning, ensures that every partner in the channel represents a worthwhile investment of time, energy, and money.

5. Build a strong channel support infrastructure

A crucial component of partner channel design involves support infrastructure: the tools and programs provided to partners to help them succeed in the market place. Specifically, a partner channel must usually be provided with *marketing support, training,* and *sales and technical support.* Each is discussed briefly below.

Marketing support

The single factor that most influences the success of a partner channel is the extent to which there is demand for its products and services. Partners cannot make the impossible happen; customers have to want to buy products for partners to be successful.

At a very minimum, marketing support for a partner channel involves all of the traditional techniques for generating demand: effective branding, aggressive advertising, and so on. In addition, however, business partners must be provided with their own tools for creating demand on a local level. Many will be unable to do this on their own, and will need support – and probably some money too.

Partner channels differ substantially in terms of the types of marketing support that they need. A simple discount coupon that can help a supermarket move products out the door obviously won't help an arms merchant who's trying to sell laser-guided missiles. Marketing support is usually less an issue of finding the perfect solution than of providing partners with a lot of different ways to attract customers. Five tried-and-true techniques that almost always deliver good results include the following:

- **Advertising allowances** Giving partners money for local advertising is one of the most effective ways to ensure that they make more sales, even though it's expensive.

- **Sales promotions** In all of their various forms – heavily-advertised special deals, rebates, etc. – sales promotions help partners move more product.
- **Demonstrators** Partners make more sales when they have products that they can demonstrate to customers. Asking partners to pony up the money for all their demonstration products is ill-advised. Many won't be able to afford to do it. The more products they can demo to customers, the better.
- **Co-branding** Allowing partners to use logos and other trademarks, and mentioning these partners in advertisements, can have a powerful effect on their prestige and ability to draw customers – assuming that your brand has prestige, of course.
- **In-store sales support** One of the authors recently went into a CompUSA to pick up a $10 box of floppy disks, bumped into a Hewlett-Packard rep, and was promptly talked into buying an $800 laser printer. Though expensive, in-store sales support is very effective in retail channels.

Training

Basic product training is absolutely essential for a partner channel. Partners should receive similar instruction, documentation and other resources as the field sales force. They should not be put (or allowed) into a selling environment until they have thorough familiarity with the product line.

In addition, partners need to know not only what they are selling, but *how* to sell it. Since many partners are smaller organizations with less experienced sales forces, a partner channel often must be provided with some basic sales training. At a minimum, this should include a seminar on customer needs analysis and should contain scenarios in which partners can test and refine their ability to sell the manufacturer's products into a variety of customer environments. Sales training is a good investment for a partner channel; in addition to increasing sales volume, it is often seen very positively by prospective partners.

Sales and technical support

Many partner channels require some degree of support in the sales process, both in closing deals (sales support) and in solving customers', and their own, technical problems (technical support). In many cases, they are given barebones resources that don't even begin to meet their needs for back-up and support.

One smart approach is to sit down with partners and determine what kinds of support they require in selling situations and in managing customer relationships. It can be a costly mistake to assume that a channel will take delivery of a product and move it into the hands of its customers without any direct selling assistance. In large, complex sales, partners should have, at a minimum, a phone number they can call to discuss sales opportunities with a seasoned business developer. Some types of sales and channels may also require the participation of manufacturer personnel on actual sales calls and in account management and development efforts.

In technical support, there is one overriding trend in leading companies: the use of technology to support partners in the field. This often includes, for example, 24x7 (i.e. all day, every day) call centres into which partners can place requests for technical data, product reference materials, pricing/quote sheets, etc. The Internet, as well, appears to be emerging as a key medium for providing technical support to partners. Companies such as Cisco and Oracle, for example, use 'extranet' web sites to link up with partners and provide them with on-line documentation, product and technical specs, troubleshooting recommendations, and, through e-mail, the ability to communicate directly in an efficient, fast manner. Any manufacturer investing in a partner channel should take a serious look at the Internet as an optimal vehicle for providing technical support.

In sum, expecting partners to take delivery of a product and sell it on their own, without a healthy support infrastructure, tends to be unrealistic and foolish. A big part of a sound channel design involves giving partners the marketing support, training, and sales and technical support they need to succeed in the field.

6. Measure and manage channel performance

The success of a partner channel is highly dependent on active performance measurement and management. The bottom line is that *partners don't work for you*. They have different objectives and different business models. They have their own ideas about how to develop business, retain customers, and sell your products – or someone else's. Their loyalties are to their own shareholders. In short, it is almost guaranteed that they won't do what you want them to do, in the way you want them to do it, without a rigorous performance management system.

One performance management issue involves setting realistic expectations for the channel, particularly at first. Most partner channels take eighteen to thirty months to achieve target levels of sales and profitability. In the first two years or so, new partners, learning how to sell new products into new markets, rarely deliver the kind of sales volume that could be expected of them once they know what they are doing. At the same time, profitability suffers due to the large start-up costs associated with getting a channel off the ground. A partner channel that might eventually consume only 12 cents of every revenue dollar will generally eat up at least 18 cents, and as much as 30 cents, during the first two years of operation.

This is an important issue because many companies set their expectations for a new channel by looking at competitors who have established and productive channels. To put it simply, asking a nascent partner channel to deliver levels of sales and profitability comparable to established industry benchmarks is like telling a four-year-old child to read and summarize a college physics textbook. It isn't going to happen.

With that caveat in mind, the key to partner performance management is to measure the right things. Choosing partner performance metrics – and getting performance data back from the channel – can be a tricky business. For one thing, it isn't always easy to get partners to cooperate; it depends on whether they've agreed to provide this information. Southland Corporation can demand, and get, all sorts of performance data from its 7–11 distributors, because they are contractually obligated to provide it. Without a contract, though, a request for even the most basic sales volume data can lead to physical injury as a result of partners falling on the floor in laughter. Manufacturers are the very *last* people on the planet surface to whom they want to disclose their financial and operational data. In most cases, whatever performance data is going to be needed from business partners should to be agreed to *in writing*.

Second, it is not always obvious what to measure. Many companies collect and process volumes and volumes of data from their indirect channels without a clear understanding of the purpose or benefit of this bureaucratic effort. Much of the time, in fact, the data is confusing and impractical. For example, does *high inventory turnover* mean that the partner is selling a lot of products quickly (which is good), or that inventory levels are so low that they are constantly reordering supplies in a panic (bad)? It's important to collect straightforward, useful data that *says* something – that tells you things you really need to know to impact channel behaviour and performance. Most companies would do well to tear up their channel reports and start over with a clean piece of paper and some simple, informative channel metrics. Figure 7.10 suggests eleven them, each of which can help pinpoint problems in the partner base and suggest areas for management attention.

Importantly, channel performance metrics must be communicated to the channel. Partners cannot and will not comply with performance measures that they have not been told about or for which they are not collecting the right data. *Sales calls per month* is a good measure of selling activity, but it will only work if partners know they have to collect this information.

Performance measures also need to be applied consistently across the partner base, and at regular intervals. For example, if customer satisfaction is key, then the channel should know that a representative sample of every partner's customers will be interviewed every six months or year to gather this information.

Finally, collecting performance data and doing something useful with it are two different things. For performance data to have utility, it must be connected to the reward (and punishment) system. Partners must understand things such as: What is the reward for achieving target levels of sales revenue? How about achieving twice the targeted sales revenue? Is there a bonus or incentive payment? Conversely: What is the sanction for failing to achieve target levels of performance? Will they lose money? New leads? Membership in the channel? Performance measurement never does any good

Metric	What It Is	What It Tells You
Sales Volume	Partner's total sales, e.g. per month.	Simplest and best indicator of partner's sales performance
Sales Growth Rate	Partner's growth rate, e.g. annual	Indicator of partner's business success -- and future importance to you
Operating Margins	Pre-tax profits, e.g. '30 %'	Partner's financial health and viability
Market Share	% of market $$$ sold by partner	Partner's market penetration and competitive position.
Partner Share	% of revenue from your products	Key indicator of partner's commitment to and promotion of your brand.
Sales Made / Sales Quota	Actual / planned sales	Partner's ability to meet its own selling targets.
Lead-to-Close Ratio	Closed deals divided by total leads	Partner's selling skills: its ability to turn opportunities into sales.
Sales Calls Per Month	Self explanatory	Simple, good measure of partner's selling activity / capacity.
Inventory Maintained	Avg. in-stock inventory, in $$$	Good indicator of whether partner can meet fluctuating local demand.
Customer Satisfaction	Various types of customer ratings	Key performance indicator for service and support partners.
Customer Complaints	Complaints/period, e.g. 5/month'	Key performance indicator and red flag for service partners.

Figure 7.10 Eleven informative and useful partner performance metrics

in the absence of a clearly-articulated relationship between performance and reward.

7. Get good channel feedback

McDonald's has had some good ideas over the years, but the Big Mac wasn't one of them. That idea, in fact, came from a franchisee. So did the apple pie, another very popular item[16]. Of course, it makes sense that people who sell food to customers everyday would have a lot of insight into what these customers might want to eat. Partners – in this case franchisees – always have a wealth of information about market conditions and customer needs. Many companies make the significant mistake of failing to extract this information from the channel. Lacking direct contact with the customer base, they become increasingly removed from the dynamics of the market place and lose touch with the needs of both their customers and their partners.

This section describes three effective tools for staying in tune with market developments and partners' needs: *channel surveys, structured interviews,* and *partner leadership councils.*

Channel surveys

Channel surveying is pretty straightforward, and it's a good place to start. A channel survey normally specifies a number of dimensions – pricing, marketing support, etc. – for which feedback from the channel would be beneficial. The survey is generally sent to a representative sample of, say, 100–250 partners. The idea is to get quantitative data that can be rolled-up to suggest widely held opinions about your performance in key areas. Many third-party consulting and research firms design and administer these surveys, and working with one of them can be helpful. A sample channel survey is shown in Figure 7.11.

Structured interviews

As useful as a survey might be, this approach has limited utility. In most cases, surveys yield volumes of data on channel satisfactions and dissatisfactions (dissatisfactions, most of the time). Yet they provide precious little insight on what are really much more substantive issues such as changes in the market place, shifting perceptions in the customer base, and sources of big new revenue growth. To get this kind of information – to gain insight into the market place – requires more than a mail-in survey form. A highly effective approach for getting this information is *structured interviewing*, or in-depth interviewing that is open-ended and yet structured around key themes – and that is also applied consistently across a group of partners. For example, the following are a dozen open-ended questions that tend to get high-impact results.

Please take a few minutes to rate our performance in each of the following areas. Be candid! Your feedback will help us address any problem areas and improve the overall quality of our distributor programs.

	Excellent	**Good**	**Fair**	**Poor**
Our Market Position				
• Brand image/ reputation	O	O	O	O
• Technological superiority	O	O	O	O
• Competitive performance	O	O	O	O
• Product quality	O	O	O	O
Channel Support				
• Marketing funds	O	O	O	O
• Sales call participation	O	O	O	O
• Technical assistance	O	O	O	O
• Training programs	O	O	O	O
Channel Programs				
• Overall quality	O	O	O	O
• Responsiveness to your needs	O	O	O	O
• Promotional events	O	O	O	O
• Loaner/demo equipment	O	O	O	O
• Partner web site	O	O	O	O
• Lead tracking data base	O	O	O	O
• Help desk	O	O	O	O
• (Etc.)	O	O	O	O

Figure 7.11 Channel survey – a sample

- Responsiveness to customers' needs:
  - How well are we meeting the needs of your (the channel's) customers?
  - What needs do customers have that we are not currently addressing?
- Competitive position and stature in the market place:
  - In general, how do you think we are perceived by your customers?

  - What is most important to your customers, and how well do they think we compare to the competition in providing it?
  - When you lose competitive bids with our products, why are you losing? What would it take for you to win more deals with our products?
- Areas of perceived strengths and weaknesses:
  - What do you think customers like most about our products and services?
  - When customers complain about us, what do they complain about?
- Changes in market conditions and customer behaviour:
  - Are customers' needs changing? What do they need that they are not getting today?
  - Are there particular markets or types of sales that seem to be growing rapidly? Or slowing down?
- New selling opportunities:
  - From your experience, where are the big selling opportunities going to be in the next couple of years?
  - What could we be doing differently – in any area – to help you drive more sales?
  - Are there any particular deals that we could help you close *today*?

An interview of this sort can reduce a lot of the market numbness and distance that typically results from selling through intermediaries. If conducted across a range of partners – say, twenty to thirty of them – it will also establish the key themes and beliefs about the market place that are shared widely in the partner community. Finally, interviewing of this sort almost always generates new selling opportunities and deal-making situations. It is wise to think in terms of conducting both surveys and structured partner interviews at least once a year.

Partner leadership councils

The third approach is the *partner leadership council*. Here, a group of prominent partners are enlisted to meet with top management periodically to represent the partner community at large. A council can consist of as much as ten per cent of the partner base, though it is more common for twenty or so top channel members to participate. Leadership councils are serious business, and successful firms use them for a wide range of purposes. Black & Decker, for example, uses its Distributor Advisory Committee to get input on everything from its distributor programs to major product design concepts. There are a few risks with partner councils, however:

- **A partner leadership council creates a new responsibility** A leadership council puts an onus on the manufacturer to deal with the many concerns and challenges that come up in the council meetings. Few things can damage the credibility of a manufacturer faster – throughout the entire partner base – than blowing off the issues of influential partners. Once major issues are put on the table, the entire partner community will be watching to see what happens. It can be a Pandora's Box for manufacturers who aren't committed to dealing honestly and decisively with partners' concerns.

- **Senior management must participate** Nothing alienates key partners faster than low-level functionaries who are unable to take real action on their concerns. For the council to have any credibility, at least some of the manufacturer's participants need to be senior decision makers.
- **Evangelizing needs to be minimized** The temptation is huge in a leadership council to try to 'pump up' the channel by talking about new products and new profit opportunities. But all the mumbo-jumbo about how everyone will become millionaires – when the new product is released in just six short months! – should be kept to a minimum. Partners don't come to leadership council meetings to listen; they come to talk. The agenda should allow plenty of time for them to do just that.

In sum, partners work on the front lines with customers, and as a result have market insights that can significantly improve a manufacturer's market position. They also have expectations and dissatisfactions that need to be explored and resolved. Part of a good channel design involves putting in place some systematic tools to extract and get value out of this information.

Summary

An indirect partner channel represents one of the more challenging components of a channel system. Partners channels come in many forms, they are complex, and they can't be controlled like direct channels. Yet the effort is often worthwhile, because business partners can deliver sales and support at a relatively low cost, and can have a dramatic impact on a company's ability to penetrate new markets and reach more customers.

This chapter looked at a group of seven best practices of partner channel design, organized loosely into a life cycle of channel development.

- It began by looking at two preliminary planning steps: *channel scoping* and *partner role clarification*. These involve determining how big the channel needs to be, and what specifically it is supposed to be doing in the sales process. This kind of planning is essential in any partner channel design effort.
- It then looked at three core elements of a sound channel design: *robust channel policies, partner recruitment tools*, and a *well-designed channel support infrastructure*.
- Finally, it looked at two issues that become central once a partner channel is up and running: *channel performance management* and *structured channel feedback*. Performance management is about setting up performance metrics and incentives to get the right behaviours and performance from the channel. Feedback is about just the opposite: getting information back from the channel about its expectations, needs, and insights into the market place.

Ultimately, the factor that most influences a company's success with a partner channel is the extent to which it views its partners not just as partners but as *customers*. Growth through partners is highly dependent on the loyalty of those partners, their willingness to represent and support the brand, and their commitment to the product line. Most partners will have plenty of other places they can go if they decide that someone else will treat them better, offer them better products, or help them make more money. Their loyalty and commitment will be in direct proportion to the loyalty and commitment shown to them by the manufacturer. It is well worth keeping this in mind when working with business partners.

Notes

[1] Much lively discussion exists about the use of the word 'partner'; whole books have been written about it, in fact. An author of this book wrote one! See Rackham, Friedman and Ruff (1996), *Getting Partnering Right: How Market Leaders Are Creating Long-Term Competitive Advantage* (NY: McGraw-Hill). In relationship management, and in lawyers' offices, distinctions between partners, allies, distributors, etc., can be important. However, the terminology can be pedantic and unnecessary when it comes to the practical task of channel design. To avoid confusion, this chapter simply refers to *all* intermediaries as business partners. Some would disagree, strenuously, with this use of the word.
[2] Snap-On also makes diagnostic equipment and tool storage products.
[3] International Data Corporation, 1996.
[4] All data as of July 1998.
[5] All data as of July 1998.
[6] They don't get paid salaries. On the other hand, they do get paid – in margin and commissions – and require partner administration programs, marketing budgets, etc.
[7] In recognition of this need, Oracle has been rapidly building a range of homegrown applications for its databases, while continuing to grow its application partner channels.
[8] Some of the numbers have been changed at the request of the company. The proportions are about right, though.
[9] This subject is discussed in much greater depth in Chapter 11, *Investing in (and across) a portfolio of channels*.
[10] Not an accurate figure, since Snap-On also sells direct, but a reasonable approximation solely for illustrative purposes.
[11] Most major Internet businesses, such as Yahoo!, Excite, and AOL, provide links to Amazon's web site as well – and earn money for what amounts to very little work: adding a link or two to their web sites.
[12] Lead adjudication is the decision as to whether a lead is worth a follow-up and where to send it.

[13] The percentage of new leads that are successfully converted into closed sales. If a partner is given ten leads and converts two of them into sales, the lead-to-close ratio is 20 per cent.
[14] Huthwaite, Inc. Study Of Channel Revenue Distribution in Eleven High-Tech Companies, 1996.
[15] Legal counsel is *mandatory* when terminating a channel partner, unless the specific conditions of termination are described in a contract.
[16] McDonald's the corporation, on the other hand, gave us the Arch Deluxe.

Chapter 8

Telechannels

When most of us think of a 'telechannel,' the first thought that comes to mind is those uninvited telemarketers who call just as we're sitting down to dinner. Cold-calling into consumers' homes, though, is just a small part of how companies use telechannels. In 1997, for example, US *business-to-business* sales over the phone totalled over $158 billion dollars and represented well over half of all telephone-based transaction volume[1]. Today, telechannels handle a diverse range of responsibilities such as technical support, customer service, catalogue sales order processing, lead generation for other channels, outbound sales campaigns, and various customer loyalty / retention programs. Far from being just another low-cost channel with limited sales and service capabilities, the telechannel is a versatile and potent way to do business, and offers its own unique brand of competitive advantage. Consider the following:

- **Marriott**, the worldwide leader in lodging, has over the past twenty years built a world-class call centre to book room reservations, corporate events and major conferences. While many regional hotel chains and smaller national players *still* book these reservations at the individual-property level, Marriott's call centre provides centralized handling of over 50,000 calls per day by over 2000 telereps to book reservations across its entire lodging network.

  In addition to being a significant source of the company's rapid expansion and growth, this call centre has enabled Marriott to launch whole new businesses quickly and cost effectively. For example, when Marriott launched two hotel chains for the lower-cost travel niche, Courtyard by Marriott (for business travellers) and Fairfield Inns (leisure travellers), these were marketed through its existing call centre, resulting in dramatically lower start-up costs as a result of the shared call centre infrastructure. In addition, in both cases Marriott used its call centre to begin booking reservations *as soon as new properties in each chain were ready for occupancy*, resulting in faster times-to-market than had ever been achieved in a lodging start-up.
- **GEICO**, originally a sleepy regional insurance company for government employees, in the late 1980s and 1990s sprinted to market leadership with a campaign proclaiming 'Give us 15 minutes and we could save you hundreds of dollars'. Breaking with tradition in the insurance industry – the face-to-face agent channel – GEICO built eight call centres to field inbound calls across forty-six states within the US[2].

These call centres enable GEICO to sell insurance at substantially lower prices than its competitors. One source of these lower prices is the considerably lower cost of doing business over the phone. Another is the ability of its telereps to view driving records and actuarial data[3] on-line while talking to new customers – enabling them to offer service only to the most insurable and lowest-risk drivers. In addition to providing a quick, efficient and less-expensive way to sell insurance, GEICO's call centre has enabled the company to develop one of the industry's most sophisticated and complete customer databases.

- **Dell Computer** has rapidly become one of the top personal computer manufacturers (as mentioned earlier in this book) and it has done so largely through its telechannel. By selling directly to customers and bypassing the more traditional retail and distributor channels, Dell has rapidly gained market share – while achieving a dramatically lower-cost structure. Indeed, Dell's selling costs are estimated to be thirty per cent lower than the average retail- or distribution based competitor[4]. In addition, because customers order Dell's products directly from the manufacturer, it has achieved inventory turns of over 30× per year – more than twice the industry average.

As these examples suggest, telechannels are used for a variety of strategic purposes. In many leading companies, they have become sophisticated organizations that enhance customer service and contribute directly to both top and bottom line growth. The next section takes a more detailed look at the purposes and benefits of a telechannel within a go-to-market system.

The business purpose – and payoff – of a telechannel

Although telechannels are used for a wide range of purposes, they are usually targeted at one or more of the business objectives suggested in Figure 8.1.

Each is discussed briefly below.

Increase revenue growth

Telechannels impact revenue growth in two ways: by providing a high-volume, low-cost means to sell to *new* customers in geographically dispersed markets, and by providing a new way to initiate more extensive and frequent contact with buyers in *existing* accounts.

Most people are familiar with the use of telechannels to acquire new buyers, particularly when used in conjunction with direct mail campaigns. It's an attractive channel for this purpose, because a telechannel rep is always just an inexpensive phone call away from a new prospect – anyplace in the world. Lands' End, the popular catalogue clothing company, is an oft-discussed example of a company that has built a dominant position in its marketplace by reaching customers through direct mail and then providing

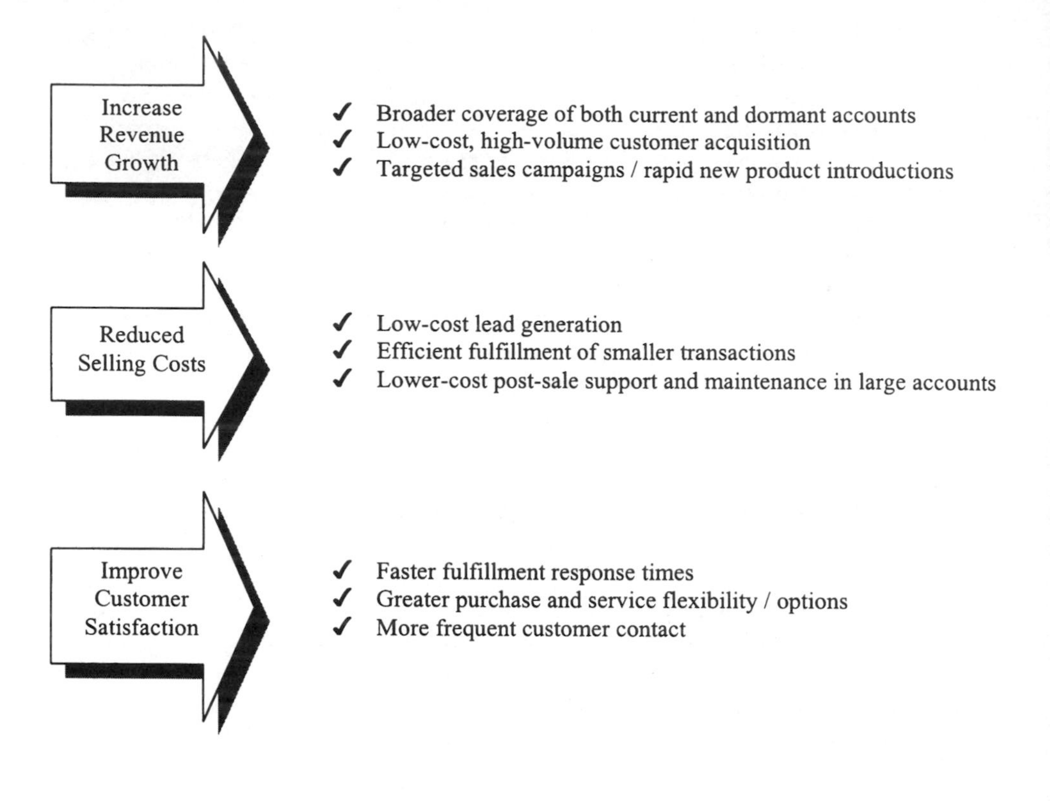

Figure 8.1 Telechannel business objectives

efficient 'inbound' call centres to process orders efficiently and inexpensively.

Telechannels, however, can also be used to increase sales growth within *existing* key accounts. Take IBM, for example, the leading supplier of information technology products and services to global corporations, and its customer Siemens, the German telecommunications giant. IBM's field reps in Munich can effectively cover all of Siemens' corporate technology buyers, but Siemens' global reach extends to hundreds of plants and offices throughout the world. The task of selling to buyers across all these dispersed offices is an impossible one with just a field sales force.

To expand its presence within these types of global accounts, IBM has established a key account 'Gold Service' telechannel, based out of centralized call centres in Europe, North America, and the Far East. Working with field sales teams, these telereps make outbound calls to identify sales opportunities within Siemens and other accounts, and take in-bound calls directly from buyers who want to make immediate purchases. IBM's Gold Service call centres thus expand the company's reach into its major accounts – and also increase the productivity of its sales force. IBM's highly skilled and highly paid field sales force can now focus on large, complex transactions, while letting the telechannel handle smaller, quicker customer orders.

Reduce selling costs

A telerep usually costs about fifty per cent less than a field sales rep, and can also make four times as many customer contacts per day – thus leading to dramatic cost savings in the sales process. General Electric's Medical Systems business provides a good example. This division decided to try call centres when it realized the unfavourable economics of having field reps selling $1.98 accessories supplies along with million dollar medical imaging systems. By transferring accessory and supply transactions to a call centre, and focusing the sales force on big-ticket opportunities, the division's was able to reduce its overall sales costs by fifty percent[5]. For most companies, cost reduction is a primary driver behind a telechannel initiative.

Improve customer satisfaction

Finally, and perhaps most importantly, a telechannel can have a significant impact on customer satisfaction and retention. Every manager understands the importance of satisfied, loyal customers. The cost of finding a new customer, as suggested in Chapter 2, can be three to six times that of keeping an existing, loyal one. Telechannels provide numerous ways to improve customer retention and increase brand loyalty, through faster customer service, more responsive technical support, and more flexible, round-the-clock assistance and order processing.

A somewhat subtler role of the telechannel lies in its ability to build strong customer relationships by maintaining a high frequency of customer contact *after* a sale has been completed. As a simple example, BMW dealers use a telechannel to follow up with every customer after the purchase of a car and whenever any maintenance work is performed. Phone interviews provide these dealers and the company with a wealth of information about customer preferences and satisfaction levels. But perhaps more importantly, these interviews increase the contact between BMW, its dealers, and its customers, maintaining an ongoing dialogue about customer needs and perceptions. The company's enhanced focus on customer satisfaction and loyalty (of which the telechannel program is a component) explains in part its resurgence from a very shaky early-1990s to a strong position of market leadership. Sales have doubled since 1993, and BMW has emerged as the third most admired automotive company in the world[6].

Certainly, not all companies achieve all of these benefits through their telechannels. In many organizations, call centres still serve as back-office operations, providing customer service and technical support while contributing little in the way of new sales or higher profitability. Indeed, many call centres still reflect their roots as small-time support operations designed to take some of the work off the backs of field reps. Most were never intended to play an active or perhaps dominant role in the realization of a company's strategic objectives – and they don't. To achieve big gains in growth, profits and customer loyalty, the average telechannel must be converted into a strategic call centre, a fully-staffed and fully-functioning organization that is tasked with some or all of the following responsibilities:

- Taking inbound customer orders.
- Handling inquiries from sales reps, channel partners and customers.
- Making outbound phone contact to existing customers as well as new prospects.
- Performing post-sale customer satisfaction interviews, both to build databases on customers' preferences and satisfaction levels, and to increase customer loyalty and retention.
- Taking on post-sale account development/maintenance tasks from a field sales force (or other main selling channel) to leverage field rep time and reduce overall selling costs.
- Leveraging an information technology infrastructure (e.g. customer databases, client-server networks, telephone switches) to manage a high volume of customer contacts systematically and productively.

This chapter provides a starting point for converting a back-office call centre capability into a real strategic asset. It begins by looking at the three fundamental applications of a telechannel in a go-to-market system: telesales, telecoverage, and teleprospecting[7]. The chapter then takes an in-depth look at a process for building a strategic call center plan – a roadmap for achieving high-impact results from the use of telechannels.

The three telechannel applications: telesales, telecoverage, and teleprospecting

The first step in building a high-impact telechannel plan is to understand how the different types of call centres provide strategic opportunity. Figure 8.2 shows a breakdown of call centres into five types of 'applications,' or uses to which they can be put.

Of the five call centre applications suggested in Figure 8.2, three in particular play a role in a company's sales process: telesales, telecoverage, and teleprospecting. Each has a different and unique role.

Telesales centres focus on completing and closing sales transactions over the telephone, with little or no support from other channels. A telesales rep for Staples, for example, will help a customer place an order for office products

❶ Telesales ❷ Telecoverage ❸ Teleprospecting	**Sales Telechannels**
❹ Customer service ❺ Technical support	**Service/Support Telechannels**

Figure 8.2 The five types of telechannel applications

over the phone, and then send the transaction to a fulfilment centre for processing. *Telecoverage* centres, on the other hand, focus on telephone-based relationship management of large accounts, usually in support of a field sales force. IBM's call centres, handling key accounts such as Siemens, are examples of telecoverage centres. Telecoverage reps generally work hand-in-hand with field sales reps to support key accounts, by making periodic outbound calls to established buyers, and by handling incoming customer inquiries. Finally, *teleprospecting* centres focus on inbound customer inquiries resulting from direct-response marketing campaigns and awareness advertising. Teleprospecting reps do not close sales over the phone; they collect and qualify incoming leads for routing to an appropriate channel. A brief summary of these three telechannel applications is shown in Figure 8.3.

Each of these three applications serves a different strategic purpose, and it's important to understand the contribution that each can make within a go-to-market system. A brief description of each application is provided below.

Telesales	Close orders (usually small, catalog products) over the phone.
Telecoverage	Maintain and nurture key account buyer relationships, in support of a primary selling channel (e.g. field sales force).
Teleprospecting	Generate and qualify new leads for closure by another sales channel.

Figure 8.3 The three telechannel sales applications

Telesales

Examples of telesales operations include direct-marketing catalogue houses such as L.L. Bean, or direct-marketing service companies such as Veritas, which advertises life insurance products in the *Wall Street Journal* and closes insurance sales over the phone. The key characteristic of a telesales centre is that it *closes sales*.

Generally, telesales reps takes orders from customers who already know what they need, and who call in response to a catalogue mailing or media advertisement. In addition to these 'inbound' calls from customers, telesales centres often engage in some 'outbound' activity. For example, many companies involved in subscription businesses, such as cable or satellite services, have built successful outbound telesales centres to call customers in pursuit of service renewals or upgrades. A telesales centre is a particularly useful channel for companies with relatively simple products and a goal of lower selling costs.

Telecoverage

Telecoverage reps are generally assigned to specific key accounts, and work alongside field sales reps to increase customer contact frequency and develop relationships with buyers. Telecoverage reps can be assigned to take incoming key account calls, but are often also responsible for placing periodic outbound calls to key buyers. Telecoverage has many benefits. It allows a company to:

- cover and penetrate more buyers within existing large accounts
- reactivate and re-establish relationships with 'dormant' buyers
- cover geographically dispersed accounts cost effectively
- pre-qualify sales opportunities for field reps

Telecoverage is a particularly effective application for companies seeking deeper penetration of existing accounts and higher sales force productivity.

Teleprospecting

The purpose of a teleprospecting centre is to generate cost-effective leads for hand-off to another sales channel, such as a field rep or distributor, for sales closure. Oracle Corporation, for example, uses teleprospecting reps to uncover new sales leads, and then hands those leads to its business partners for closure and fulfilment.

Inbound teleprospecting centres take incoming leads resulting from direct mail or marketing campaigns, qualify them, and pass them on to field reps or partners. *Outbound* teleprospecting centers are used for high-volume, low-cost demand generation in support of other channels. In both cases, teleprospecting tends to be an effective approach for companies with complex products and for whom the goal is to increase the volume of qualified, new leads for its primary sales channel.

As suggested, each of the three types of telechannel applications can combine both *inbound* calls (for example, in which a customer calls a toll-free number) and *outbound* calls, in which a telerep makes a proactive call to a customer. Inbound call centres are generally targeted at cost reduction, by handling catalogue orders and routine customer supply reorders efficiently and quickly. Outbound call centres, on the other hand, are usually targeted at sales and market share growth: they provide a low-cost means to reach and sell to thousands of customers across dispersed markets and territories. As many companies are beginning to focus on call centres as a source of growth and profit – and not just cost reduction – it comes as no surprise that outbound telchannels are growing much faster than inbound telechannels. Indeed, outbound teleselling has been growing at about thirty per cent per year for the past fifteen years.

A summary of the roles, responsibilities, and characteristics of each type of telechannel, for both inbound and outbound customer contact, is shown in Figure 8.4.

The distinction between the three call centre applications provides a useful starting point for evaluating which types of telechannels are needed and why. Of course, it's only a starting point. The larger task at hand is to build a sound strategic plan for designing and implementing the right mix of call centres.

Building the strategic call centre plan

This section describes seven key steps for building a strategic call centre plan. The seven steps are shown in Figure 8.5 (on p. 139).

1. Develop telechannel business objectives

As suggested earlier, telechannels can achieve a variety of objectives, from cost reduction in the sales process, to increased growth in revenues and market share, to increased customer loyalty and retention. While all of those objectives can be achieved with telechannels, they cannot necessarily all be achieved at the same time – or with the same types of call centres. In fact, failure to align the choice and design of a telechannel with the overall goals for which it is intended can lead to unexpected and poor results.

One financial services client determined in 1995, for example, that significant expansion in future sales and profits required aggressive growth of its existing customer base – to be achieved primarily through the cross-selling and up-selling of new financial services[8]. The company decided that a vast majority of this growth could be achieved through its existing call centre. The company moved quickly and decisively to arm its call centre with product brochures and

Telesales	Telecoverage	Teleprospecting
'End-to-end channel that books orders'	'Account and buyer relationship management'	'Fields and qualifies new leads for hand-off to another channel'
Characteristics of Operation		
• Small, off-the-rack products • Orders placed by existing customers or sometimes a field rep • Lead generated by catalog or direct mail • Customer knows what they want • Rep books complete order and sends to fulfillment • Requires product knowledge • Cross-selling opportunities improve productivity	• Handles return calls from buyers • Interacts frequently with field sales reps *(outbound)*	• Gets leads from mass-marketing programs and toll-free number inquiries • Qualifies leads as far as possible, trying to resolve simple inquiries in one call • Hands off most promising, qualified opportunities to another channel • Tracks opportunity-to-close process (sometimes)
• Product-specific campaign (e.g. service renewals) • Existing customers • Leads from an internal database of buyers • Requires minimal customer education • Rep books complete order	*(inbound)* • Teams with field reps to support their accounts • Telecoverage reps are assigned accounts and specific buyers • Buyers contacted 3-6 times per year • Understands customers' needs • Typically covers all products • Hands large $$$ opportunities to field reps • Can book small transactions or hand over to a telesales specialist	• Targeted at a qualified prospect list (new and some existing customers) • Typically, large dollar or high-margin products • Most campaigns involve generating leads for another channel • In some cases, can book an order off a cold call

Figure 8.4 Profiles of the three telechannel applications. *Source:* Oxford Associates

the names and numbers of seventy per cent of its existing customers.

After six months, the initiative was judged an abject failure. Sales generated by the call centre barely covered its higher costs (in new telereps and new call centre infrastructure). More importantly, closed accounts had risen by an

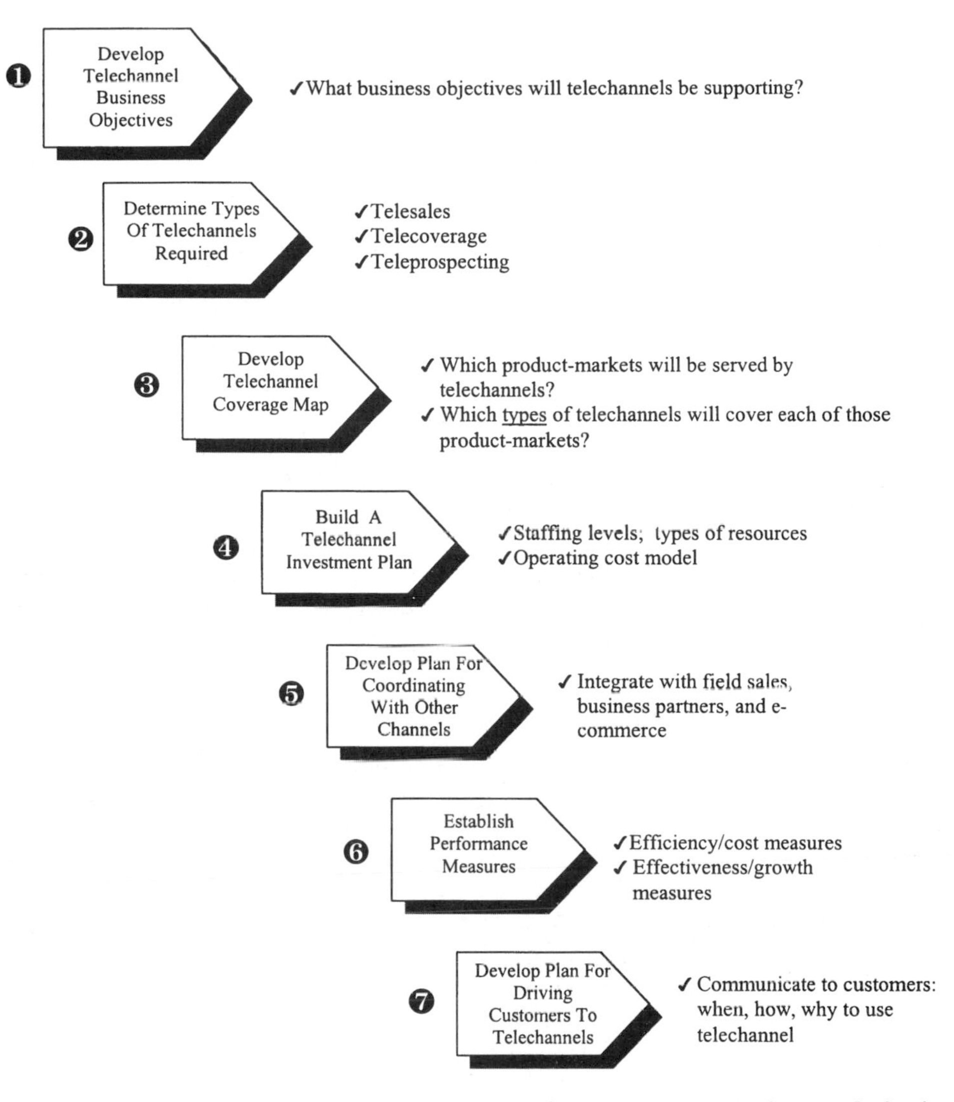

Figure 8.5 Building the strategic call centre plan – seven steps. *Source:* Oxford Associates

alarming sixteen per cent over the six-month period. The call centre, it turned out, was ill-equipped for key account development. Its telereps, measured and rewarded on the basis of the number of calls made each day, were highly motivated to get customers off the phone as quickly as possible – thus creating problems in terms of customer satisfaction. In addition, telereps, who until this initiative had been responsible for cold-calling into small businesses and low-end accounts, had been trained for 'quick kill' closes that were very ill-suited to the development of long-term relationships with existing customers. In short, the company had attempted to use its existing telesales operation to achieve the kinds of account growth that typically require a skilled, well-trained telecoverage centre. It was a basic mismatch between corporate objectives and the design of the telechannel.

In short, it's important to step back, *before* investing in a telechannel, to consider the business purpose of a telechannel in light of larger corporate goals such as growth, profitability, and customer retention. At a minimum, managers should address four questions:

- Is the fundamental goal to retain existing customers or to acquire new ones?
- Is the purpose of the telechannel to make new sales independently, or to increase the productivity and capacity of another sales channel?
- Is the purpose to generate lots of easy sales, or to increase customer loyalty and foster the development of deeper account relationships?
- Is revenue growth more important than selling profitability – or vice versa?

These questions provide a starting point for articulating and clarifying the basic business purpose of a telechannel. Answering them is the first step in building a sound strategic call centre plan.

2. Determine types of telechannels required

This next part of the planning process involves identifying the types of telechannels that can best support a set of business objectives. Figure 8.6 pro-

Business Objective	Telesales	Telecoverage	Teleprospecting
Increase existing account penetration	✓✓	✓✓✓	✓
Increase new account acquisition	✓		✓✓✓
Reduce selling costs	✓✓✓	✓	✓✓
Increase sales rep productivity	✓	✓✓✓	✓✓
Improve customer response times	✓✓	✓	
Increase customer satisfaction	✓	✓✓	

Figure 8.6 Aligning telechannel choices with business objectives

vides some guidelines for identifying how each type of telechannel might best fit with a particular type of business objective.

Of course, most companies that launch telechannel initiatives have more than one business objective in mind. At a minimum, many managers want to increase overall revenues while also reducing selling costs. Multiple business objectives can require multiple telechannels. For example, a telesales centre that is trained for efficient catalogue-based order taking will rarely be able to support a goal of long-term key account relationship development; that might require a telecoverage centre. Managers investing in telechannels thus need to think in terms of using different types of call centres for different objectives in different product-markets. The next section describes this process of targeting call centre applications at specific opportunities in the market place.

3. Develop the telechannel coverage map

Very few telechannels are applied across an entire market place; most perform a speciality function, such as lead generation, within a limited set of product-markets. As a result, it's important to consider which product-markets represent the best opportunities for each type of telechannel. Specifically, two questions must be answered:

- Which customers will each telechannel application target?
- Which products will each telechannel promote or sell?

To answer these questions, it's useful to take a look at a typical mapping of telechannels against product-markets. Generally speaking, telechannels are mapped against product-markets as follows:

- **Telesales** centres typically work in markets in which simple products are sold. Reps in these centres are skilled at closing easy, fast deals with customers who know what they want and are ready to buy. The emphasis here is on the simplicity of the product, not the type of customer. In fact, telesales channels can often be very effective at selling simpler products to large customers who also purchase more complex products through another channel.
- **Telecoverage** centres tend to focus on providing support to field reps and distributors in large, complex accounts. Telecoverage centres focus more on a type of customer – large, key accounts – than on a particular type of product. Indeed, telecoverage reps often represent a company's entire product line to a group of assigned buyers in a set of key accounts.
- **Teleprospecting** reps focus on the development of leads for another channel. Usually, the emphasis is on finding and qualifying sales opportunities that will justify the time and expense of a more expensive channel's efforts. This often means mid- and large-size accounts, and more expensive products or solutions.

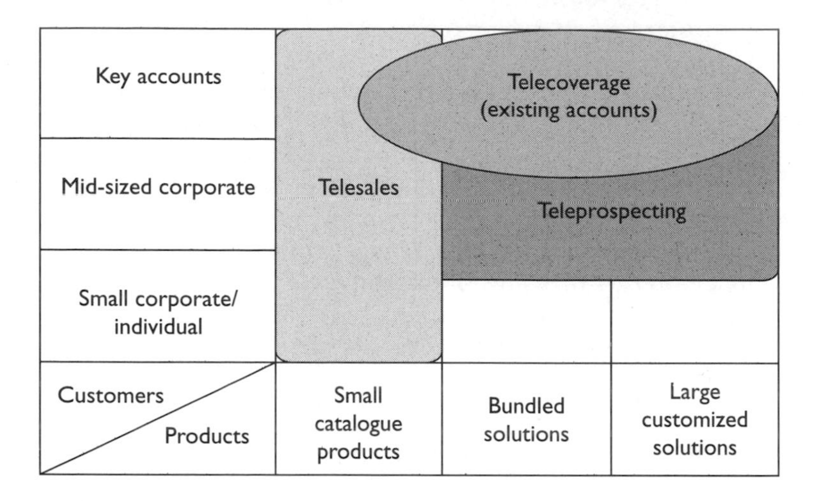

Figure 8.7 Typical telechannel coverage map

The telechannel coverage map in Figure 8.7 provides an example of how these guidelines can play out when a company seeks to map multiple telechannels against its overall market space.

This step in the planning process should be considered complete only when there is a clear picture that describes the product-markets to which each type of telechannel will be assigned.

4. Build a telechannel investment plan

Telechannels are expensive. Large ones can require millions of dollars of investments in technology and people, and in addition, can require their own buildings and other physical infrastructure costs. Even small call centres must be staffed and provided with expensive telephony and technology systems. When designing a telechannel, it is crucial to understand its cost structure and investment requirements.

There is no magic answer for designing a telechannel investment plan. Telechannels range from the very simple – a few inside sales reps sitting near some phones – to very complex telechannels consisting of global call centres with thousands of telereps spread across acres of buildings. It's an area where expert advice from an experienced call centre designer is essential. This section describes an approach for 'ball-parking' a telechannel's costs in the strategic call centre plan, as a basis for down-the-road detailed financial planning – most likely in conjunction with outside call centre experts.

Most telechannels share common categories of expenses. These include

Labor	Telerep salaries/benefits/bonuses Directors (salary/benefits) Managers (salary/benefits) Supervisors (salary/benefits) Administrators (salary/benefits) Recruiting Training
Technology	Telerep workstations Software (e.g. databases) Hardware (servers, etc.)
Telephony	Telephone equipment (e.g. headsets) Recurring telephone charges
Overhead	Infrastructure start-up (e.g. new buildings) Recurring facilities operating costs General overhead allocation

Figure 8.8 Call centre cost/investment categories

labour costs, technology costs, telephony equipment costs, and overhead/ facilities costs. Figure 8.8 suggests how these four basic categories of expenses can be subdivided into more detailed cost items.

As suggested in the figure, many of the costs associated with a telechannel boil down to *people* – call centre reps, managers, administrators, and so on. Indeed, as a general rule of thumb, about eighty per cent of a call centre's cost structure consists of telereps' salaries, benefits, recruiting and training. This is a very useful benchmark, because it is not that hard to estimate a telechannel's total cost once labour expenses have been estimated.

To take a simple example, consider a new call centre with a revenue target of $10 million. Assume it is staffed by telereps who are each expected to generate $1 million in sales (a reasonable benchmark for many telechannels). That suggests a total staffing of ten telereps. A telerep's fully-loaded salary is generally in the neighbourhood of $70,000. So the basic labour cost for the call centre would be 10 × $70,000, or $700,000. Now add twenty-five per cent for technology, telephone equipment, and facilities costs – another $175,000. This would yield a total call centre operating cost of $875,000, or 8.75 per cent of revenues – which, in fact, is usually about what a call centre costs to operate on an ongoing basis.

	1999	2000	2001
Forecasted telechannel revenue	$50 m	$250 m	$325 m
Productivity per telerep	$1 m	$1.75 m	$2.2 m
# of telereps required	50	115	150
Fully-loaded cost per telerep	$70,000	$75,000	$80,000
Infrastructure cost-per-station (telerep)	$20,000	$20,000	$20,000
- information technology			
- technology equipment			
- data bases, etc.			
Total telechannel operating costs	***$4.50 m***	***$10.93 m***	***$15.00 m***

Infrastructure cost-per-station: normally about 25 % of fully-loaded cost-per-rep

Figure 8.9 Summary telechannel 'pro forma' income statement

This kind of loose estimating of costs, though obviously inexact, can help to establish the order of magnitude of a call centre's operating budget. Let's take it a step further. Consider a company that's planning to grow aggressively through telesales: next year's forecasted revenue is $50 million, but the company is seeking $325 million in telechannel sales within three years. How much would something like that cost to support? Figure 8.9 shows how the cost can be ball-parked with just a few simple assumptions.

As the figure suggests, a telechannel's revenue projections can easily be translated into an operating budget by making some assumptions:

- **Revenue-per-telerep** Here, it is estimated in Year 1 at $1 million, gradually increasing to $2.2 million as telereps become more experienced and productive.
- **Fully-loaded cost-per-telerep** Salaries, benefits, etc. Here, it is shown as $70,000 to $80,000 – which is often a good approximation.
- **All other combined costs** Call centre management, facilities, technology, etc. – which, as stated earlier, are usually about twenty-five per cent of telerep labour costs. In the example, it is shown as a flat $20,000 per telerep to keep the example simple.

A little number crunching, as shown in Figure 8.9, suggests that a company seeking $325 million in telesales could anticipate operating costs of about $15 million. This kind of basic financial modelling is an essential component of a strategic call centre plan, although, of course, more detailed financial planning will be required later on.

5. Develop a plan for coordinating with other channels

Telechannels rarely operate independently within a go-to-market system. More often, they rely on and support a variety of other channels throughout the sales process. The quality of a telechannel's coordination and integration with other channels can greatly influence its performance and success. The strategic call centre plan should account for channel coordination issues and attempt to minimize problems before they happen. This section takes a look at the coordination issues that typically arise between a call centre and three other channels: field sales forces, business partners, and e-commerce channels.

Coordination with the field sales force

In large accounts, call centres can provide support to a sales force in some or all of the following areas:

- lead generation
- pre-sales support
- post-sales support
- small-order processing
- relationship management

In addition, large account customers often like to 'surf' back and forth between field sales reps and telereps, asking field reps to handle their complex transactions while calling on telereps to handle routine reorders or simple purchases. All of this creates the potential for channel confusion as field reps and telereps try to figure out who's supposed to be doing what in different selling situations. Tight integration between a telechannel and a sales force is mandatory when the two channels will be working together – or even working independently in the same product-markets. The strategic call centre plan should:

- Identify which types of sales or customers should be handled or supported by each channel.
- Establish clear roles, responsibilities and hand-off points for sales in which both channels will be involved.
- Suggest two to three 'pilots' (controlled tests in low-risk accounts) to complete a proof-of-concept test and to iron out any potential integration problems prior to broad-scale implementation.
- Establish performance metrics that motivate telechannel reps and field reps to work cooperatively together within accounts. For instance, sales revenue credit may need to be double-counted to encourage reps across the two channels to work together in the larger interest of key customer development and satisfaction.

Coordination with business partners

Telechannels can provide substantial lead generation and sales support to business partner channels. For example, IBM supports its business partners in the small and medium size business (SMB) market by advertising heavily to generates calls into its SMB call centre. Telereps in this centre qualify incoming leads and route them to appropriate partners. Partners then take these leads, close the sales, and provide post-sale fulfilment and support. This is an increasingly popular selling model in the high technology industry; for the cost of a little lead generation and some coordination with business partners, companies such as IBM are rewarded with substantial sales revenues and well-supported customers. However, telechannel-partner coordination is not without its problems, including channel conflict, dissatisfied partners, and sales opportunities that fall through the cracks between the channels. To prevent these problems, the strategic call centre plan should include the following:

- **A realistic assessment of the telechannel staffing levels needed to make business partners successful.** Partners quickly sour on lead generation programs that fail to deliver a reasonable number of qualified leads – and they begin to look elsewhere (i.e. competitors) when they feel lead-deprived. So if you have 100 partners, and each has been promised five good leads per month, you have to put in place the call centre personnel to come up with 500 good leads per month – at a minimum. The strategic call centre plan should clearly specify the number of telereps needed to deliver the quantity of leads that has been promised to business partners.
- **A 'closed loop' performance measurement system that tracks end-to-end sales.** The big risk in telerep–partner integration is the 'missing-in-action' sale: the opportunity that falls through the cracks for lack of an effective hand-off between channels. To avoid this problem, it is essential to track leads from the moment they come in the door, to the hand-off between channels, to the completion and support of the sale. End-to-end management of leads is essential to monitor the performance and success of both telereps and business partners – and to keep track of sales opportunities. The call centre plan should clearly define who is responsible for recording lead data and how this data will get tracked, updated and reported from the initiation to the completion of a sale.
- **A compensation plan to encourage telechannel cooperation with business partners.** As in the case of integration with a direct sales force, a compensation system must be designed to ensure that telereps and business partners cooperate in the sales process. Telereps' compensation plans should reward them for delivering leads to partners and for sales that are closed by those partners. Most of the time, the compensation plan should also provide disincentives for telereps who close their own sales rather than pass those leads to business partners. Competition between lead-generating telereps and business partners should be avoided in almost all cases.

Coordination with e-commerce

In many industries, customers are beginning to use call centres and e-commerce channels (such as the Internet) interchangeably. Book orders, flower orders, personal computer orders – all are simple examples of products that are sold in both channels, either channel, or a combination of the two channels. Customers today increasingly research their purchases on the Internet, place orders to buy products over the phone, and then use the Internet to check the status of their orders. These channels, in short, often share the same customers and types of transactions – and often share pricing structures and promotional campaigns too. The integration of these two channels – sometimes called *Teleweb* – is a big part of cutting-edge channel strategy, and it requires that the two channels be coordinated closely throughout the sales process. The strategic call centre plan should establish:

- **A joint marketing campaign strategy.** For products or services that can be sold over the telephone or the Internet, marketing campaigns should be designed to educate customers about the availability of *either* channel for a purchase or inquiry. Advertisements, promotions, etc., should be planned with an eye toward presenting these channels as interchangeable to customers – so they can choose whichever channel they prefer to use.
- **Business-process and technical links between telechannels and e-commerce channels.** Seamless customer service between a telechannel and an e-commerce channel requires strong technology and business process links. At a minimum, telereps in most companies should have the ability to monitor customers' online activities during inbound telephone calls, in order to assist these customers in their web-based orders or inquiries. More advanced technologies include tools such as *screen synchronization*, in which on-line customers call into telereps, who can then take control of their screens and talk them through order processes while these customers are on the telephone. Whichever technologies are selected, the call centre plan should identify the required process and technology links needed for telereps and e-commerce channels to provide a seamless buying experience to customers.
- **Common customer database.** Finally, it's important to keep in mind that telechannels and e-commerce channels often serve the same customers in the same markets with the same products. As a result, it makes sense that both channels would work off the same databases of customer transaction histories. As a simple example, a customer who requests information six times on a specific product over the Internet is an excellent candidate for a follow-up outbound telesales call – but this only works if the call centre has access to web transaction data and knows that the customer has placed those half-dozen online inquiries. The strategic call centre plan should clearly specify what types of data the two channels will share – and how that data will be collected, aggregated, and made available to the telechannel for outbound sales efforts.

In sum, channel integration is a serious issue in a call centre initiative. Telechannels generally work hand-in-hand with other channels, and thought must be given to how, when, and where a call centre will interact with those channels throughout the sales process. In the case of e-commerce, it's important to keep in mind that telechannels and web sites are becoming interchangeable – in the minds of customers – and require shared systems, processes and technologies.

6. Establish performance measures

As with any channel, ongoing performance measurement is the backbone of superior channel performance. The issue with telechannels is not often one of a lack of metrics. Quite the opposite! Providers of call centre telephony equipment – the telephone switch vendors – have all built strong capabilities into their products to measure and report telerep performance along dozens of dimensions. The question is whether they are measuring the right things.

Typical monitored call centre activities – inbound and outbound call volumes, average inbound call wait times, abandon rates, cost per call, etc. – tend to provide a wealth of information to help companies gauge and understand telerep *operational efficiency*. The problem, as suggested earlier, is that many companies are trying to figure out how to manage their call centres for greater *effectiveness*, or contribution toward strategic goals such as revenue growth, profitability and customer satisfaction. That is a different animal than operational efficiency, and requires different performance metrics. For example, telesales channels are often measured in terms of calls per day and the average cost per call. But what if a company's primary goal is to increase customer satisfaction and develop a smaller number of high-volume customer relationships? It may make more sense to measure things such as customers' satisfaction with call centre service, customer reorder rates, and average order size. In short, effectiveness metrics are just as important as efficiency metrics. Indeed, for companies that are primarily seeking revenue and market share growth, they can be more important. Figure 8.10 suggests a handful of solid metrics, for both efficiency and effectiveness, across the three key telechannel applications.

While looking over the various and many options for measuring and tracking call centre performance, managers should resist the temptation just to measure the easy stuff that comes preloaded on telephony equipment vendors' products. This data can provide little information on how well a call centre is actually supporting a set of strategic business objectives. A small number of well-chosen *effectiveness* metrics can say a lot more about a call centre's overall contribution to growth within a go-to-market system.

7. Develop a plan for driving customers to telechannels

It may sound banal, but here's the essential truth about call centres: they only work if customers use them. Particularly in the case of inbound call centres, cus-

Measurement Type	Telesales	Telecoverage	Teleprospecting
Effectiveness Metrics (increase revenue growth and customer satisfaction)	✓ Revenue per rep ✓ Average order size ✓ Customer satisfaction rate ✓ Customer reorder rate	✓ Account 'share of wallet' ✓ Customer purchase frequency ✓ Average order size ✓ Customer satisfaction	✓ Number of leads generated ✓ Lead-to-close rate ✓ $$$ of opportunities generated ✓ Prospect perceptions of telereps
Efficiency Metrics (increase productivity and reduce costs)	✓ Cost per order closed ✓ Orders per rep per day	✓ Number of buyers per telerep ✓ Increase in sales force productivity	✓ Calls per telerep per day ✓ Average cost per lead generated

Figure 8.10 Telechannel performance metrics – a short list. *Source:* Oxford Associates

tomer awareness programs – organized efforts to encourage customers to work through telechannels – are an essential part of a call centre launch. Aside from the obvious – making sure that telephone numbers are prominently displayed on brochures, advertisements, etc. – a customer awareness program should:

- **Communicate *when* to use the telechannel (versus other channels).** It can be very unclear to customers when they are supposed to use a telechannel versus, say, a field sales rep. Large account buyers may be accustomed to working with field reps, and they may not understand that they should call in orders under $250 to a telerep for faster processing and delivery. A telechannel launch should be accompanied by an education program for large accounts that explains the circumstances in which those customers should use a call centre as opposed to another channel.
- **Communicate *why* they should use the telechannel.** Telechannels are often readily accepted by customers, who like the convenience and self-service of doing business over the phone. Not all customers, however, can be migrated easily to a telechannel. Large corporate buyers, accustomed to hand holding from field sales reps, can find call centres more impersonal and limited than a face-to-face rep. Thus, the benefits to customers of using a telechannel – lower costs, faster service, more efficient order processing, etc. – need to be communicated in advance of a new call centre launch. Customers generally use call centres only when they understand the advantages of doing business through this channel and believe it to be preferable to other available alternatives.

In sum, a customer awareness program is an important component of a strategic call centre plan. Customers must know how to get in contact with a call centre, and must understand when, how and why they should use telechannels alongside or in replacement of other available channels.

Summary

Many companies still view the call centre as a back-office organization whose responsibility is to handle customer complaints and, perhaps, take a few direct mail orders. This chapter presented an alternative view about telechannels: that they can be high-impact components of a go-to-market system, and can produce dramatic gains in revenue growth, profitability and customer loyalty. Certainly, companies such as Marriott, GEICO, Dell and other market leaders have exploited the potential of telechannels to achieve these goals. Now, other companies must make the choice to convert back-office call centre operations into true strategic assets.

This chapter examined three types of telechannels: telesales, telecoverage, and teleprospecting call centres. *Telesales* centres focus on smaller, simpler products, and take complete responsibility for sale closure. *Telecoverage* centres, on the other hand, focus on the penetration of large accounts, and generally work hand-in-hand with field reps to develop and grow key buyer relationships. Finally, *teleprospecting* centres find and develop well-qualified leads for follow-up by another channel – usually a field sales force. Each type of channel can make a unique contribution to a company's overall go-to-market success and performance.

Several underlying themes drive the successes of leading companies that have achieved competitive advantage through telechannels. Three are particularly important:

- **Strategic focus** Telechannel design must be a 'top-down' process that begins with overall corporate objectives, and then identifies telechannel solutions which can best support those objectives in the market place. Only after the business purpose of a telechannel has been clarified does it make much sense to worry about detailed design.
- **Long-term perspective** Telechannel implementation is a big investment. Companies spend millions of dollars designing, building, and implementing telechannels. This is not a responsibility that should be assigned to 'quick fixers' within an organization – people looking for easy, painless solutions. Call centres can take two to three years to reach peak performance, and always require substantial planning and careful execution. Executives should think in terms of assigning long-range thinkers, and committing the right levels of resources and investments, before launching a major telechannel initiative.
- **Technology bias** Successful telechannels are always supported by well-conceived and well-designed information systems and customer databases. Activities such as account telecoverage, end-to-end telesales order processing, and targeted teleprospecting all require robust information systems to succeed. Managers must look at technology not just as a capital expense, but rather as a key source of competitive advantage and productivity in a telechannel.

Finally, it is always worth remembering that a telechannel's key strategic asset is the quality, training, and professionalism of its telereps. Good telereps are hard to find, and they're easy to lose; the teleservices business has high attrition and turnover. As a result, it's crucial to spend sufficient time and effort figuring out how to attract, train, and hold onto high-quality high-performers to staff a telechannel organization. Without those people, no telechannel initiative can succeed.

Notes

[1] Direct Marketing Association, 'Results of WEFA Study', 1997.
[2] To handle inquiries from both new and existing customers.
[3] For example, automobile type, insurance regulations, zip code, driver demographics, etc.
[4] Various industry sources – 1998 data.
[5] Richard J. Heuther, 'Developing Business to Business Teleprospecting in GE', quoted from Call Center Managers Forum (www.callcentres.com.au), 6 October 1998.
[6] Sources: *Fortune*, 6 October 1998, press release; BMW Annual Report 1997.
[7] Teleprospecting is often called 'telemarketing'; we prefer 'teleprospecting' for clarity in relation to other types of telechannels.
[8] Cross-selling: leveraging established customer relationships by selling existing products and services into accounts that have not already purchased them. Up-selling: leveraging established customer relationships by moving them up the 'food chain' toward more comprehensive (and expensive) products and solutions.

Chapter 9

The Internet

The Internet, without a doubt, is having a profound effect on how companies go to market. Unheard of until a few years ago by anyone except scientists and technologists, it has already become an important medium of exchange. The numbers speak for themselves. On-line shopping – just one component of Internet commerce – hit $12.4 billion dollars in 1997 and is projected to reach $425 billion by 2002[1]. That's an abstract number, so let's think in terms of specific companies. This year, Cisco Systems is selling $20 million worth of product *every day* over the Internet[2]. Car-buying service AutoByTel has processed 1.5 million online purchase requests in its three years of operation, and now handles over 100,000 customer requests per month[3]. Online bookseller Amazon.com, launched in June 1996, has already sold books to over 3.1 million customers, and has an annual sales rate of almost a half billion dollars[4]. As far as how many people are on the Internet in total, no one even really knows, and in any event the number increases by thousands on an hourly basis. Figure 9.1 provides as good an estimate as any, from a leading research firm[5].

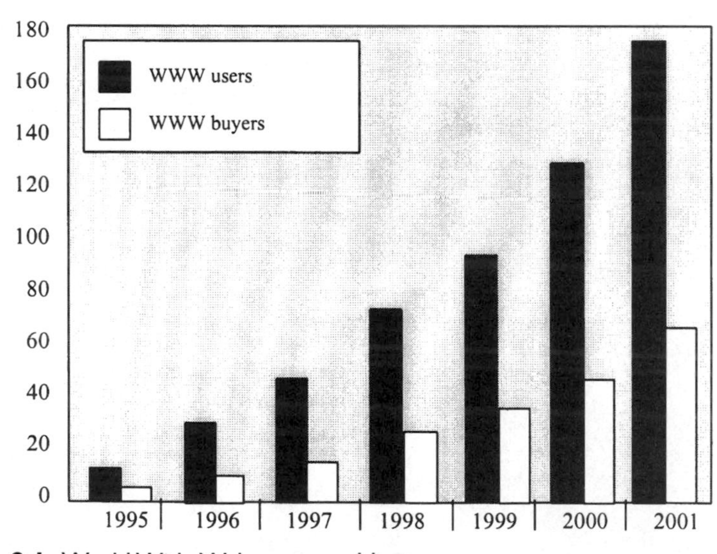

Figure 9.1 World Wide Web users and buyers

There is simply no historical analogy to describe the speed at which the Internet is growing and becoming woven into the fabric of commercial activity. There is also no historical analogy to describe the hype that has accompanied this growth. The Internet has been described as everything from a major 'paradigm shift' (whatever that means) to a digital revolution that will fundamentally reshape our lives, to a new medium that will drive traditional media, such as television and newspapers, into the dustbin of history. All of that may or may not pan out.

The future of technology is not the subject of this chapter, though. We leave the paradigm shifts and digital revolutions to others, and deal with the Internet on a more prosaic and grounded level: as a *sales channel*, a route through which companies can do business and build relationships with their customers. The Internet's capabilities are only now becoming known, and much remains to be learned, explored, and developed over the next decade. Even at this point, however, it's clear that as a sales channel the Internet offers four important benefits:

- **Lower sales costs** On a cost-per-transaction basis, the Internet is, simply, the lowest-cost route to market. An Internet transaction usually costs no more than a quarter as much as one made by a telechannel, and is often orders of magnitude cheaper than a transaction made by a field sales rep or a business partner. Figure 9.2 provides an illustration of just how large the cost-savings can be (this is basically the same as Figure 5.2, reprinted here for convenience).

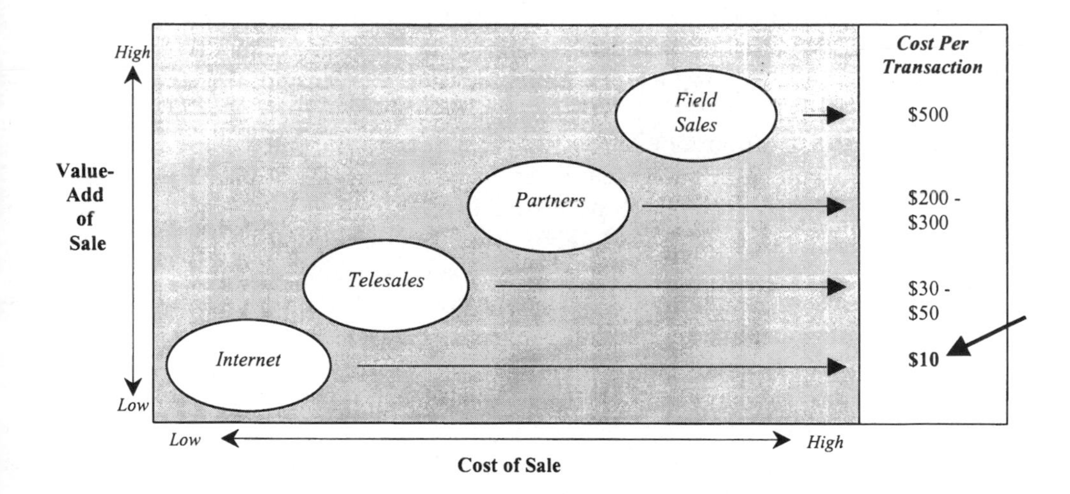

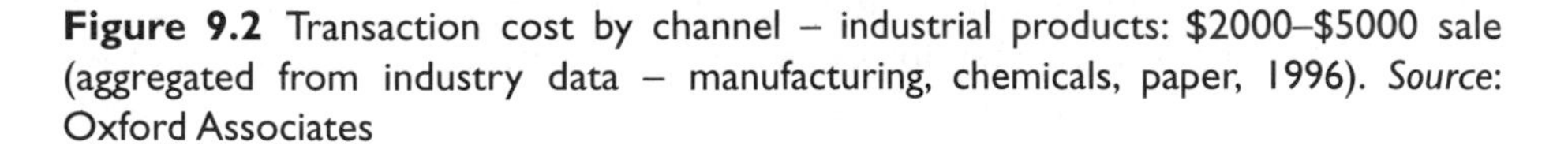

Figure 9.2 Transaction cost by channel – industrial products: $2000–$5000 sale (aggregated from industry data – manufacturing, chemicals, paper, 1996). *Source*: Oxford Associates

- **Expanded market reach** The Internet provides the means to reach untold numbers of people – some of whom might actually be potential buyers – at little or no incremental selling cost. Unlike any other channel, *the cost of getting in touch with ten million people is about the same as the cost of getting in touch with a thousand.* Not every company has yet been able to translate this unique capability into a real selling advantage, but those that have, such as Amazon.com, have built customer bases in months that took other companies years or decades to build with other channels.
- **Increased customer loyalty** To date, most managers have thought of the Internet in terms of its ability to make sales of simple, low-cost products to consumers. Yet its real power may be in high-end business-to-business account development. This involves its ability to provide large accounts with a combination of self-service, lower prices, in-depth purchasing assistance (through on-line help facilities), product training, round-the-clock availability, interaction through e-mail and discussion boards, and pushbutton connection to another channel (e.g. a call centre). Companies such as Cisco and Netscape are already incorporating many of these features into their e-commerce systems to achieve tighter coordination with their large customers as well as their partners and vendors. The bottom line is that the Internet can be a powerful source of enhanced customer service as well as increased contact frequency.
- **Leverage for other sales channels** Like a call centre, the Internet can be a tool for increasing the productivity of other, more expensive channels such as field sales forces and distributors. It can generate low-cost leads for follow-up by another channel. It can take care of many types of low-end, routine transactions such as simple supply replenishment orders. It is also proving to be a pretty good channel for some types of technical support and customer service. In short, the Internet can be used to free up the time and energy of other channels so they can focus on higher-end strategic opportunities and new business opportunities.

Perhaps the most important fact about the Internet is that customers are getting used to it. They *like* this channel. It offers them fast, efficient service, the ability to do their own research and purchase on their own schedules, and often substantially lower prices. Internet usage will undoubtedly increase, in both consumer and business-to-business markets, as more people go on-line and become accustomed to doing business through this medium. In short, for many companies, the Internet is not exactly an option anymore. It's become a necessary addition to the channel portfolio for organizations that want to stay in tune with evolving customer preferences and buying behaviors.

In sum, evidence is accumulating that the Internet is here to stay, and that it is rapidly evolving into a real commercial medium. The challenge is to get beyond the hype, and to examine the Internet as a viable sales channel – one with limitations but also with unique capabilities. That is the purpose of this chapter. It looks at a process for building an e-commerce strategy, from the initial definition of an Internet market coverage plan to the difficult challenge

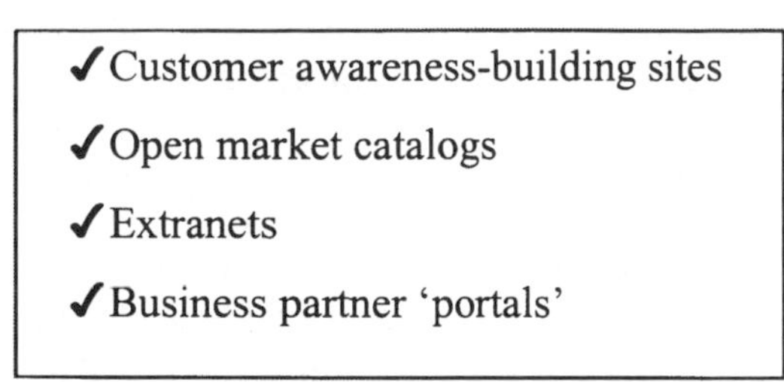

Figure 9.3 The four types of e-commerce sites

of driving customers and new prospects to the web to do business. We begin with a simple primer that describes the four basic types of Internet commerce sites.

Doing business on the Internet – a primer

Not everything that happens on the Internet is a sales transaction. Companies, academic institutions, government agencies, and all sorts of other organizations and individuals use the Internet for a wide range of purposes. Most *commercial* Internet sites focus on some combination of the following activities: generating customer awareness; creating demand for products and services; processing sales transactions; and providing technical support and customer service. These commercial 'applications' of the Internet are often collectively referred to as *e-commerce,* although the definition is a little hazy and is still evolving[6]. E-commerce sites come in four basic flavours, as shown in Figure 9.3.

Each type of e-commerce site is discussed below.

Awareness sites

Many companies already have some type of 'awareness-building' web site, and it's a reasonable prediction that within a couple of years, *every* company, from a billion-dollar multinational corporation to a local retail shop, will have one. An awareness site is the standard *www.mycompany.com* web site that provides basic information about a company's background, products and services, locations, etc. In general, an awareness site is best understood as an electronic version of a company's product brochures, annual reports, public relations announcements, recruiting materials, etc. Sometimes referred to as 'brochure-ware,' these sites typically contain:

- A solid overview of the company – without great depth in any particular area
- Static or infrequently-updated content

- An ability to personalize the visitor's experience to a minimal extent
- Limited or no ability to give price quotes, or to recommend or sell products

Awareness sites are used primarily to stimulate interest in a brand, to educate customers about products and services, and in some cases to generate inbound e-mail inquiries that can be forwarded to another sales channel.

While these sites do not have the ability to close deals, they are nevertheless very valuable to customers and to the companies that build these sites. The explosion of awareness sites has dramatically increased the volume and flow of information across many markets. These sites give customers the ability to view product and service information, and to compare and contrast offerings across competing suppliers. Awareness sites contribute to customers' lasting images about suppliers, and help to shape their preferences for different companies' offerings. As a result, it has become increasingly critical for *every* company – particularly those in highly competitive markets – to develop clean, professional awareness sites that communicate a positive image. The cost of designing and implementing a high-quality awareness site varies, but for large, complex organizations it is generally estimated to be in the range of $200,000 to $1,000,000.

Open market catalogue sites

The next step up in web site functionality is the *open market catalogue* site. In addition to providing corporate and product information, these sites allow customers to make purchases over the web from an on-line catalogue (i.e. something comparable in nature to the direct mail catalogues of an L.L. Bean).

The best-known and most easily understood open market catalogue site is that of Amazon.com. The leading retailer of books over the Internet, Amazon.com offers over three million book titles. With an easy-to-use and entertaining site, Amazon allows customers to search for books by subject matter, title, author, etc., and then to place orders with a credit card. Amazon ships most orders within three business days by drawing on its network of book stocking distributors. As of mid-1998, Amazon was taking over 10,000 orders *per day* on its web site.

Amazon's success – and the success of other, similar sites – hasn't gone unnoticed, of course. Many companies are now pursuing the development of their own open market catalogue sites. If Wave I of the Internet was about getting on the web with some brochureware – some corporate information and perhaps an e-mail response form – Wave II is clearly about offering customers a site with a catalogue of products and services so they can make actual purchases.

The performance to date of various open market catalogue sites suggests that they work best with:

- Off-the-rack or minimally-customized products
- Standardized, competitive pricing structures
- Readily-available product inventory
- Educated customers who know what they need

Eventually most companies will offer some sort of on-line catalogue to their customers, at least for their lower-cost and less-customized products. As many Internet managers have realized, however, it may take several years to work out the various technical, product packaging and pricing, and customer education issues to make this type of site work optimally as a sales channel.

Extranets

Extranets are secure, customized sites that companies set up for their large customers (and, sometimes, suppliers too). These sites are usually accessible only by designated buyers within key accounts. They offer all of the functionality and services of awareness sites and open market catalogues, and also allow customers to do some or all of the following:

- Review contracts and discount agreements on-line
- Place orders for standard products
- Configure customized products, get price quotes, and in some cases, place on-line orders for these customized or unique offerings
- Receive order confirmations and track order and shipping status
- Access information and content specifically relevant to their account
- Identify and e-mail the specific individuals (sales reps, telereps, customer service professionals) assigned to their account
- Review content specifically developed and updated for their needs

Extranets have been around for nearly twenty years; they used to be called electronic data interchange (EDI) systems. But while EDI was limited mostly to non-graphical, structured data (e.g. product codes and price lists), web-based extranets provide a much broader range of information and services that can greatly solidify the relationship between supplier and customer.

Dell Computer is one example of a company that has emphasized extranets. Dell's extranets are called 'Premier Pages' and are basically customized web sites for over 10,000 of the company's largest customers. These sites reside inside the secure firewalls of Dell's customers and allow individual executives to purchase customized personal computers at discounted and pre-negotiated prices. In addition to providing individual corporate buyers with this easy-to-access channel, Dell's Premier Pages reduce the amount of time their high-value sales reps have to spend on small, simple transactions. Once an extranet is established within an account, Dell's sales reps are able to devote more time to customer relationship development and problem solving. Importantly, these extranets have proven to be strong barriers to entry for competitors. Once corporate buyers get accustomed to doing business over a proprietary extranet – and get comfortable with a set of products, prices, and extranet site functions – they tend to stick with a supplier. Dell's extranets, in fact, have helped build 'sticky' customer relationships that have contributed to its industry-leading account retention and growth rates.

From a customer's perspective, well-designed extranets increase the ease of doing business and ensure that they are getting special price discounts as well as the service levels negotiated in the overall supplier contract. From the supplier's perspective, the benefits include more than just customer satisfaction. By providing an extranet with a robust set of capabilities, suppliers can dramatically reduce sales and service costs, increase customer sales growth rates, and gain share within large accounts.

Business partner 'portals'

In the world before e-commerce, a business partner was an independent third party who represented, and sold, your products on your behalf. The value of a business partner, such as a retail store, distributor, or manufacturer's agent, was (and still is) its ability to:

- offer your products along with the complementary products of other suppliers
- reach and penetrate dispersed markets
- provide additional value-added services (e.g. financing, customer education, etc.)
- complete sales at a lower selling cost

Put simply, most companies enlist business partners to reach more customers, sell more products, and make more profit.

Business partnering in the world of e-commerce is no different. What has become known as 'portals' are actually – from a sales channel perspective – third-party web sites with which a company can partner to promote its products. The most commonly known portals are Internet access points such as Yahoo!, Excite and America Online. These companies, along with other portals, provide vendors with banner advertising space as well as customized 'hot links' to corporate web sites. In a narrow sense, these portals are the on-line equivalent of print magazines, in which a company can buy space to promote its services and offer a toll-free number for customers to place in-bound enquiries and orders.

But a new, and perhaps more compelling, type of Internet portal is emerging – and it looks remarkably like the traditional business partner channel. These business partner portals include companies such as Computer Data Warehouse (CDW) in the high tech industry and Charles Schwab in financial services. Some of these companies offer their own product lines, but most serve primarily as electronic distribution channels for other vendors. CDW, for example, offers 20,000 computer products and supplies from vendors such as Microsoft, IBM, Hewlett-Packard, Apple Computer, and many other high tech manufacturers. For many small high tech companies, CDW's direct marketing channels, including its e-commerce site, account for over twenty per cent of all sales volume. Even larger high tech firms rely heavily on this new type of channel. Apple Computer, for example, does not sell any of its products directly on its Apple.com web site – but it has a very strong e-commerce channel consisting of representation on the third-party sites of companies such as CDW.

Here's the important point: *to sell products over the Internet, companies do not necessarily have to set up their own fully-functioning e-commerce sites*. Indeed, just as it is generally less expensive to sell through distributors than a direct sales force, in the same manner it can be far more cost-effective to build a solid awareness site and yet leave the actual selling of products to an e-commerce partner. This approach has the added benefit of being attractive to customers, who generally prefer the variety and enhanced service provided by business partners – whether electronic or otherwise. In addition, this approach requires far less start-up e-commerce investment than an approach centred on direct-to-customer e-commerce site development.

These four types of e-commerce sites provide a starting point for thinking about the kind of 'web presence', or participation in e-commerce, that might make sense – depending on what you're trying to achieve on the Internet and in the market place. It should come as no surprise that the more time, energy and money you are willing to invest in e-commerce, the larger the potential gains can be. A basic awareness-building site can be put on the Internet at a fraction of the cost of a complex open market catalogue that's linked to a series of extranets. More complex sites that close large deals over the Internet, however, can offer larger potential returns in terms of sales growth and business development.

Building an e-commerce strategy

This section describes a simple process for putting together a coherent and sound strategic e-commerce plan. The emphasis is on identifying the web site business applications, investments, and performance measures needed to deploy the Internet as a real channel within a go-to-market system. The process is shown in Figure 9.4.

1. Develop an e-commerce coverage map

There are two fundamental issues that must be dealt with at the beginning of an e-commerce initiative:

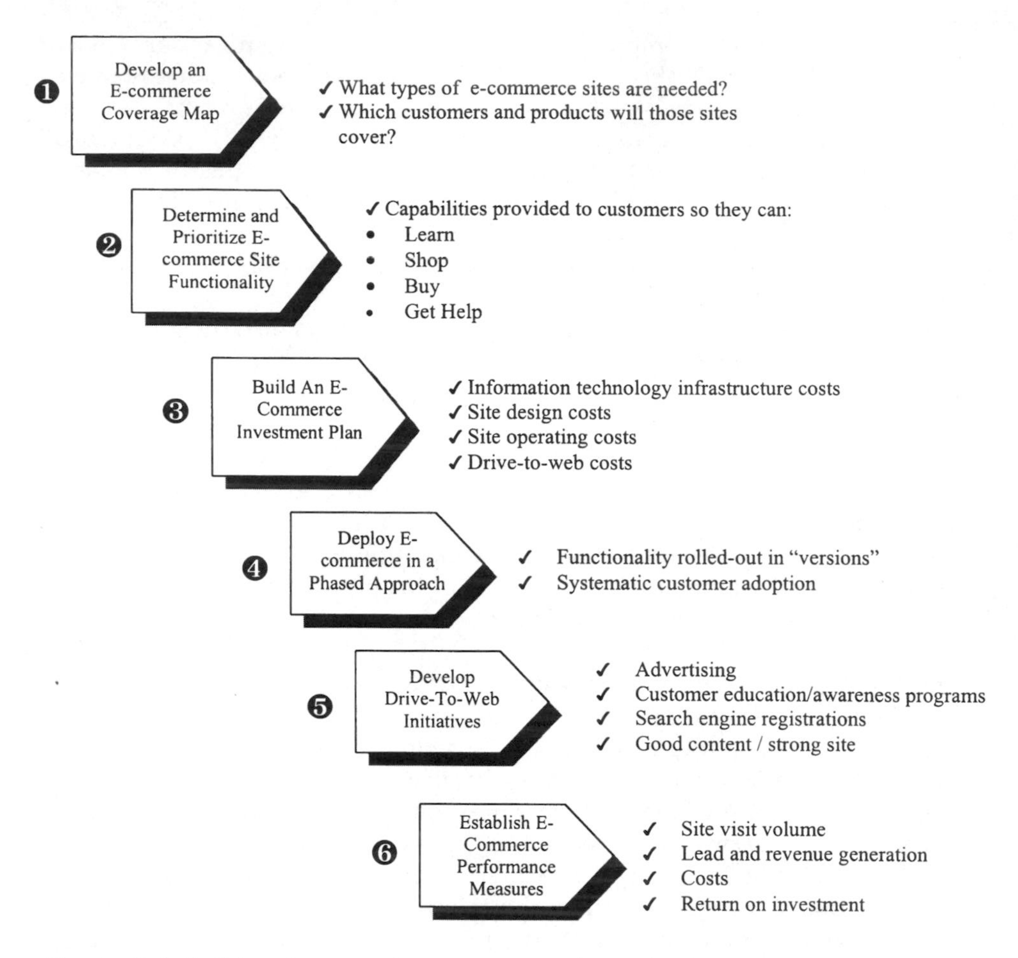

Figure 9.4 Building the strategic e-commerce plan – six steps

- 'Which customers are we going to try to attract through e-commerce?'
- 'What kinds of products and services are we going to promote or sell to them?'

For most companies, the best starting point is to think in terms of using this channel to serve the low-end segment of the market: simple, off-the-rack products to consumers and small businesses. Certainly, this is the segment where most of the big names on the Internet, such as Amazon.com and 1-800-Flowers, have made their mark. This approach would suggest a coverage model that looks like the one shown in Figure 9.5.

As suggested in the figure, the basic approach is to get started with a site that enables small customers to purchase simple, off-the-rack products on-line through, for example, an open market catalogue. The challenge with this

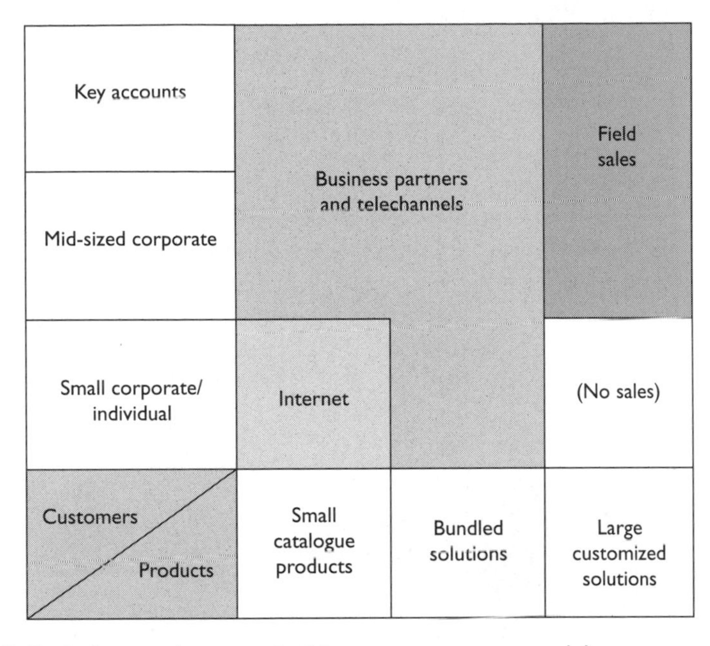

Figure 9.5 Basic 'low-end transaction' Internet coverage model

approach – at least for companies with broad product lines – is to exert some discipline in choosing products for inclusion on the site. A simple on-line catalogue of thirty to fifty off-the-rack products can be far more effective than an ambitious but misguided effort to stuff a larger number of more complex product into the catalogue. This type of web site is best seen for what it is: a channel that will serve a defined and limited subset of the overall market.

If the goal is to serve a broader range of product-markets with the Internet – for instance, medium and large-sized customers who buy more complex solutions – it may be necessary to invest in more complicated, expensive web sites. A coverage map should be developed that directs these different types of web sites toward specific product-markets within the overall market place. A sample of this approach is shown in Figure 9.6.

As Figure 9.6 suggests, a company that intends to serve a wide range of product-markets must begin to think in terms of a larger set of web sites. Large account transactions – particularly those involving complex products – may require specialized extranet sites to handle pricing flexibility and product customization. Middle-market development will require high-quality awareness-building sites. Finally, cost-effective, high-volume business in the small transaction segment will require open market catalogues or business partner portal arrangements.

While an Internet coverage map could certainly be developed at a high degree of complexity, with dozens of web sites covering discrete product-markets, the truth is that it often better to identify a good e-commerce opportunity and go

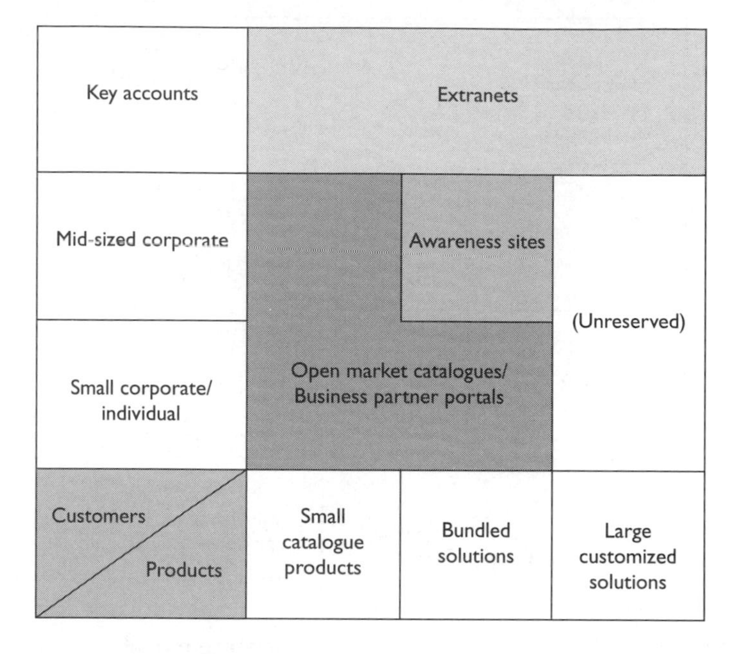

Figure 9.6 Example of multiple site e-commerce coverage map. *Source*: Oxford Associates

after it with a single, well-designed web site. The Internet is a new medium, and for most companies it makes sense to get on the Internet with an awareness site and a small catalogue, and then take some time to learn about this channel and see what develops. In fact, a simple coverage model that targets a small and manageable segment of the market place (e.g. small customers, simple products) is almost always the right answer for companies that are new to the Internet.

2. Determine and prioritize e-commerce site functionality

After choosing a product-market and an appropriate type of web site, the obvious question is: what kinds of functions and capabilities should be put on the site? Selection of site functionality can be a confusing and difficult matter; this section provides an approach for getting started.

Web site functionality should reflect what people will want to *do* once they get to your site. An airline company investing in a web site, for example, would have to offer trip ticketing and fare comparisons, because that is a large part of what people do on airlines' web sites. A consulting firm, on the other hand, wouldn't necessarily want to offer *any* products; people visit those sites to get information and learn about the capabilities of different consulting firms. It's important to figure out *why* people would visit a new web site. Generally, they visit sites to do one or more of the following things:

- **Learn** Some people visit web sites to learn about companies and their capabilities.
- **Shop** Sometimes people visit a web site to figure out what a company has to offer, and to get a detailed understanding of different products and services. If they find something they want, they may want to buy.
- **Buy** Here, customers place orders for products online, often making payment electronically (e.g. with a credit card).
- **Get help** Customers may also visit a web site to get help – with a purchase, with post-sale support, or with customer service.

Each of these different uses by customers implies a different set of site functions, as shown in Figure 9.7.

When identifying a target set of web site functions, it's important to keep in mind the value of simplicity. Many companies have discovered the hard way that clean web sites with fewer, yet easier-to-use, functions can attract more

Customer Activity	Customer Requirement	Sample Site Functions
Learn	Easily retrieve information about company, products, technologies, intellectual capital	• Corporate overview/history • Online publications and reports • Product line browsing • Search for product by name • Warranty and service option descriptions • Email form for information requests • Lead-routing to another channel
Shop	Determine product needs, pricing, and availability	• View product descriptions and sample applications/uses • Retrieve market-level or specially-negotiated price quotes • Configure solutions online • Determine product availability and ship times • Review financing options • Create a 'shopping cart'
Buy	Place an order	• Sign and execute contracts online • Confirm order placement and delivery time • Periodically review order status • Retrieve an account summary and order history
Get help	Get resolution to a problem, or get information on other resources (e.g. phone support)	• Frequently asked questions (FAQ) lists • Online product documentation • Support information (phone numbers, etc.) • Decision tree automated help queries

Figure 9.7 Determining web site functions and capabilities.

customers and keep them on the site longer than feature-rich, yet overly-complex, sites. Particularly with newer sites, it makes sense to limit functionality to a carefully chosen handful of key business capabilities and then to see how well the site responds to customers' and prospects' needs. It is quite a bit easier to add new functions to an existing site than it is to redesign a complex site for greater simplicity and ease of use.

3. Build an e-commerce investment plan

After identifying the basic functionality of an e-commerce site, the next step is to figure out how much it will cost. E-commerce channels can vary dramatically in cost, from a simple homebrew $1,000 web site to a multi-million dollar extranet system that coordinates the activities of suppliers, customers and partners.

The cost of an e-commerce channel has two components: fixed start-up costs, such as the purchase of computer hardware and software; and operating costs, such as the payment of web administrators' salaries and the costs of ongoing web hosting services. A lot of money tends to disappear into a black hole when a company first ventures into the world of e-commerce. Unnecessary equipment is purchased, and money is spent on consultants and designers who encourage larger expenditures on technological gadgetry than is really needed. As a result, it's smart to add an Internet expert to the team who can objectively evaluate equipment and service expenditures against specific business requirements. As a starting point, investments and operating costs should be estimated for each of the items shown in Figure 9.8.

One crucial component of an e-commerce investment plan is an e-commerce governance committee. This committee should be tasked with identifying and documenting the projected costs of an e-commerce initiative, monitoring development activities against an e-commerce budget, and ensuring that development and operating costs stay within established guidelines. It is unwise to invest in something new and unpredictable, such as the Internet, without proper management controls and accountability.

4. Build and deploy e-commerce in a phased approach

As suggested earlier, it usually makes sense to start slowly with e-commerce, by launching an Internet presence with minimal (though well-designed) functionality and then adding to it over time. First, e-commerce is evolving rapidly, and large investments in cutting-edge technology may quickly become obsolete. Many companies, for example, are now stuck with multi-million dollar investments in old electronic data interchange (EDI) systems that have been made completely worthless by the rapid adoption of the Internet as an e-commerce standard.

Second, it is impossible to predict in advance how and when customers will use an e-commerce site. For example, when car-shopping service AutoByTel

Information technology infrastructure	• Hardware (e.g. server, network equipment) • Software (e.g. platform, user interface)
Design costs	• Graphical standards / site layout and design • Content development • Application development (e.g. online order-placement capabilities)
Operating costs	• Labor (webmaster / site administration marketing personnel, etc.) • Web site hosting and maintenance • Content maintenance and updating • Ongoing facilities expenses
Drive-to-web costs	• Media buys to promote e-commerce site • Brochure/marketing collateral updates • E-commerce availability communications to existing accounts • Search engine registrations • Purchased links from other sites • Online advertising (e.g. banner ads)

Figure 9.8 Building the e-commerce investment plan. *Source*: Oxford Associates

was launched, most observers figured that visitors would use the site primarily to find the lowest-available price on a specific car. While users *did* use the service for that purpose, it turned out that they were also looking to perform competitive feature comparisons across cars, as well as to get general advice on purchasing a vehicle (leasing versus buying, etc.). Today, AutoByTel has evolved into a multifaceted car advice and purchasing service, in response to customer needs that have evolved and solidified over the last few years. In general, web sites follow a consistent pattern of evolving over time in response to visitors' needs, and few, if any, look the same as they did a year or two ago. As a result, it can be counter-productive to invest heavily in a full-featured 'steady state' e-commerce site. It makes much more sense to phase in the functionality of a site, thus giving customers' needs an opportunity to emerge.

As an example, Figure 9.9 provides a sample phase-in approach to e-commerce site development, from a machine parts manufacturer.

As the figure suggests, this company opted to roll out its e-commerce site in three phases, starting with basic get-on-the-net functionality and gradually

	Phase I (0-12 Months)	Phase II (12-24 Months)	Phase III (24-36 Months)
Site Capabilities			
Learn	Basic product-line descriptions	Add detailed descriptions of all products and services	Add capability for visitors to compare products against the competition
Shop	Catalog of 50 simple off-the-rack products	Expand catalog to 200+ products	Add capability to configure multiple-product solutions on-line
Buy	Buy products with credit card, at market price	Allow select customers to buy products with pre-approved credit at negotiated discount prices	Link e-commerce site to customers' inventory and procurement systems, to signal buyers when they need to replenish products
Customer Access	• 10 major accounts • 20 mid-sized accounts	All major accounts	All customers and new prospects

Figure 9.9 Sample e-commerce rollout plan from a machine parts manufactuer

progressing over a period of two to three years toward new features and more sophisticated e-commerce capabilities. In almost all cases, this is a more productive approach than the launching of an e-commerce site with expensive, complex functions that may or may not be accepted and used by customers.

5. Develop Drive-To-Web Initiatives

In the movie *Field of Dreams,* Kevin Costner's character builds a baseball diamond in the corn fields of Iowa because he is told to 'build it and they will come.' Unfortunately, this approach works better in the movies than it does in e-commerce. For every Amazon.com, there are probably a thousand web sites that have never, ever been visited. One of the authors, for example, doing some research on vintage cars, came across a web site with a little counter indicating the number of visitors who had stopped at the site. Counting the author's visit, the number was 00000004 (presumably the extra zeros represented room for traffic growth). You are much more likely to get that kind of traffic than the traffic of an Amazon.com or an AutoByTel – unless you develop a *drive to web* plan that pulls Internet users to your site.

Companies with high-traffic sites generally approach the drive-to-web issue systematically, by engaging in the six activities suggested in Figure 9.10.

❶ **General Site Promotion**	Inclusion of Internet addresses (e.g. 'www.mycompany.com') in all marketing collateral. brochures, print advertisements, media campaigns, etc.
❷ **E-commerce Campaigns**	Launching of targeted marketing campaigns (such as direct mail) specifically to promote web site awareness/usage.
❸ **Education Initiatives**	Investment in the education of customers, field sales reps, business partners and telereps to help them understand the availability and purpose of e-commerce sites.
❹ **References On Other Sites**	Placement of 'hot links' on the related sites of business partners, trade associations, buying groups, etc., often in return for reciprocal links to those organizations' sites
❺ **Search Engine Registrations**	Registration with all of the major search engines, and use of appropriate domain names and terminology on the site (to ensure that search engines find the site when users do relevant searches).
❻ **Good Content**	Site appeal above and beyond the ability to read corporate information and place orders for products: in other words, content that will draw visitors back to the site multiple times.

Figure 9.10 Six approaches for driving customers to web sites

A company that is serious about e-commerce must think in terms of doing all, or at least most, of the approaches shown in the figure. It's worth pointing out that drive-to-web activities can be expensive, and in fact can cost more than a web site itself. It may be necessary to prioritize a little – for example, by focusing initially just on making sure an e-commerce site is mentioned in existing marketing materials and campaigns. Eventually, however, every company must deal with the fact that an e-commerce site is only as good as the number of visitors it gets and the number of those visitors that it is able to bring back a second, third and fourth time.

6. Establish e-commerce performance measures

As of 8 October 1998, Internet portal company Yahoo! had a market capitalization of $10 billion dollars on last-quarter earnings of $16.7 million[7]. We should all be so lucky! Most companies with annual profits in the $67 million range (i.e. $16.7 million × 4 quarters) sport market capitalizations of about $1.3 to $2 billion. Welcome to the strange world of e-commerce performance measurement (and compensation, if you happen to be a shareholder). Here's the basic story:

No one yet understands how to measure e-commerce success.

E-commerce is the only channel that is measured in terms of things like 'eyeballs' and 'page views', while other channels fuss with mundane metrics such as sales and profits. Sarcasm aside, that there is some logic in these neuvometrics. The Internet is growing fast and has a lot of potential. Getting a horde of people to visit your site may not have much value now – it depends on whether they're buying anything – but as companies eventually figure out how to do business in this medium, the ability to attract large numbers of people will likely translate into sales and profits. That's why Yahoo! and other Internet companies have such high valuations – and it's also who companies need to think in terms of new types of performance metrics for this channel. Revenue and profits are still important – but so are new measures that indicate how well the site is doing at attracting and registering visitors and getting them to come back a second or third time.

Most companies should think in terms of measuring e-commerce performance along four dimensions that, collectively, combine traditional channel metrics with new e-commerce performance indicators:

- **Site volume** The popularity of the site – how well it's doing at pulling in new visitors and bringing back the old ones.
- **Leads and revenue generation** The site's success in generating leads and sales.
- **Costs** The investment and operating costs associated with the site.
- **Benefits** The payoff, measured in return on investment and customer satisfaction.

Figure 9.11 suggests some metrics for assessing e-commerce performance along each of these dimensions.

Of course, a list of this length needs to be prioritized. No one has the time or energy to measure a channel along so many complex dimensions – nor is it necessary. Managers must consider the basic business objectives underlying their e-commerce initiatives and measure things that directly impact the achievement of those objectives. A web site targeted at consumer awareness may, indeed, be best measured on new metrics such as site visits and page hits. Alternatively, a company that's really trying to sell products in volume over the Internet may do better to avoid those metrics and focus on traditional measures of revenues, costs, and profits. Either way, the key is to measure *something*. Most e-commerce initiatives today are not measured along any meaningful dimension, and as a result it is impossible in most cases to gauge whether these initiatives are succeeding or failing. As with any other channel, sound performance measurement provides the means to fix problems, make new high-impact investments, and establish channel accountability.

E-Commerce Site Volume	
✓ Site visits per day or month	Total visits per day or month. A common metric, but not necessarily the most useful one.
✓ Number of registered users	Number of site visitors choosing to 'register' (I.e. sending in their names, addresses, etc.). A more powerful metric than site visits for measuring the success of building a potential lead stream.
✓ Page hits by type	Tracks visitors' navigation paths (I.e. the pages they choose to view within an overall site). Yields powerful data about visitor preferences and interests.
✓ Revenue generated per day	Total revenues / # of days in operation -- should be compared in weekly or monthly roll-ups to yield data on increasing/decreasing sales through e-commerce.
✓ Site revisit rate	Revisits by same customer. A key metric for determining the ongoing value of a site to customers and prospects.
E-Commerce Lead and Revenue Generation	
✓ Leads generated	Total number of visits that result in booked orders or follow-up customer inquiries.
✓ Number of orders booked	Total volume of orders placed on the Internet; some companies count transactions completed by another channel but originated or supported online.
✓ Average transaction size	Size of average order, in $$$ or units sold
E-Commerce Costs	
✓ Cost per visit	Total cost of e-commerce (start-up investments, operating costs, and drive-to-web activities) divided by the number of visits
✓ Cost per lead	Total cost of e-commerce divided by number of new leads generated
✓ Cost per order	Total cost of e-commerce divided by number of orders booked
E-Commerce Benefits	
✓ Site cost displacement savings	Dollar value of labor savings from site (e.g. reduced time of field reps, telereps, or technical support personnel)
✓ Site return on investment (ROI)	Combined revenues generated + costs saved, divided by total e-commerce investment and operating costs
✓ Overall customer satisfaction	Overall customer satisfaction as well as quality of e-commerce site visit

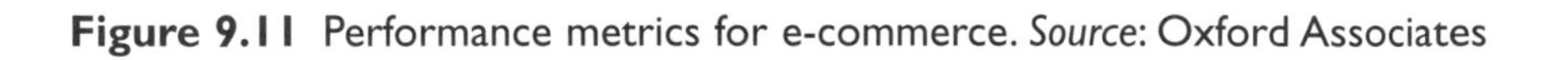

Figure 9.11 Performance metrics for e-commerce. *Source*: Oxford Associates

Summary

In some companies, the Internet is seen as a tsunami that is rolling over and crushing every established business practice. In others, the Internet has been viewed as a rather scary and unfamiliar medium with very unclear benefits or purposes. For most of us, the truth lies somewhere in the middle. The Internet hasn't solved world hunger yet, but it can be a powerful component of a go-to-market system, one that can reduce sales costs, reach new buyers, tighten up relationships with customers, and provide leverage to other sales channels.

Most executives would benefit by thinking more rigorously about what they really are trying to use the Internet to accomplish. E-commerce comes in many flavours, from the mundane corporate-awareness site all the way to complicated extranets that link customers, suppliers and partners in proprietary e-commerce environments. Executives must understand what their e-commerce objectives are *before* making choices from among these various alternatives.

This chapter presented a simple process for developing an e-commerce strategic plan, one that is focused less on technology than on basic business issues such as channel coverage, investment planning and performance management. In some ways, the Internet differs from other channels, but in the end, it really *is* just another channel to connect products with customers. Like any other channel, it must be designed, implemented, and managed thoughtfully against clear corporate objectives. And like any other channel, its success depends on the extent to which managers can identify a unique, well-defined, and value-added role for it within a broader go-to-market system.

Notes

[1] *Source*: International Data Corporation, as mentioned in Kristin Roberts, *Small business markets on Net as online use grows*, Reuters, 28 September 1998.
[2] *Source*: Cisco web site, 15 October 1998.
[3] *Source*: AutoByTel web site, 18 October 1998. Also mentioned in Chapter 1.
[4] Amazon.com data as of 21 October 1998.
[5] *Source*: IDC, July 1997. Not all estimates are as optimistic. Forrester Research, for example, estimates a total of 100 million Internet users by 2003.
[6] Some use 'e-commerce' to refer only to *business transactions completed electronically*, and would not include, for example, customer awareness-building in the definition.
[7] Not counting non-recurring charges.

Part Three

Managing Channels for High Performance

Chapter 10

The art of channel mix and integration

Not long ago, organizations generally sold their products and services through a single channel. A large, established company such as an IBM or a Xerox, for example, would sell everything from mainframe computers to typewriters, or from huge photocopiers to toner replacement cartridges, through one channel – the direct sales force. A consumer-oriented company such as Kodak sold products through retail distributors. A few direct marketing companies such as Avon sold through door-to-door neighbourhood sales agents. 'Go-to-market strategy' usually meant building a good channel and making it work.

Today, all of those companies – IBM, Xerox, Kodak and Avon – go to market through some version or another of a 'hybrid' channel model: a mixture of field sales forces, the Internet, telechannels, direct mail, business partners, and so on. These are just a few miscellaneous examples of a much broader trend. In financial services, for example, and particularly in the brokerage business, the *entire industry* has migrated over the past decade to a hybrid channel model. In telecommunications, shipping and high technology, an executive suggesting that his or her company go to market through one channel would probably be fired – if not just taken out back and shot.

The reason for this migration toward multiple channels is simple. Hybrid channel models deliver results – the kinds of tangible results that show up on income statements and affect stock prices. A hybrid mix of channels working well together can reduce selling costs by twenty to thirty per cent, and in some cases, can cut them in half. For example, a $1000 order that costs $300 to close with a direct sales channel can often be closed for $200 or less with a mix of channels. That kind of improvement in selling profitability can fundamentally improve and reshape a company's competitive position, as well as make its shareholders much more wealthy.

In addition to higher profitability, hybrid channel models deliver growth. In many markets, no single channel captures more than half of the available transaction volume anymore, and often it's considerably less than that. Two, three, or more channels may be required to access the critical mass of transaction volume, the seventy or eighty per cent of business, taking place in a market. The trend, in fact, is toward a greater dispersion of transactions across an ever-wider range of channels; customers are increasingly promiscuous in their use of multiple channels as they seek out lower costs and improved purchasing flexibility. As a result, growth in revenue and market share is becoming increasingly dependent on the use of a hybrid mix of channels.

The development of a sound hybrid, multiple-channel model is a serious undertaking. A number of key questions must be raised, such as: Should channels overlap with each other and compete for the same customers, or should each channel be assigned its own unique product-market? Should channels each serve end-to-end sales, or should each channel serve a specific function (such as lead qualification or post-sale support) within a larger sales process? These are important questions. It is one thing to identify a few channels that potentially could serve a market; it is quite another to figure out how to use those channels *together* to achieve superior performance.

This chapter addresses the issue of bringing channels together into a *system*, and looks at the issue from two angles: channel mix and channel integration. Channel *mix* entails the use of multiple channels, each serving sales opportunities more or less independently, to increase growth in sales and market share. Channel *integration*, on the other hand, involves the tight coordination of channels *within a single sale* to improve selling profitability and to service complex transactions. Both approaches are often used together, but not always. Channel mix is a little easier to design and implement; channel integration is more complex but can sometimes deliver stronger bottom-line results. The two approaches, and more generally the use of multiple channels as parts of a coherent selling system, are discussed below.

Channel mix

Channel mix is about the coverage of a company's overall market with multiple channels. Channels in a mix can be independent of each other, and may not interact at all within any particular sale. They just coexist, each providing a different route to customers. The purpose of a channel mix is to intercept a broad range of purchasing transactions, and thus to increase sales growth and market share.

Examples of channel coexistence within markets are abundant. Motorola sells cellular telephones through cellular service providers, retail stores (e.g. Wal-Mart), and car mobile phone installation shops, among other channels. Barnes & Noble sell books through retail stores as well as over the Internet. WD-40, the lubricant, is sold through just about every retail channel known to mankind. Ernst & Young, the account firm, offers 'direct sales' partners to sell to and manage large consulting clients – but also an Internet consulting site called Ernie for smaller businesses. Fedex sells through Fedex retail stores, indirect retail outlets (such as Parcels Plus), call centres, and account reps, among other channels. In all of these cases, channels coexist in the market place, sometimes serving discrete product-markets and often overlapping in their service of the same customers. The goal, in all cases, is the same: to make it easy for more customers to do business in whatever ways they choose, and thus to increase growth in market share and revenue.

Channel mix comes in two flavours: *intensive* and *selective*. Intensive channel coverage involves the use of multiple channels within a product-market, overlapping and sometimes competing with each other. Selective coverage is the assigning of individual channels to specific product-markets without channel overlap or competition. These two fundamentally different approaches are shown in Figure 10.1.

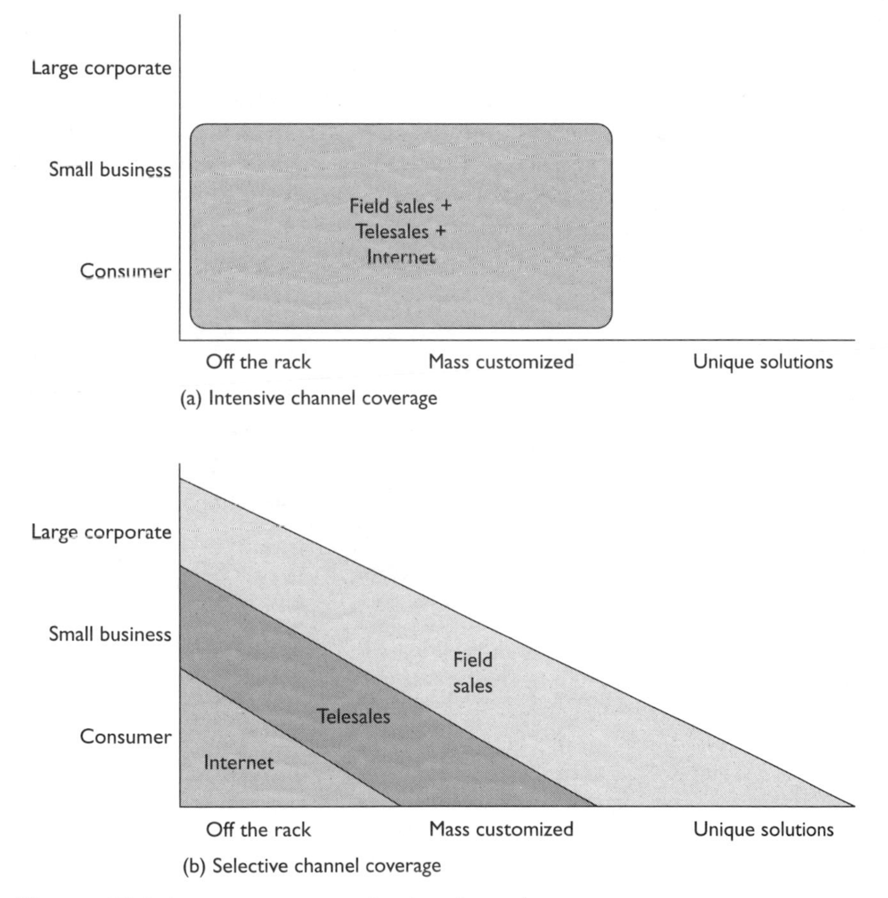

Figure 10.1 Intensive versus selective channel coverage

Most companies do not pursue either a pure intensive coverage strategy or a pure selective coverage strategy. A hybrid of the two is far more common. A hybrid strategy typically involves the assignment of a single channel to one or a few high-priority product-markets, separate from a group of overlapping channels that serve the larger market mass. An example is shown in Figure 10.2, in this case for British Airways. British Airway's goal, of course, is to fill its planes with people, which requires that a variety of services, such as ticketing and travel planning, be provided to a range of customers, from individual travellers to large corporations. To serve these different product-markets, the company offers a number of direct channels (Internet, telechannels, and retail shops) as well as an indirect (travel agents) channel.

As Figure 10.2 shows, British Airway's approach is a hybrid of intensive and selective coverage. It serves its broad base of individual travellers and small businesses with multiple, overlapping channels. Almost any customer can use any channel; the goal is to intercept as many transactions as possible. At the same time, the company maintains a direct sales force to serve a unique product-market: specialized services provided to large corporate accounts. The goal in this product-market is not massive coverage, but rather the controlled delivery of high-quality, highly customized account services.

This hybrid approach – selective channel coverage in key product-markets and intensive channel coverage across the broader market – is very powerful. This is a channel strategy that can deliver high sales growth while retaining a unique channel focus on a core group of customers. Most companies sell into markets where a hybrid channel model is appropriate. Good hybrid systems are based on four principles:

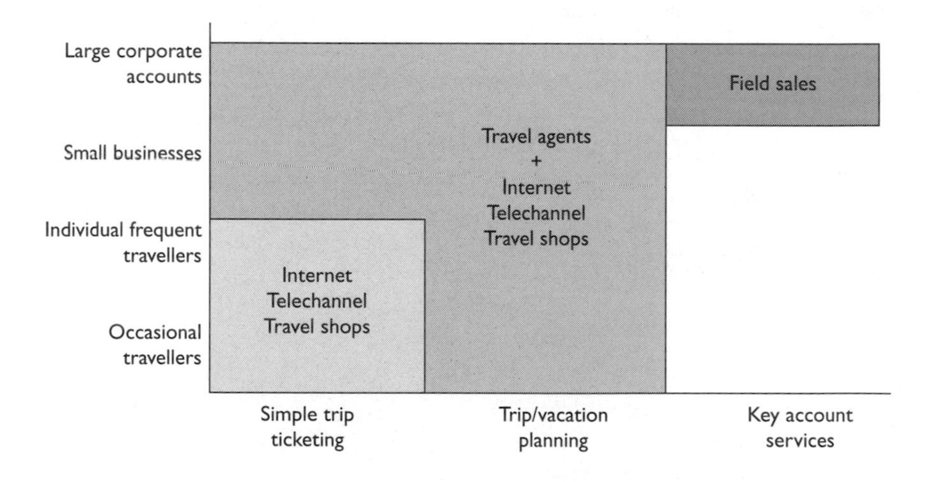

Figure 10.2 British Airways – hybrid channel coverage map

Channel	Share of Market
Dealers	45 %
Retail Stores	18 %
Direct (Field) Sales	15 %
Buying Consortia	4 %
Direct Mail/Response	3 %
Value-added reseller	3 %
Unknown/other	12 %
	-------
	100 %

78 % combined share (Dealers, Retail Stores, Direct (Field) Sales)

Figure 10.3 Office equipment market in Germany, 1994

- Align intensively-covered markets with the 'critical buying mass'
- Manage the channel mix for profitability, not just sales
- Save selective coverage for when it really counts
- Beware of conflict, particularly with indirect channels

Align intensively-covered markets with the 'critical buying mass'

Customer behavior, as noted earlier in this book, is a bedrock principle of channel selection. It is also a bedrock principle of channel mix. The channels added to a mix should be those that, collectively, will be best able to access the bulk of the available transactions in that market: the *critical buying mass*.

Figure 10.3, for example, shows a breakdown of channel usage for customers buying office equipment in Germany. As the figure shows, the critical buying mass for office equipment is in the dealer, retail and direct sales channels; together these channels 'own' seventy-eight per cent of the total transaction volume. No other named channel has more than a four per cent share.

If you had some office equipment to sell, and wanted to compete in this market, which mix of channels should you use? It depends on your business strategy, of course. But here's one good answer: *any* channel mix that accesses the critical mass of buyer activity. Just about any combination of dealers, retail and direct sales could work. That's where the bulk of transaction activity is taking place. All other channels *combined* account for less than a quarter of the market. You could add one or two of those channels to the mix to pick up some sales at the margin, but those channels are hardly a foundation for a robust business base. Generally, there is no benefit in over stuffing a market with channels that will subsist on the occasional offbeat purchase, delivering two or three per cent of the potential sales volume. Put simply:

A mix of channels should collectively be targeted at the critical mass of business activity taking place in a market.

Of course, many companies employ channels to capture marginal or low-volume business. Even in the German office equipment market, for example, almost a quarter of the market is available to a company providing a channel outside the critical mass. It doesn't hurt to have a marginal channel to tag along with other channels in serving a market. Sometimes a new low-share channel, such as a web site, can be a valuable hedge against future migrations in customer behavior. The success of a channel mix, though, ultimately depends on its ability to access the critical mass of business taking place in its market. Every channel added to the mix should be a worthy contributor to the cause.

Manage the channel mix for profitability, not just sales

Intensive channel coverage of a market almost always leads to higher sales. More channels cost more money, however. It can be a Faustian bargain to use a channel mix to drive up revenues and market share: sales may go up but profits can go down. Profitability should always be a consideration in constructing a channel mix:

Multiple independent channels may end up chasing the same sales

Coverage of a market by multiple channels may involve channel 'shift' – customers moving from one channel to another – without channel 'lift' – new sales. Thus, an Internet site may simply steal sales from a telesales operation, or a field rep may take sales away from a distributor, in both cases yielding no *new* revenue – at a higher selling cost.

From a profitability perspective, unless revenue is going to increase faster than channel costs – and not just shift around from channel to channel – it may make sense to limit channel expansion within a product-market. A $40 million market that can be served by a channel which costs $10 million to operate makes more sense than a $40 million market served by two channels at a combined cost of $20 million.

The key is to determine just how much *new* sales revenue will actually be produced by the addition of a new channel to a product-market. None? Some? A lot? Sales volume may not ride on this question, but profitability certainly will. Channel shift versus channel lift can be very difficult to assess. It is not easy to distinguish between really new business, on the one hand, and already-captured business shifting around from channel to channel, on the other. It is well worth the effort, though. Channel *shift* yields lower overall profitability: flat sales, at higher selling costs. Channel *lift*, on the other hand, yields sales growth and thus at least the potential to maintain, or improve, the profitability of a channel mix.

Not all channels will be profitable in every product-market

A channel mix should consist of channels that individually represent profitable business opportunities for a *specific product-market*. A market that involves selling $100 toner cartridges for laser printers cannot profitably be served by a sales force of $150,000-per-year sales reps, although the sales force may be profitable in other markets with larger order sizes. It's important to draw a line in the sand for each product-market: a level of selling expense that will not be exceeded by any participating channel. Take as an example a commercial kitchen equipment supplier that makes its profit target by maintaining an overall corporate *E*/*R* ratio of twenty per cent[1]. Figure 10.4 shows how this plays out in terms of channel selection in one of the company's smaller, lower-order-size markets.

What Figure 10.4 shows is that the company cannot use all of its existing channels profitably in the ExecuChef (small–medium-sized customer) segment. Given the small average order size of $2,000, an *E*/*R* ratio of twenty per cent – the company's target selling expense – allows only for a $400 cost per transaction. Any channel requiring more than $400 to complete a transaction will exceed the company's selling expense guidelines. Note that only three of the company's five channels can profitably serve this market; the other two are not worth considering for the channel mix in this product-market.

Note also that Figure 10.4 does not say the company *should* use all three of the channels with transaction costs less than $400. It may be impossible to sell a commercial kitchen appliance over the Internet, for example. What the figure shows, simply, is a group of channels each of which can deliver a profitable transaction. As a result, *any* mix of these channels, regardless of which ones are chosen by customers, will result in a profitable sale.

It is not always possible for every channel in a product-market to deliver a maximally profitable transaction. For instance, direct sales force participation

- *Product-Market: ExecuChef Kitchen Series (For Small Restaurants)*
- *Average Order Size: $2,000*

Channel Options	Cost Per Transaction	
Internet	$40	
Direct Mail/Fax-back	$180	
Telesales	$320	↑ < 20 %
		$400 = 20 %
Distributor	$410	↓ > 20 %
Field Sales Rep	$760	

Figure 10.4 Commercial kitchen equipment supplier

in a product-market will always drag down the profitability of a channel mix dominated by direct marketing channels. Sometimes, however, the sales force (or another relatively expensive channel) is needed to access the critical mass of buying activity. High average profitability across channels, in these cases, will depend on the extent to which the more expensive channels can be assigned to a finite number of discrete product-markets and used sparingly in the overall channel mix. The more expensive the channel, the more sense it makes to put boundaries around the types of transactions in which it is involved.

Save selective coverage for when it really counts

As noted earlier, it is atypical for a company to apply an intensive multiple-channel mix to its entire range of product-markets. A hybrid approach – involving a mix of channels in most markets, and yet the selective assignment of a unique channel to a few product-markets – is more common. For most companies, the trap lies in over-engineering the markets that will be assigned unique channels.

For example, one medical supply client of ours identified five discrete product-markets and, in a fit of channel frenzy, five different channels, each of which would be assigned to a different product-market. What was the point of all that market engineering? Most of the client's customers bought through distributors, a few large accounts had been reserved for the field sales force, and many customers were interested in alternative channels (such as teleservices) for routine reordering activity. Clearly its major 'house' accounts deserved a field sales force presence, but the rest of the customer base was a prime candidate for a flexible channel mix. The client was stuck on the idea of aligning discrete channels with discrete product-markets, but for all except its largest customers, an intensive channel mix would have resulted in higher sales volume at a lower average transaction cost[2].

In most cases, companies are better off identifying one or two high-priority product-markets that really do warrant the assignment of a single channel. The rest of the market – the broad, diverse territory of dispersed customers – is almost always better served through a flexible set of alternative channels.

Beware of conflict, particularly with indirect channels

In a market covered by multiple independent channels, channel conflict – competition between channels for sales opportunities – is as certain as death and taxes. It needs to be managed.

Channel conflict between a company's *direct* channels – the sales force, call centres, Internet, direct mail, etc. – is a manageable problem, if a problem at all. Conflict between direct channels is just another way of saying that customers are being provided with multiple purchasing options by the manufacturer. A direct channel that 'steals' a sale from another direct channel (channel shift) has no net negative effect on revenue. Thus, channel conflict is not really an issue (though profitability may be). Competing direct channels, in fact, can often create some synergy as they work together to increase overall market exposure and take on specialized functions. Dell Computer recently discovered, for example, that half of its customers buying computers over the telephone had visited their web site first. Presumably, these customers are drawn to the web site to take an unhurried look at Dell's products, and yet are more comfortable talking to an actual human being when making the purchase. Each of these two channels serves a purpose in the sale; the two together, though 'competing' in a narrow sense, result in increased overall sales volume. Competition between direct channels can have profit implications but rarely does it result in lower sales. Sometimes, as in the case of Dell, competing direct channels can work very effectively together increase sales.

Conflict between a manufacturer's direct channels and its indirect partners is a whole different story. This is the era of the Angry Sales Conference, wherein executives try to explain to their irate distributors why the new direct channels they want to build – Internet sites, call centres, etc. – are actually a better deal for everyone. Most of the time, they aren't a better deal. A manufacturer can always price lower and, in fact, in some cases can provide more efficient service than a distributor. As a result, sales will tend to migrate from distributors back to direct channels. This is why distribution channel members, such as Compaq's partners, get hostile when a manufacturer such as Compaq entertains the notion of adding direct channels into a crowded channel mix.

When indirect channel partners are involved, three issues must be taken into account:

- **Pricing** Are prices for the same products the same across different channels? If not, customers will migrate to whichever channels offer more competitive prices. This can be acceptable, as long as the migration isn't away from channels you value and want to keep – such as a loyal network of business partners and distributors. In addition, customers are generally confused by channel pricing differences. They will need to be told why they are paying more or less than they could through another channel. One way out of this trap is to give both customers and partners a reason to accept different prices in different channels: namely, channel-specific product configurations.
- **Product configuration** Channel conflict can be minimized through product variation – even slight variation. Pens can be sold in boxes of ten over the phone, boxes of 100 by distributors, in premium versions – attractive cases and a company's logo – by field reps, and so on. Same pen, different version – and different pricing structure. Minor differences in configuration can help price differentials work in a channel mix, and can also make it easier for customers to understand when and why they are supposed to use one channel instead of another.

- **Market growth** In evaluating potential conflict with partners, market growth is a key variable, as is the existing coverage of that market by indirect partners. A market growing at twenty per cent per year, in which business partners are only involved in half of the available transactions, is a good candidate for another direct channel or two. Everybody will have lots of room to grow. A market growing at four per cent, in which business partners do ninety-five per cent of the transactions, however, is a different story. Every single sale in a direct channel will come at the expense of a business partner. Something has to give: fewer partners, fewer direct channels, or lots more partner conferences with expensive hors-d'oeuvres and happy speeches about channel synergy.

Channel conflict assumes that the different channels in a market are acting independently and are selling against each other. That is not always the case. In fact, a far more productive approach can be to use each channel for a different activity in the sales process, and thus to bring channels together into an integrated system. Channel *integration* can reduce conflict, and more importantly, can lead to significant improvements in both selling profitability and customer service.

Channel integration

Channel integration involves the use of multiple channels, each performing different functions *within a single sales process*. The primary outcome (and for most companies, the goal) of channel integration is improved selling profitability. A secondary outcome (and goal) is increased market coverage: integrated channels can usually provide access to a broader range of customers. With some strategic effort and fortitude, most companies can realize significant profitability and market coverage gains with an integrated channel model. It is a powerful, although more complex, way to go to market.

There are many types and varieties of channel integration. A few examples that illustrate the range of complexity are provided below:

- **Staples**, in the simplest and most common type of channel integration, uses a direct mail operation to send out product catalogues to customers and local businesses. Customers who want to buy products phone in to a call centre to place their orders. Thus, the direct mail operation and telechannel work together to generate leads and close sales.
- **IBM** periodically launches SMB (small-to-medium business) initiatives, such as campaigns into the community banking market with specialized software applications for the AS/400 computer. These campaigns begin in IBM's direct marketing department, which sends out brochures containing an 800 number. A call in to the 800 number goes to IBM's call centre, where the lead is qualified. Qualified leads are then routed to business partners for sale closure. Once the deal is closed, IBM ships

the equipment to the customer site. Business partners then take over and provide on-site installation and support.

- Data base company **Oracle** uses many forms of channel integration in its different markets. One is based on the highly effective multi-customer seminar model. Here, Oracle culls prospects from a database and sends out direct mail brochures inviting potential customers to attend a local Oracle seminar. Attending the seminar along with those customers are Oracle's local business partners. At the seminar, an Oracle sales rep makes a pitch on the company's software products. Interested customers are then connected with local business partners for pre-sales configuration, sale closure and post-sale support[3].

  In a different twist on channel integration, Oracle's direct marketing division sent out brochures with a toll-free call-in number to 12,000 companies between August 1996 and January 1997. Lower-cost telereps were instructed to take incoming calls and close any sales opportunities under $65,000 – while routing larger transactions to a field sales rep. The campaign resulted in 150 closed sales and over $15,000,000 in new business.

What these and all other examples of channel integration have in common is an underlying principle that a sales process consists of a number of different tasks, each of which can potentially be assigned to a different channel based on what that channel is capable of doing best. A sales process normally consists of around five discrete tasks, as shown in Figure 10.5[4].

Why have one channel perform all five of these tasks? A more profitable approach can be to create a division of labour within the sales process: to have different channels take on different functions within the overall sale. For instance, an outbound call centre can usually generate leads and qualify them at a far lower cost and in a far higher quantity than can be done by a field sales rep. As Oracle did, why not have inexpensive telemarketing reps generate and qualify leads, close the easy ones, and pass the complex ones off to field sales reps? That would lower the total cost-of-sales, as well as free up the time of field reps to pursue more and larger opportunities.

In short, channel integration involves the 'pushing down' of tasks within the sales process to channels that are better able to perform them at a lower cost – and perhaps in higher volume too. The tasks in the middle of a sales process – face-to-face selling and sale closure – are usually the only ones that really require an expensive field rep or value-added business partner. At the

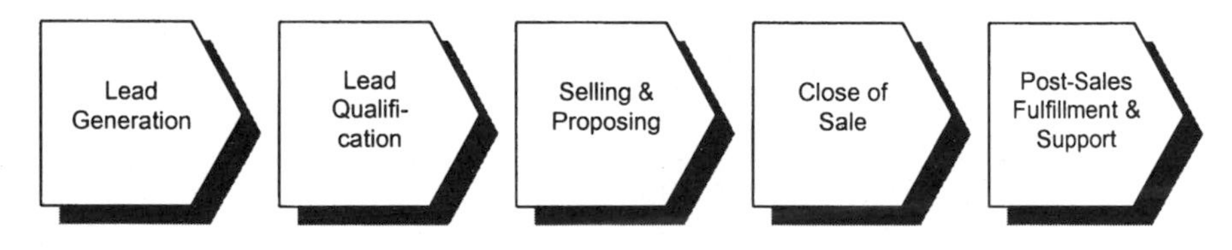

Figure 10.5 Typical sales process

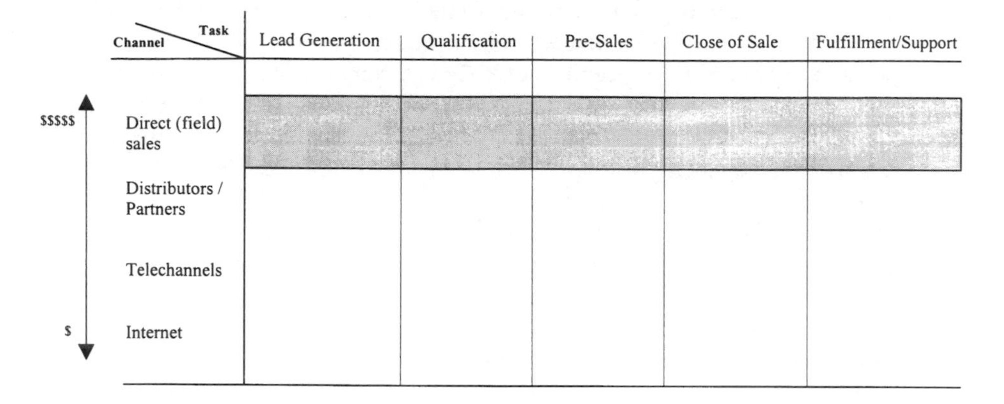

Figure 10.6 Single-channel sales model

beginning of the sales process (the initial lead generation and qualification) and at the end (the support provided to the customer after the sale) lie opportunities to migrate tasks to lower-cost channels. Thus, a company that starts off with a single channel as shown in Figure 10.6 might push down tasks within the selling process toward lower-cost channels, as shown in Figure 10.7[5].

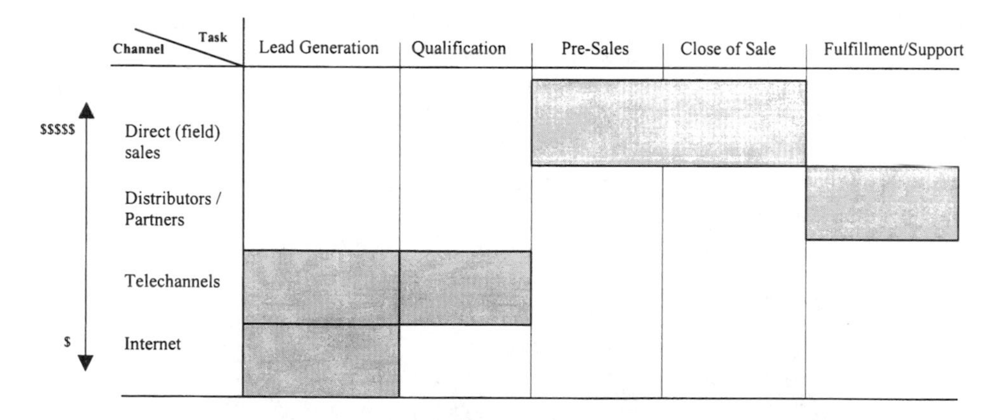

Figure 10.7 Hybrid (multiple) channel sales model

This kind of structure – low-cost channels at either end of the sale, with an expensive channel used only where it really counts – can typically reduce the cost of a sale by a third to a half. Why? Because the highest-cost channel required at any point in a sale, such as a field rep or business partner, will yield a higher overall sales cost if it is used throughout the entire sales process than if it is used only in the discrete tasks where it is truly needed. A blended channel cost – a mix of higher and lower-cost channels – will *always* be less costly than the sole use of the highest cost channel needed in the sale.

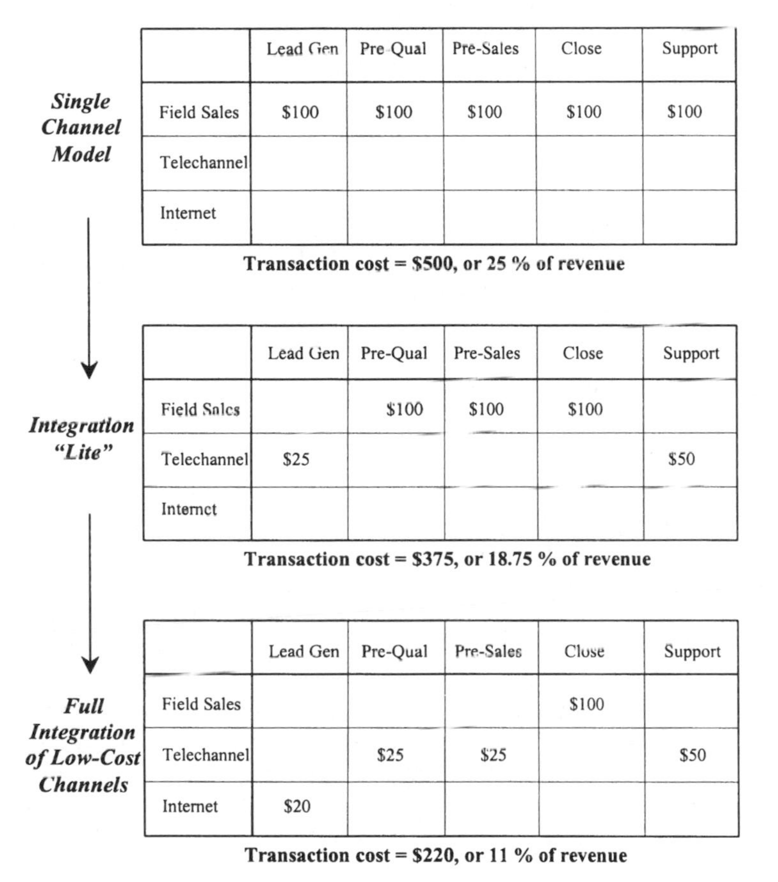

Single Channel Model

	Lead Gen	Pre Qual	Pre-Sales	Close	Support
Field Sales	$100	$100	$100	$100	$100
Telechannel					
Internet					

Transaction cost = $500, or 25 % of revenue

Integration "Lite"

	Lead Gen	Pre-Qual	Pre-Sales	Close	Support
Field Sales		$100	$100	$100	
Telechannel	$25				$50
Internet					

Transaction cost = $375, or 18.75 % of revenue

Full Integration of Low-Cost Channels

	Lead Gen	Pre-Qual	Pre-Sales	Close	Support
Field Sales				$100	
Telechannel		$25	$25		$50
Internet	$20				

Transaction cost = $220, or 11 % of revenue

Assumptions:

- Field sales: Salary $100,000/yr. 250 selling days. 4 contacts/calls per day. Result: $100 cost per contact
- Telesales: Salary $50,000/yr. 250 selling days. 8 contacts/calls per day. Result: $25 cost per contact.
- Internet: Rough estimate. $1000/month maintenance. 200 inquiries/month. 4 inquires per lead. Result: $20 per lead.
- Post-sale support: 1 contact by direct field rep, or 2 contacts by telerep.
- For illustrative purposes only, all channel costs are unloaded. Fully-loaded channel costs (e.g. marketing and start-up investments allocated across transactions) would lead to higher transaction costs in each channel

Figure 10.8 Higher profitability through blended channels – example based on a $2000 sale

A somewhat simplified example of how this works is shown in Figure 10.8.

What the figure shows is a transaction cost of twenty-five per cent in the single (direct sales) channel model, with a reduction to just under nineteen per cent, and then to eleven per cent, as more aggressive uses of less expensive channels are included in the mix. In other words, the cost-per-transaction can be reduced by twenty-five per cent through some minor migration of tasks to less expensive channels, and then cut by more than fifty per cent with a more aggressive blended model. These are not unusual outcomes in an integrated channel model. This has *serious* implications for companies presently oriented toward using one or two high-cost channels. No one can afford to pass up the opportunity at least to evaluate whether an integrated channel model might be appropriate for certain markets or types of sales.

Channel integration is profitable, but that does not make it easy. Everyone would already have a fully integrated model if it were a matter of taking out a sheet of paper and drawing a few charts. In fact, channel integration brings with it a number of complexities, and is thus often reserved for complex sales with long sales cycles. It is not usually worth the hassle to integrate channels for simple, short-cycle sales. For sales that are worth the effort, effective channel integration depends on three factors:

- Appropriate channel-task alignment
- Management of channel hand-offs
- Effective assignment of 'account ownership'

Appropriate channel-task alignment

Channel integration is seductive – who doesn't want to slash their selling costs in half? – but it can become risky without some channel assignment discipline. Not every channel is suitable for every selling task. Judgement is required in aligning channels with different selling tasks.

In the sale of a $500 photocopier, for example, many tasks, and perhaps all of them, can be pushed down toward lower-cost channels. This sale could be made by using direct mail and the Internet to generate and qualify leads, and then low-cost distributors and retail shops to sell and service the product. That is quite a bit different than selling a $200,000 office automation solution. In this more complex sale, low-cost channels can (and should) be used to generate and qualify leads, but it is unrealistic to expect the sale to be closed and supported without more expensive channels such as field reps or value-added partners. Disaster would result from over-migrating key selling tasks – specifically, the high-value tasks in the middle of the sales process – to lower-cost channels. People do not buy $200,000 business solutions over the telephone or in an Office Depot.

It's important to determine which channels can realistically perform which tasks in the sales process. As a starting point, Figure 10.9 shows how channels

Channel \ Task	Lead Generation	Qualification	Pre-Sales	Close of Sale	Fulfillment/Support
Direct (field) sales	✓	✓	✓✓✓	✓✓✓	✓
Distributors / Partners	✓✓	✓✓	✓✓✓	✓✓✓	✓✓✓
Telechannels	✓✓✓	✓✓✓	✓	✓	✓✓✓
Internet	✓✓✓	✓✓	✓	✓	✓

✓✓✓: unique contribution, i.e. best performance or lowest-cost alternative
✓✓: capable of performing
✓: unsuitable or uneconomical

Figure 10.9 Channel specialization in the sales process

typically can be aligned with sales process tasks *in a typical large, business-to-business sale.*

The figure makes two important points:

- Each channel in a sales process will either be uniquely superior at performing a task, about as capable of performing a task as another channel, or just unsuitable for that task. For example, call centres are very strong in lead generation and qualification, but weaker in sales closure. Again, this figure is oriented toward larger order sizes in business-to-business sales. In small order sales or consumer sales, a call centre may be perfectly sufficient for sales closure. Thus, channel-task assignments need to be designed with a specific type of sale in mind.
- In an ideal integration of channels, you would push each selling task down to the lowest-cost channel in which the channel still earns high grades for performance. This will result in a high-performance zone (shaded in the figure) in which each channel is doing what it does best, and in which the overall cost of sales has been driven down to the lowest possible level. This is where the profitability improvements come from in channel integration.

Management of channel hand-offs

There is more room for error in a sales process served by three or four channels than in a sales process served by one. Specifically, the errors pop up in the hand-offs between channels: the transition points where one channel, for example, hands-off a raw lead for qualification to another channel, or perhaps hands off a closed deal for post-sales support.

Hand-offs are the critical risk areas in channel integration. One company discovered, for example, that out of the 300 leads generated by its telemarketing reps and given to its sales force in March of 1996, only eleven had resulted in sales. This close rate of less than four per cent contrasted with the twenty-one per cent close rate achieved by the sales force in other markets – with no help from any other channel. After a great deal of hand wringing, the company figured out that its telemarketing reps had been told to give the sales force good leads, but also had informally been told not to take it upon themselves to make 'go – no go' decisions over leads. The somewhat-confused telemarketing reps, in fear of throwing out good potential business, had dumped just about every new lead into the hands of the sales force. Every single one of those leads was then pursued by the sales force, leading to a huge amount of wasted time and money. The hand-off between telemarketing and direct sales, in short, was being made too soon and with insufficient lead qualification, driving down the efficiency (and profitability) of the integrated sales process.

Prevention of that kind of problem requires active, hands-on management, as well as:

- **Precise definition of task completion points** At what point is a lead considered 'qualified'? When it comes in the door, when it feels like an opportunity, or when the customer's budget and purchase date has been formally confirmed? As another example, is a sale 'closed' when a customer gives the nod, or when a purchase order has been received? Precise definition of task completion points is critical, because these are the points at which sales opportunities are handed over from one channel to the next. Each task in the sales process must be defined clearly so each channel understands what it is supposed to complete before it moves a sale down the pipeline.
- **Definition of *how* hand-offs are supposed to be made** Is the sales rep supposed to call a business partner within two days of a sale closure, or log the closure in a database for a follow-up call, or just scribble a note in a day planner to himself or herself as a reminder? The more rigorous and formalized are the hand-off procedures, the more likely will be the individual channels to execute them properly. Documented, specific hand-off procedures are a must in an integrated channel system.

Effective assignment of account ownership

Anarchy doesn't work in a multiple-channel sales process. Much is at stake – both sales and profits – and it is not the time for new-age-style empowered work teams, each doing their job independently. Leads get lost, and so do customers, when no one is in charge. Someone has to 'own' the overall account relationship when multiple channels are working together in a sale.

Account ownership involves several important responsibilities in multiple-channel sales:

- Ensuring that everything that is supposed to get done gets done correctly – throughout the entire sale.
- Solving any problems, such as poor hand-offs between channels, that could threaten the sale or the account relationship.
- Making sure sales opportunities are successfully converted into closed deals.
- Finding new opportunities within the account for future sales growth.

Account ownership is an important and big job. One approach is to assign it to the person or channel responsible for closing the actual sale. For instance, a direct field rep – the closer of the sale – may be given responsibility for making sure a lead is converted into a sale, and then that post-sales support is provided to the customer, and then that new opportunities within the account are identified and converted into new sales. This approach has several merits, the most important one being that the channel responsible for closure is often the one with the most at stake – a sales commission – riding on the smooth continuity of the sales process and the growth of the account relationship. In fact, companies just getting started in channel integration could do far worse than simply to assign account ownership to whichever channel is responsible for closing deals.

However, the channel assigned to sales closure is not *always* the most appropriate one for account ownership. It depends on the type of sale involved. In short-cycle, simple sales, most of the activity and customer contact take place early in the sales process: lead generation, qualification, and closure. However, in more complex, longer-cycle sales, most of the activity – and customer contact – takes place *after* the sale: in fulfillment and post-sale support. As a result, in complex sales, it may make more sense to put account ownership into the hands of a fulfillment or post-sales support channel, such as a business partner, after the initial sale into an account. A post-sales support channel will likely be much closer to the customer and more on top of new selling opportunities than the closer of the sale; in fact, the sales closer may have moved on to entirely new selling opportunities. In short, in complex, lengthy sales, a post-sales support channel can be a better choice for account ownership than the deal-closing channel.

When a variety of sale types are involved – at varying levels of complexity (e.g. simple, complex), a smart approach is to put accounts into different tiers, each of which is owned by a different channel. Hewlett-Packard, for example, has five tiers of accounts, owned, depending on complexity and type, by the direct sales force, business partners, or distributors. When you use selling tiers, you can apply a different type of owner to different accounts, based on their unique requirements. An example of this approach is shown in Figure 10.10.

As shown in the figure, sales can be owned by different channels, depending on how complex (and important) the sale is. Top-tier accounts – the most complex, important relationships with the most after-sale support and selling activity – should be owned by trusted resources such as the field sales force or value-added partners. Conversely, simpler sales with few post-sales activities can be owned by an alternative, lower-cost channel such as a call centre. No matter who is in charge, though, account ownership over the sales process is an essential ingredient of an integrated channel model.

Well-defined account ownership goes along with proper channel-task assignment and channel hand-off management as three prerequisites of a successful integrated channel model. All three bring structure and clarity to what is often a complex and error-prone process. The potential payoff of channel integration is huge, but to achieve that payoff, multiple channels must be managed and controlled as a single smoothly functioning system.

Summary

Most companies cannot serve an entire market place with a single channel anymore. A single-channel approach is usually too expensive, as well as too limited in terms of market reach and growth. A hybrid channel model is often a better alternative. Hybrid channel models can deliver impressive gains in profitability, revenue growth and market share. However, hybrid channel models are more complex than single-channel models. They need to be managed as *systems*.

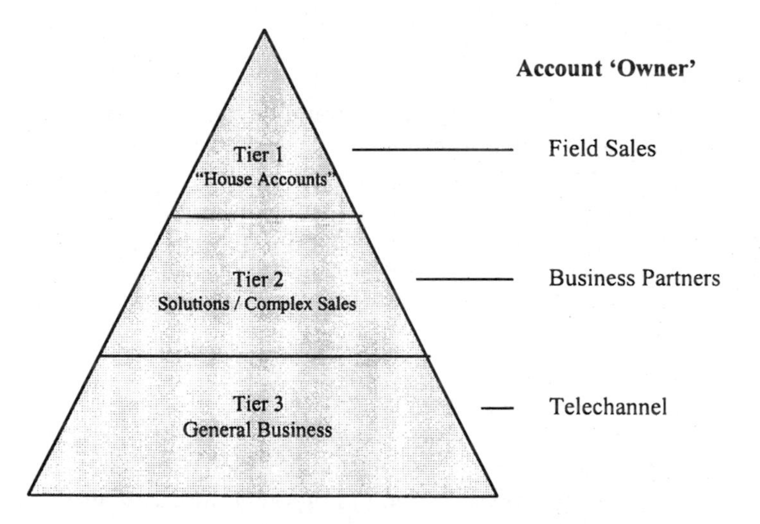

Figure 10.10 Aligning ownership with account complexity – sample three tier approach. *Source*: Oxford Associates

This involves careful structuring both the overall channel mix in a market as well as the integration of channels within the sales process.

Channel mix begins with a decision about whether to apply intensive, selective or hybrid channel coverage to a market. In most cases, companies are best off looking to a hybrid model, in which some product-markets are intensively covered by multiple channels, and yet in which others are served by a unique channel in a more focused manner. Sound hybrid models are based on four principles:

- **Align intensively covered markets with the critical buying mass** The mix of channels chosen to cover a product-market should collectively be targeted at capturing the critical mass of transaction volume – the bulk of the available business.
- **Monitor profitability** Multiple-channel mixes can exert downward pressure on profitability. One way to avoid this problem is to ensure that the channels added to a mix are each independently capable of turning a profit. A more difficult type of analysis – but perhaps more valuable – is to assess how a group of channels will affect sales 'lift' – new sales – versus 'shift' – sales moving around from channel to channel. Profitability in a channel mix is highly dependent on the extent to which new channels bring in *new* sales.
- **Save selective coverage for when it really counts** The tendency is often to assign discrete channels to each and every product-market. Selective coverage, however, is usually better left to a handful of product-markets. Most product-markets will experience faster growth as well as happier customers when provided with a mix of channels.
- **Beware of channel conflict** Channel conflict can erode profits and alienate key business partners. Pricing consistency across channels and the development of channel-specific product configurations are two helpful tools for managing channel conflict. The more extreme strategy is to limit channel participation to a smaller number of channels that can live comfortably off the available business base.

When *integrating* channels within a single sales process, the key is to use each channel for the parts of the sales process that it is uniquely able to perform. Some channels – telecentres, the Internet, etc. – are low cost and yet perfectly able to perform functions such as lead generation and qualification. Higher value-added functions, such as sales closure, will typically require more expensive resources such as field sales reps. Companies can often reduce the cost of sales dramatically by pushing various sales process tasks to lower-cost channels. However, success depends on careful management of:

- **Alignment of channels with the right sales tasks** It's possible to make an educated guess about which channels should be assigned to which sales tasks. However, that guess should be validated in a low-risk market before rolling out an integrated channel system to the broad market. Ultimately, channel-task suitability is highly dependent on the specific nature of the sale involved.

- **Hand-offs** The hand-off points at which leads or sales are given from one channel to another are the key risk areas in an integrated channel system. One requirement is a precise definition of when each task in the sales process is 'complete'; another is a clear set of procedures for *how* each channel should hand off a lead or sale to the next channel.
- **Account ownership** Overall coordination across all selling tasks is mandatory for an integrated channel model to work effectively. Thus, someone has to 'own' a sales opportunity from the minute it comes in the door to the conclusion of the transaction and the support of the account. Different channels can play this role depending on account complexity; the obvious choice – the sales closer – is not always the best one.

Channel mix and integration are the first major management challenges associated with bringing channels together into a coherent, high-performance system. The next chapter takes it a step further, by looking at what it takes to make a group of channels successful *in the field* – specifically from the vantage point of the *investments* and *resources* that each channel will need to do its job and deliver optimal results.

Notes

[1] Meaning the company can hit its profit targets when twenty per cent of revenue is spent on selling costs.
[2] As a result of blending lower-cost channels in with its relatively expensive distributor channel.
[3] Microsoft uses a similar model for small- and medium-size customer sales. It's a good strategy in the software business, where the goal is frequently to generate a lot of leads and get them into the hands of business partners for sale closure and fulfillment.
[4] There is no 'standard' sales process; every company's process is unique. The one shown is a typical major account sales process, give or take a task or two.
[5] For an in-depth understanding of hybrid marketing, see: Moriarty, Rowland and Ursula Moran (1990) Managing hybrid marketing systems, *Harvard Business Review*, November–December. This is the seminal article that kicked off much of the current interest in integrated channel systems.

Chapter 11

Investing in (and across) a portfolio of channels

Let's say you have $30 million to spend on sales and marketing this year. Should you invest it in the field sales force, a shiny new call centre, an improved and expanded reseller channel, or perhaps on a superbowl advertising blitz? Maybe the money should go into a new strategic alliance program or an experimental channel such as the Internet. What is even the basis for making this kind of decision? Is it:

- The anticipated revenue contribution of each channel?
- The expected cost of each channel?
- Funding levels carried over from last year, along with a small amount of 'entrepreneurial capital' thrown at new, alternative channels?
- A 'gut feel' about where to spend the money, based on historical experience?

As this simple question suggests, investing in a multiple-channel system is a complex activity. And it is getting more complicated every day. Organizations have more choices than ever before about where to spend their sales and marketing dollars. Figure 11.1 illustrates this basic challenge.

Investment planning wouldn't be a big deal if companies had unlimited funds and resources to throw at their channels. But they don't. Budgets are always finite and resources are always scarce. As a result, it's imperative to use investment dollars and resources where they really count: where they will do the most good, and where they are most needed in the light of market and revenue opportunities. Both under-funded and over-funded channels can have a serious nega-

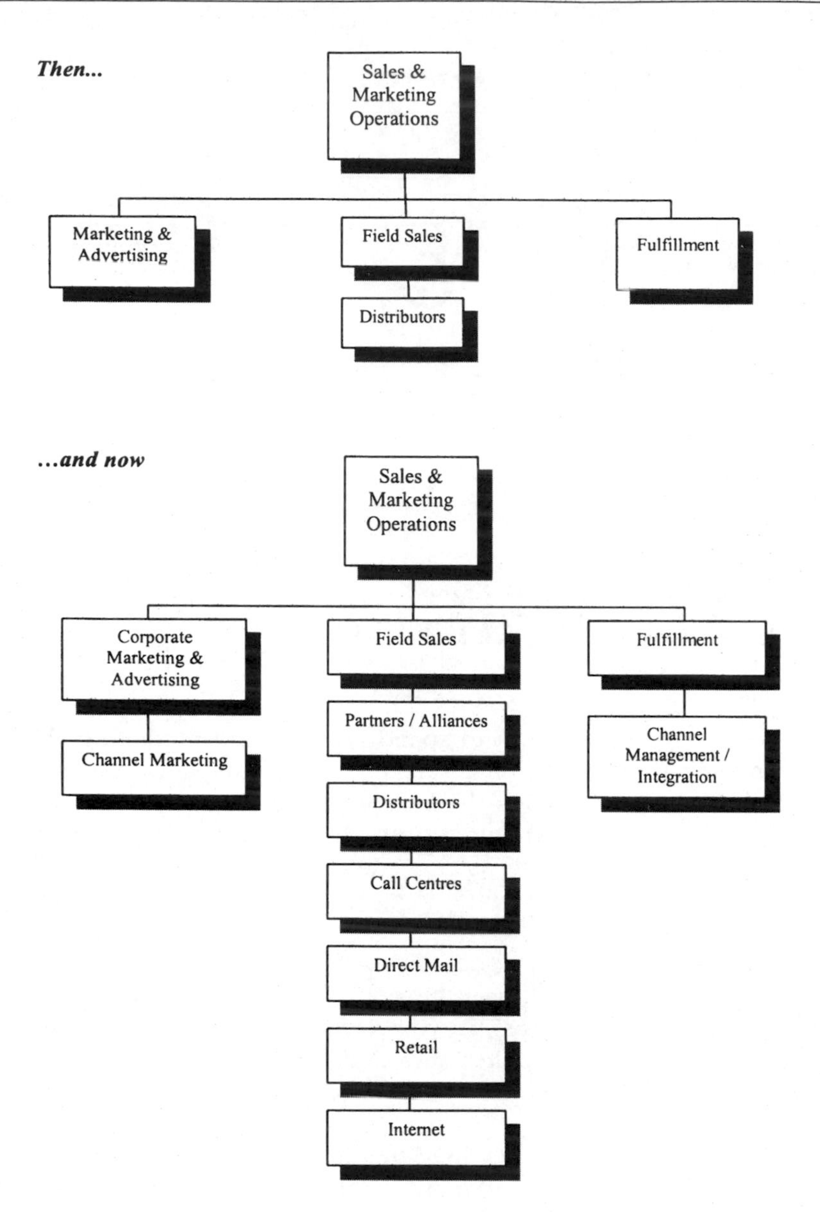

Figure 11.1 Increasing go-to-market investment complexity

tive impact on sales performance. A sales force that requires 200 field reps to make its numbers will miss those numbers by quite a margin if it is only given enough money to support 100; conversely, if given the money to hire 400 field reps, it will squander investment dollars that could have been used to support another channel's needs. Similarly, a web site that is under-funded will lack the quality of design or back-office integration required to make it work as a real sales channel; an over-funded web site will become an investment black hole (as indeed many of them have become). To avoid these kinds of problems:

> A company must have a rational and market-driven plan for assigning investment funds and resources optimally across a range of channels.

Very few companies have such a plan in place today. Most organizations tend to take last year's cost numbers and adjust them incrementally upward or downward depending on which sales and marketing activities are doing well or poorly. A successful advertising campaign may get some extra money this year; the floundering international branch takes a ten per cent cutback until it proves itself. This kind of conventional, incremental budget planning may work acceptably with a single channel but it doesn't work with multiple channels, for two reasons:

- **Lack of market and revenue focus** Conventional budgeting often begins with how much each channel is expected to *cost* this year – e.g., by looking at last year's costs – rather than with the *revenue* which can be realized by each channel and then the specific investments that are needed to capture that revenue. In a multiple channel environment, revenue is everything; it is the foundation for setting channel investment levels and establishing investment trade-offs across channels. In other words, 'a call centre will cost about $25 million' is not a very useful piece of information. How much revenue will that call centre contribute? Half a million? Ten billion? What are other channels expected to bring in? Half as much? A hundred times as much? Channel revenue is the only sensible basis for determining how much of the total pool of sales and marketing investment money each channel should receive. Revenue, not cost, is the starting point of an effective multiple-channel planning process.
- **Piecemeal channel planning** Conventional budgeting often deals with each sales and marketing expense individually, rather than as part of a collective portfolio of go-to-market investments. This is a recipe for disaster in a multiple-channel environment. Budget season comes along, and all of the various channel managers submit their requests for funds and resources. Most of these existing channels are given at least modest funding increases to accommodate their new initiatives and requirements. At the same time, nothing ever gets cut from the budget, because every dollar, resource and activity in every channel is seen as tied to a potential sale. New channels may also be added, each of which entails a significant new expense. As a result of all this spending, overall selling costs increase – faster than sales in many cases. In short: lower selling profitability.

Multiple-channel budgeting requires a different approach. This chapter describes one with a strong track record in many leading organizations: *enterprise-wide sales and marketing planning*. Enterprise-wide planning is based on two simple ideas. First, complex multiple-channel systems must be managed and funded against specific revenue and market projections, to ensure that channel spending doesn't become a runaway train dissociated from real selling targets. Second, channels should be invested in collectively, with scarce resources allocated across the full range of channels to ensure that each gets exactly what it needs to meet its objectives. Enterprise-wide planning has four steps:

- **Define the revenue opportunity** How much sales revenue is 'out there' to be captured? In which market segments?
- **Build a revenue forecast by channel** Which channels will be used to capture the revenue in each of those market segments? Thus, what is the total revenue expectation for *each channel*?
- **Estimate channel resources** How many resources will be required by each channel, given its revenue projection?
- **Build the go-to-market cost model** Given that number of channel resources, how much will the channel cost to operate – and what will be the total go-to-market cost (and budget)?

The process is shown graphically in Figure 11.2.

The outcome of enterprise-wide channel planning is a channel investment budget that is pegged to real opportunities in the market place, and that allocates funds and resources to channels based on their specific revenue contributions and resource requirements. This chapter describes the nuts and bolts of building this management tool.

Step 1 – Define the revenue opportunity

Every dollar invested in a channel should be spent in support of a revenue opportunity. The existence of 'off line' or 'back office' channel investments – money spent on activities only vaguely associated with revenue production – is the surest sign that a channel will fail to meet its profitability targets. Even 'non-selling' channel investments, such as sales training seminars or channel marketing trade shows, should eventually tie back to and exist in support of actual revenue targets.

The traditional tool for holding the line on wasteful channel spending is the red pen, a wonderful device for reviewing the go-to-market plan and crossing out silly-sounding or extravagant budget requests. The red pen approach is always helpful, but it's a reactive and inexact tool. A more proactive and precise approach begins with a good revenue forecast: a top-line assessment of sales opportunities. A revenue forecast establishes a sense of direction for channel planning: a market-focused purpose against which investments and resources can be committed to individual channels. The first step in enterprise-wide channel planning is thus to:

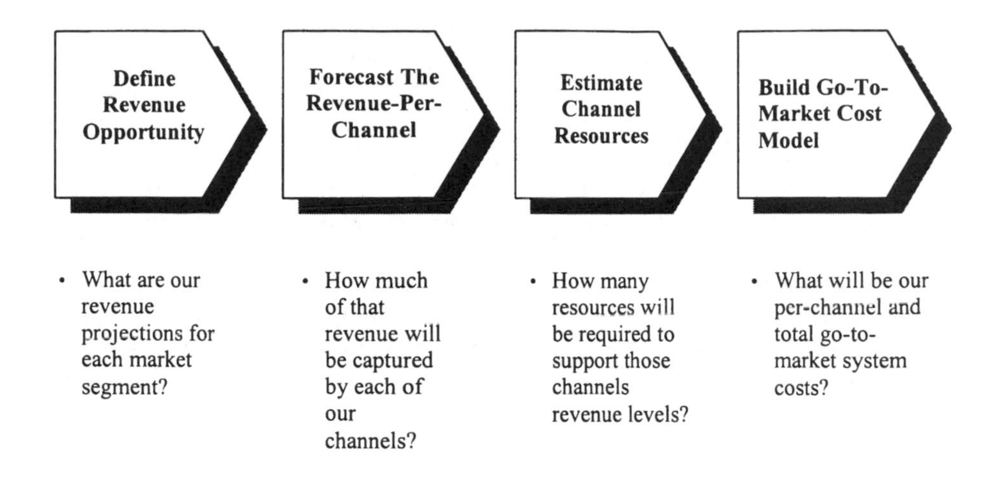

Figure 11.2 Enterprise-wide resource planning process for multiple-channel systems. *Source*: Oxford Associates

> Define the revenue forecast, and specifically, in terms that can be used for evaluating and allocating channel investments.

The most common approach to revenue forecasting is to build a model from the ground up based on sales expectations in vertical markets and across product lines. A typical example is shown in Figure 11.3, in this case for Meridian Solutions, a $57 million application software firm[1]. Meridian divides

1998 Revenue Projection By Vertical Market And Product Line

Markets / Products	Supply Management Software	Account Management / Support Software	Budget Planning / Financial Software
Legal Services	$0.0m	$4.8m	$3.0m
Accounting	$0.4m	$5.2m	$3.0m
Medical / Hospital	$6.8m	$10.1m	$5.0m
Other	$4.0m	$9.0m	$6.0m

Total Revenue Forecast 1998 = $57.4 m

Figure 11.3 Revenue forecast – Meridian Solutions

its market into three key 'verticals': legal services, accounting and medical/hospital. In addition, although the company has a wide range of products and services, it has grouped its offerings into three categories for planning purposes: supply management software; customer/account planning software; and budget/financial software.

Like Meridian, many companies set revenue targets in terms of vertical markets and product lines. This approach works particularly well for:

- **Product development** A segmentation of revenue by product line is a useful and necessary piece of information for setting R&D objectives and budgets.
- **Marketing/'message' positioning** Understanding where the revenue will come from in terms of vertical markets is important in developing the 'message' for prospective customers in those markets.

Unfortunately, where this approach doesn't work so well is in channel planning. In most cases, neither vertical markets nor product lines correspond very well to channel usage. For example, at Meridian:

- Large, corporate accounts *across every vertical market* expect to be sold to and serviced by a Meridian national account manager.
- Meridian's shrink-wrapped software products are sold through distributors, *regardless of the product line.*
- Mid-sized accounts can usually be qualified and pre-sold over the phone, *regardless of vertical or product line.*
- Unique client development projects require a national account manager and a selling team, *in any market segment.*

In short, Meridian's vertical markets and product lines have little to do with its potential use of (or investment in) channels. Some channels (national account managers) operate across all verticals, while some customer types (large corporate accounts) have specific channel expectations regardless of their industry. There is simply a low correlation between Meridian's existing segments and its channel usage.

In fact, segmentation by vertical market and product line generally has limited utility in channel planning. Take the computer industry as an example. For years, channel marketing managers in high-tech firms have spent their time and energy designing complex segments and subsegments of vertical markets that cut across multitudes of products, services, and solutions, resulting in indecipherable market strategy presentations that make the Rosetta stone seem like an easy exercise in translation.

Then came Dell Computer, which proceeded to aggregate customers across market segments with blatant disregard for the usual vertical marketing schemes in the industry. The company sells a computer to anyone who wants one, through channels – such as the Internet and telephone – that are suited to the complexity of its various products and its customers' buying preferences. Big, key accounts get direct reps; smaller, mass-market customers get low-cost channels. Nowadays, the top players in the industry all have recognized, in fact, that channel usage cuts across vertical markets and product lines. Customers' channel preferences aren't based on the vertical they're in or which product they are buying, but rather on the types of transactions in which they participate. As a result, many high tech firms have had to go back to the drawing board and reclassify their sales forecasts into new types of segments that correlate better with how customers actually want to do business.

Figure 11.4, for example, shows how Meridian has resegmented its revenue base along two dimensions that are closely aligned with channel usage: customer size and product complexity:

As the figure shows, Meridian has taken its overall revenue projection of $57.4 million and developed new market segments, based on customer size and product complexity, that are closely aligned with channel usage. For example:

- Meridian's large corporate account segments demand and need a direct sales force presence.
- Volume is low in the SOHO (small office/home office) market, and most of the sales involve off-the-rack software products. Any sale into this base of customers is ripe for migration to a lower-cost alternative channel.
- The company's middle-market accounts – its core business, the Fortune 250–1000

Revenue Projection 1999 By Customer Type and Product Type

Customers / Products	Off-The-Rack	Customized Applications	Unique Client Development Projects
Large Large Corporate	$2.0m	$12.4m	$5.6m
Mid-Sized	$4.0m	$19.0m	$12.0m
Small SO-HO	$2.2m	$0.2m	$0.0m
	Simple		*Complex*

Figure 11.4 Resegmented four distribution strategy – Meridian Systems

– is now separated out more clearly from its other business, and segmented in terms of the complexity of products offered to this market. As a result, Meridian has been able to identify opportunities to use lower-cost channels for some of these sales (simple products) while also gaining clarity about which sales in this market require the direct sales force.

Meridian, in short, has developed a *distribution-based revenue forecast*, one that looks at revenues primarily in terms of how (through which channels) they will be captured. A re-categorization of revenues along these lines, into market segments that closely reflect channel usage, provides a basis for figuring out which channels will capture which revenues. As a result, it becomes possible – and perhaps even easy – to break down the overall revenue forecast into a forecast of *revenue by channel*, the key metric required for effective channel investment planning.

Step 2 – Forecast the revenue by channel

After building the revenue forecast, the next step is to convert it into a forecast of the revenues that will be captured by each channel. This calculation requires two pieces of information:

- From Step 1, the overall revenue forecast, parsed into distribution-oriented market segments.
- A channel coverage map, showing which channel(s) will 'cover' each market segment.

Once both of these pieces of information exist, calculating the revenue by channel is a matter of *overlaying the coverage map onto the revenue forecast*, or put another way, adding up all the revenues in each segment that are assigned to a particular channel.

Take as an example Meridian's channel strategy redesign for 1998. In an effort to reduce selling costs and reach new customers, the company developed a new coverage plan that looked as shown in Figure 11.5.

Meridian's new coverage plan reflected several of the core design points discussed earlier in this book:

- Low-end transactions (small customers, simple products) can and should be migrated to low-cost channels to reduce costs (and increase transaction profitability).
  - In Meridian's case, this meant starting up a small telemarketing operation to sell shrink-wrapped software to small office customers.
- Complex products sold to large corporate accounts generally require field reps and value-added partners.

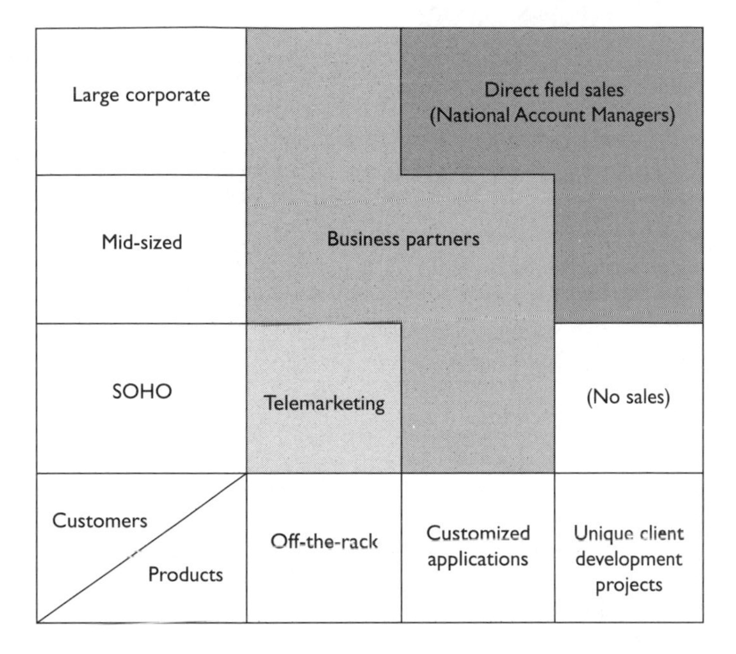

Figure 11.5 Meridian Systems market coverage redesign for 1998

- Meridian's national account managers would continue to sell to and manage most large corporate relationships as well as highly-complex solutions in the middle-market.

- Most middle-market opportunities can be handled by business partners and other mid-cost, mid-touch channels.
  - In Meridian's case, the vast bulk of middle market – mid-sized customers buying off-the-rack or mass-customized products – would be migrated to the business partner channel.

Given that Meridian already had a revenue forecast, the company, with its new channel coverage plan, had everything it needed to build a model of its revenue forecast by channel. It simply overlaid its channel coverage map on top of its revenue forecast, as shown in Figure 11.6.

It's worth noting that Meridian had a somewhat easier calculation to make than many other companies, as a result of its decision to assign one unique channel to each product-market. More often, two or more channels 'share' a product market, and as a result, the revenue in that segment must be divided up between the channels to forecast per-channel revenues accurately.

A slightly larger software firm, for example, Microsoft Corporation, sells operating systems to consumers through OEMs (original equipment manufacturers), retail stores, application developers, and systems integrators, among other channels. To calculate its revenue per channel, Microsoft thus has to

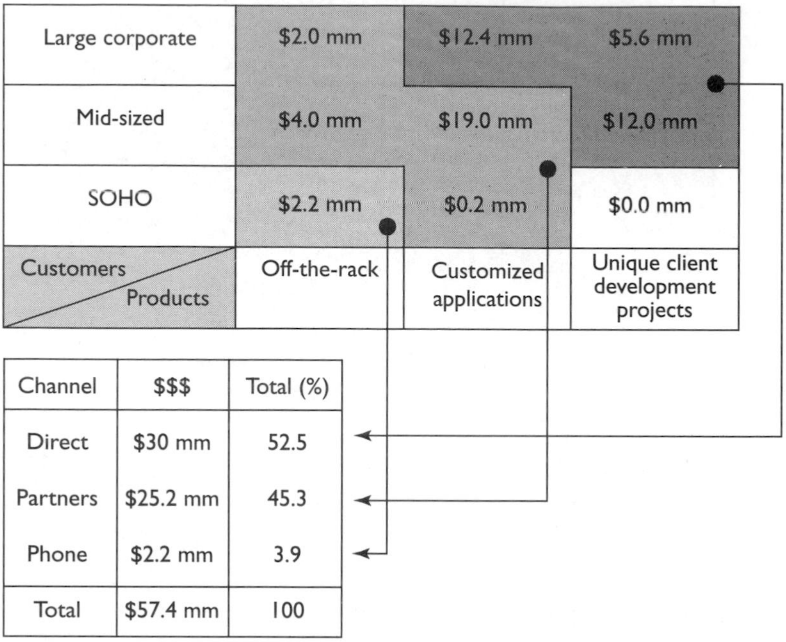

Customers / Products	Off-the-rack	Customized applications	Unique client development projects
Large corporate	$2.0 mm	$12.4 mm	$5.6 mm
Mid-sized	$4.0 mm	$19.0 mm	$12.0 mm
SOHO	$2.2 mm	$0.2 mm	$0.0 mm

Channel	$$$	Total (%)
Direct	$30 mm	52.5
Partners	$25.2 mm	45.3
Phone	$2.2 mm	3.9
Total	$57.4 mm	100

Figure 11.6 Revenue by channel forecast 1998 – Meridian Systems

figure out how much revenue will be captured by each channel within each market segment. It is more typical for companies to have to assign the revenues within a single product-market to multiple channels than it is for a company to have as clean a calculation as the one shown in Figure 11.6.

The output of this step in the enterprise-wide planning process is a revenue forecast for each channel in the go-to-market system, as illustrated in Figure 11.6. This key piece of information is the foundation for estimating channel resource requirements, as described in the next step.

Step 3 – Estimate channel resource requirements

The relationship between a channel's revenue target and the resources it needs to reach that target is straightforward. If a field sales force's revenue target is $100 million, and each resource, or sales rep, brings in an average of $1 million, then it will take 100 field reps to achieve the revenue target. Of course, if you could somehow double the productivity of the average rep to $2 million, you'd only need fifty reps. Conversely, if the productivity per resource were to decrease to a half million, you would need to hire another

Channel revenue = Number of resources x Contribution per resource
Example: Field sales force with 100 reps, at $1 million per rep Total channel revenue = $100 million

Or put another way...

Number of resources required = Channel revenue forecast / Contribution per resource
Example: Channel revenue forecast is $100 million, each rep brings in $1 million on average Number of resources = 100

Figure 11.7 Determining channel resource requirements – the basic formula

hundred reps to achieve the same revenue goal[2]. In short, a channel's ability to hit a revenue target is a function both of the average revenue contribution per selling resource as well as the number of resources, as shown in Figure 11.7.

Accurate resource estimation by channel is an essential part of the planning process for two reasons:

- **Budgeting** Resources – people, that is – are usually the most expensive components of cost in any channel. You can't get a good fix on how much a channel will cost until you determine how many people will be needed to achieve the channel's revenue target.
- **Staffing** In almost every case, a new revenue forecast will impact the number of resources needed by various channels, as well as the overall allocation of resources *across* channels. People will need to be hired or fired or shifted between channels to support the revenue plan. Resource analysis involves figuring out where people need to be added, subtracted, or shifted to optimize their allocation in pursuit of a revenue target.

Meridian Solutions provides a good example of how all this plays out in a real environment. Meridian's new revenue forecast by channel, as depicted earlier in Figure 11.6, suggested a substantial shift of revenue from its direct sales force to new business partners as well as a telemarketing operation. To make

Channel	Revenue Target	Existing Resources	Productivity Per Resource	Revenue Capacity	Resources Needed*	Headcount Addition or Subtraction
Direct Sales	$30m	54	$1.19m	$64.3m	26	- 28
Partners	$25.2m	11	$0.75m	$8.25m	34	+ 23
Telereps	$2.2m	3	$0.55m	$1.65m	4	+ 1

Revenue capacity = existing resources x productivity per resource: what the channel could deliver at today's staffing levels.

Resources needed = Revenue target / productivity per resource: the new staffing level required to hit the revenue target.

Figure 11.8 Meridian Solutions channel resource requirements analysis

this shift work, Meridian had to review its current channel resources and make some additions and subtractions to its various channels. The results are shown in Figure 11.8.

As shown in the figure, Meridian's direct sales force had fifty-four reps, with a revenue capacity of over $64 million (based on per-rep revenue production of $1.19 million). That staffing level made sense in light of the company's $57 million size – when it was thinking mainly in terms of direct (field) sales. But given Meridian's goal of reducing sales force-initiated transactions to $30 million, the sales force was clearly too big. In fact, the $30 million sales force target could be achieved easily by only twenty-six sales reps.

So why not just keep all fifty-four reps and make more sales, instead of reducing sales force headcount? After all, more sales are always better than fewer sales. The answer cuts to the core of the planning challenge in a multiple-channel environment – in a word, *trade-offs*. The investment dollars that support those 'extra' direct sales reps are needed elsewhere now: to support the business partner channel. The partner channel needs thirty-four partners to achieve its $25.2 million target, and, at present, has only eleven. Another twenty-three need to be recruited, trained, and supported in the field. The money to do that has to come from someplace. In addition, another telemarketing rep is required; that costs money too. Multiple-channel budgeting is all about allocating scarce investment dollars to the channels that need them – and away from the channels that don't. The only alternative, unfortunately, is to keep adding more and more money to the budget of every channel. That only works if you don't care about making a profit.

The output of Step 3 is a clear picture of the resource requirements, as well as the resource gaps – the surplus or deficit of resources – that currently exist in each channel. This information will determine who needs to be hired, let go or reassigned. It will also establish the foundation for building a cost model to determine how much money needs to be invested in each channel, as described in the next step.

Step 4 – Build the go-to-market cost model

The end-game in channel investment planning is a clear picture of how much money needs to be invested in each channel to achieve the overall revenue target. The output of Step 3 – an estimate of the resources, or people, required by each channel – is a good starting point, because resources often account for well over half or more of a channel's cost structure. Unfortunately, though, resources don't account for all of a channel's cost structure. This last step in the process completes the investment picture; it converts resource levels into cost levels, and also fills in the other missing pieces required for building the cost (and investment) model.

The starting point in this step is to build a bottom-up model of all of the various costs that will or can be incurred by different channels. Salaries of sales reps are the most obvious expense, but what about distributor margins, telephone bills for the call centre, technical support resources, or perhaps an allocation of corporate overhead to the sales channels? All of these items need to be accounted for in the cost model. A basic framework for building the model was presented in Chapter 5, and for convenience is shown again, in Figure 11.9 below.

Figure 11.9 provides an overview of the various types of expenses that different channels can incur. Of course, not every channel will incur every type of expense; the value of the framework lies in establishing a uniform, consistent and fairly inclusive set of cost factors across all channels.

So how does a model like this play out in a real sales environment? Again, Meridian Solutions provides an instructive example. The company had looked at its $58.7 million revenue target for 1998 and assumed that about eighteen per cent, or about $10.5 million, would be spent on sales and marketing. Great start – but how much of that $10.5 million should go to each channel, and was the $10.5 million figure an accurate and realistic one in the first place?

To figure this out, Meridian built a cost model for each channel. The company, unfamiliar with the intricacies of two of its new channels – business partners and telemarketing – opted to 'ballpark' some of the figures rather than to shoot for exact cost levels. It used the following assumptions:

- **Direct field expenses** A field rep earns an average of $130,000 in salary, bonuses and commissions.
- **Indirect field selling expenses** About three per cent of revenue is spent on

1. Direct Selling	Sales rep salaries and commissions Indirect field expenses (travel, site demos, etc.) Sales management allocation
2. Distributor Costs	Distributor or partner margins Indirect channel program costs Indirect channel marketing and promotion costs
3. Telemarketing / Telesales	Telerep salaries and commissions Phone costs Computer and systems costs Sales management allocation
4. Electronic Commerce / Internet	E-commerce start-up (design/build) E-commerce operating (maintenance) costs Fulfillment system linkage costs
5. Marketing and Advertising	Channel-support marketing and promotions Advertising and media support Corporate marketing allocation
6. Fulfillment	Shipping Order processing Inventory carrying costs Financing / Risk assumption
7. Overhead Allocation	G&A corporate overhead allocation Other allocated expenses

Figure 11.9 Basic framework for establishing channel expenses

sales rep travel expenses, and another four per cent of revenue is spent on technical support. Sales management eats up twelve per cent of total sales force compensation.

- **Call centre** A telemarketing rep makes about $50,000 in salary and bonus.
- **Business partners** Partners are paid eleven per cent of sales. An expanded partner program would also require a partner training and management program, estimated at $450,000 by looking at a few competitors, as well as a technical support budget (two and a half per cent of revenues) and some co-op marketing funds (another two per cent of revenue).
- The company decided to 'charge' each channel three per cent of revenues to pay for office administration and overhead. However, the decision was made, wisely, not to try to pass along this cost to its business partners.

Channel Expense	Direct Sales Force	Business Partners	Telemarketing
Revenue Forecast	**$30,000,000**	**$25,200,000**	**$2,200,000**
Direct Selling			
• FTEs / Resources	26	34	4
• Salaries & Commissions	$3,380,000		
• Field expenses (3 % of Revenue)	$900,000		
• Sales management (12 % of salaries)	$405,600		
• Sales/tech support (4 % of revenue)	$1,200,000		
Business Partners			
• Margins (11 % of revenue)		$2,772,000	
• Channel programs/ training		$450,000	
• Channel mktg (2 % of revenue)		$504,000	
• Sales/tech support (2.5 % of revenue)		$630,000	
Telemarketing			
• Salaries & Commissions			$200,000
• Phone/facilities costs			$34,000
• Telemarketing Management (12 % of salaries)			$36,000
Corporate Allocation			
• General & administrative (3 % of revenue)	$900,000		$66,000
Total Channel Cost	**$6,785,600**	**$4,356,000**	**$336,000**
Loaded Cost Per FTE/Resource	$260,985	$128,118	$84,000
Revenue Per FTE/Resource	$1,154,000	$741,177	$550,000
Channel E/R	*23 %*	*17 %*	*15 %*

Total go-to-market cost: $11,477,600

Figure 11.10 Meridian Solutions – channel cost model (1998)

Although certainly not exhaustive, these assumptions by Meridian's management team provided a reasonable basis for constructing a channel investment model, as shown in Figure 11.10.

Here is what the company's management team learned by going through this admittedly difficult exercise:

- **Revised sales and marketing budget** Their estimates weren't too far off in terms of the intended $10.5 million channel budget. However, by building a cost model for each channel, the management team was able to create a more realistic estimate of $11.4 million. Now they have the option either of pushing for $900,000 in cost savings to stay within budget, or increasing the budget to reflect the realistic investment levels required to capture $58.7 million in sales with this mix of channels.
- **Revenue-based channel allocations** Meridian is now positioned to allocate its total investment budget across its three channels, based on what each channel needs to deliver its revenue target. The sales force needs about $6.79 million to deliver $30 million in sales, and the business partner channel needs about $4.36 million to deliver $25.2 million in sales. The smaller, newer telemarketing channel requires only $336,000 to generate its $2.2 million[3].

In sum, this step in the enterprise-wide planning process involves building cost models for each channel in the go-to-market system – and then rolling all these costs up into an overall sales and marketing investment budget. This process will establish both:

- The overall sales and marketing budget level.
- The allocation of the right portion of that budget to each channel in the go-to-market system based on its needs.

Importantly, this last step will suggest investment levels based fundamentally on the amount of revenue that each channel is projected to deliver. It is a thus a highly useful tool for determining how to commit scarce resources across an entire channel system to achieve optimal market results.

Summary

Channel 'management' is often thought of in terms of partner recruitment programs, call centre performance management, web site integration, and other tactical, daily operational issues. That's because many channels are still young, and to date many managers have been focusing mainly on getting them up and running. Management of a channel portfolio, however, is broader than the operation of any one particular channel. As a company expands its channel mix, it becomes increasingly necessary to put planning tools in place to manage channels *collectively* as a go-to-market system. Trade-offs must be made between competing channel needs, and scarce investment dollars and resources must be put to use in the best places. As a result, a key component of effective channel management is to build a solid *enterprise-wide* investment plan, one that identifies the optimal levels of investment dollars and resources each channel needs to achieve its market objectives.

This chapter looked at one type of enterprise-wide management approach based on 'top down' budget planning. In this approach, top-line revenue is the starting point – projected revenue, parsed into revenue expectations for each market segment (Step 1). By mapping these revenue expectations against the channel coverage map, it becomes possible to develop the key metric for channel budget planning: the revenue forecast by channel (Step 2). The revenue forecast by channel can then be translated both into the resources needed by each channel to support the revenue target (Step 3), as well as the investments that will be required (Step 4). This approach, in its simplicity and structured methodology, can eliminate some of the havoc and chaos that is typically present during budget season in multiple-channel systems. Most importantly, it can help establish go-to-market resource and investment levels that are pegged to specific revenue opportunities and that are allocated optimally across all channels in the system.

Of course, effective go-to-market management requires more than a sound resource and investment plan. Sound investments ensure that channels have the *potential* to reach their objectives, but don't guarantee that channels will *achieve* that potential. For that, you have to look toward active channel performance management: the ongoing measurement and monitoring of channels against their objectives. Performance measurement and monitoring become more complicated in multiple-channel systems. With one channel, the goal is usually to 'sell a lot, fast' and the performance of the channel is relatively easy to measure. In multiple-channel systems, some channels may be primarily responsible for selling, while others are responsible for support, lead generation or fulfilment. Getting each channel to do what it's supposed to be doing, and monitoring its performance in the light of its specific charter, can be a significant management challenge. That is the subject of the next chapter, 'Measuring and managing channel performance'.

Notes

[1] The name has been changed at the request of the client.

[2] This can and does happen, for example, when new, complex products are introduced to a sales force; productivity per rep can decrease substantially until the sales force learns how to position and sell the product.

[3] As of publication of this book, the company had actually spent $520,000 on its call centre. But that is part of the investment challenge – learning from experience. A call centre with four telemarketing reps is too small an operation to cover the large, fixed costs.

Chapter 12

Measuring and managing channel performance

There's an old story about performance management, in which an archer is trying to get his young son ready for his first match. The archer carefully positions the target fifty feet out, blindfolds his son, and says 'see if you can hit the target'. His son dutifully fits an arrow into the bow and fires away, missing the target by twenty feet to the left. The archer laughs, good-naturedly. 'You'll have to do better than that. Give it another try.' The son, still blindfolded, manages to send off another arrow, this time missing the target by thirty feet to the right. The archer, now a little perturbed, says sharply, 'This kind of sorry shooting will ruin our family name. Now hit the damn target already!' Unable to see what he's doing, the son tries again and sends the projectile twenty feet over the target and into the woods beyond. Angry, the archer grabs his walking stick and hits his son in the side, knocking him to the ground. 'A man must be able to hit a target with an arrow to survive in this world. Now get up and do it right!' The son climbs to his feet painfully, fits his very last arrow, and facing in the wrong direction, fires it into the archer's prize mare, killing the horse. Exasperated, the archer cries, 'This is a disgrace. Get in the house and try making some dresses or something. Go on!' The son, unable to see where he is going with the blindfold on, wanders off into the woods, never to be seen again.

The moral of the story is as follows: yelling, cajoling or even beating people with a stick doesn't make them hit a target. In general, people – or organizations, or channels – achieve the right results only when they can see clearly:

- what they are trying to hit;
- how well they are doing over time in hitting it.

In short, in any ambitious endeavour, there is just no substitute for a clear set of goals and good performance measurement.

This simple wisdom is especially important in the management of multiple channels. In every respect, multiple-channel systems are more complex than their single-channel counterparts: more people, more activities, more investments, more initiatives, and to be candid, more room for screwing up. So how do management teams even *begin* to put the processes in place to ensure that each channel performs well and does what it's supposed to be doing? In many cases, the answer is: they don't. Multiple-channel management often falls flat on three fronts:

- **Disconnect between corporate goals and channel activity** As channel systems become more complex, companies often experience a *disconnect* between their key corporate goals and the activities of their various channels – sometimes resulting in absurd channel behavior that directly contradicts their intentions in the market place.

  For example, most pharmaceutical companies – the Pfizers and Mercks – have come to believe that targeted growth, in key $500,000 plus per year accounts, is central to their future success. Yet average account size has actually *decreased* in many of these companies[1], primarily because their sales forces show no sign of migrating away from low-dollar 'hunt and pray' sales calls on small customers (doctors offices, pharmacies and the like). Similarly, large technology firms such as IBM have concluded that sustainable future growth requires the acquisition of new 'super-accounts': large customers with the potential to deliver years of consistent, high revenue streams. Yet they struggle year in and year out – unsuccessfully, in many cases – to get their sales reps out of existing, penetrated accounts and onto the street where these reps should be building the customer bases of the future.

  Why the disconnect between corporate goals and channel activity? Primarily, it's because channels are often measured and rewarded on the wrong things. High tech and pharmaceutical reps, for example, are often rewarded for revenue production of any sort, which encourages them to pursue the 'low hanging fruit': incremental sales to familiar customers. It is easier for those reps to call on a friendly doctor or a familiar technology customer than it is to get out there and find new key accounts.

  There is only one known method for getting a channel off its path of least resistance and focused on activities that align with the corporation's goals: its metrics and rewards must be redesigned to encourage the right kinds of activities and performance. Put simply:

  > *The use of performance metrics to bring channel activity in line with specific corporate goals is the cornerstone of effective channel management.*

- **Failing to account for the channel's unique role in the sales process** What should be the measure of success of, say, a web site? One option is to gauge its success in terms of the revenue it generates. But what if the purpose of the web site isn't to close deals, but rather to generate leads for the sales force? A far better metric might be the number of visitors who register at the site, or perhaps the percentage of those visitors who request information or a follow-up call. More generally, in a go-to-market system, not every channel is responsible for performing every selling task. As a result:

  It is essential to define performance measures that are consistent with the roles and responsibilities of each channel in the sales process.

- **Out-of-control complexity** Performance measurement and reporting tend to take on a life of their own in a multiple-channel system. Not a pretty little life, like that of a daisy, but a life more akin to a giant ugly sea squid. It starts off innocently enough, with a single channel measured against twenty or thirty performance indicators. As the system expands to five or six channels, though, the life force of middle management gets sucked out trying to keep up with a hundred or more data points, reports, and performance indicators. Then, more channels get added, and with an ever-increasing arsenal of performance metrics, the system gets better and better at describing everything – and saying nothing. Thus:

  In most cases, a handful of well-chosen metrics, each of which truly says something important about channel performance, can be far more effective than an endless, growing management reporting behemoth.

In short, the end-game in a strategic channel initiative should be to put in place a set of channel performance targets and metrics that:

- Guide each channel toward performance that is consistent with corporate goals.
- Push channels toward the things they are supposed to be doing in the sales process – and discourage them from doing things they shouldn't be doing.
- Are simple, and easy to use and interpret.

This chapter lays out a process for achieving these objectives, as shown in Figure 12.1.

1. Define/confirm overall sales objectives

The first order of business is to take a careful look at corporate goals and translate them into a set of focused sales objectives. A simple example of this translation is shown in Figure 12.2.

Why are sales objectives – selling targets that apply across all channels – so important in a multiple-channel system? The reason is that channels cannot

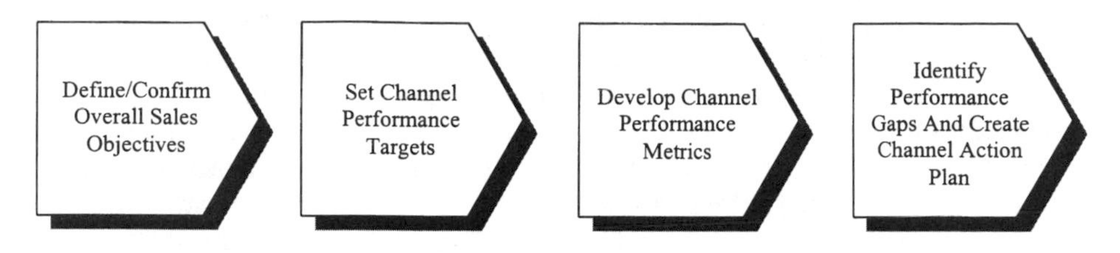

Figure 12.1 Performance measurement process for multiple-channel systems

usually interpret and act on high-level corporate goals. For example, what exactly would a sales force need to do to help its company increase earnings per share or become number one in its markets? Make more sales to more customers? Make fewer sales to more profitable, key accounts? Put more emphasis on customer retention and satisfaction, even if costs go up? Streamline processes to serve accounts more efficiently? It's hard to say. A corporate goal can be a confusing source of information about what sorts of activities a channel should emphasize. Many executives, in fact, get tired of trying to interpret their corporate goals for their sales channels, and resort in the end to injunctions such as 'Sell as much product as possible, now!' The result: frenzied selling activity that sometimes has little or nothing to do with what the company is trying to achieve in the market place.

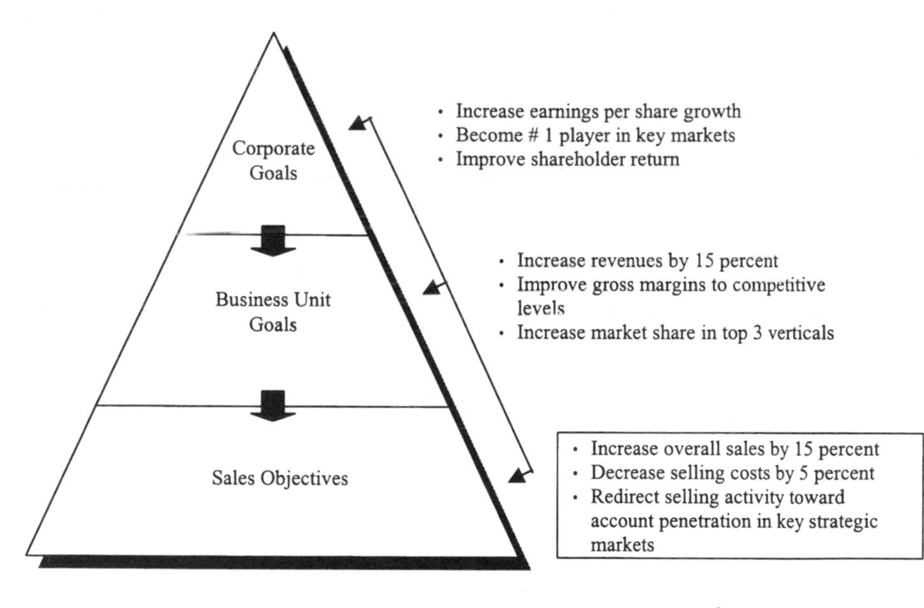

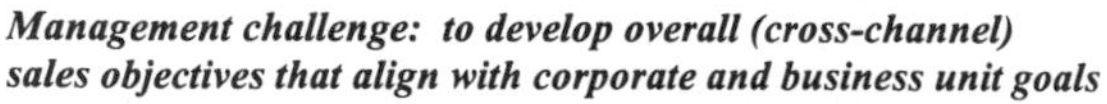

Figure 12.2 Translating corporate goals into sales objectives

As Figure 12.2 suggests, the way to bring about a tighter alignment between corporate goals and channel activity is to translate those goals into a set of tangible, focused sales objectives. While it may be difficult to figure out what a call centre should do with a corporate goal such as 'improve operating margins', it is much easier to act on a sales objective such as 'reduce transaction costs by five per cent'. Sales objectives provide baseline expectations around which performance targets and metrics for any channel can be developed.

It is worth noting that not everyone needs to go through this exercise. Some companies already have strong sales objectives that effectively communicate their corporate goals to their individual channels. But in many cases, management teams – particularly those with complex, multiple-channel systems – lack a fundamental answer to the question:

> What are all channels – collectively – supposed to be accomplishing in the market place?

The following techniques are helpful in answering this question:

- **Translate each corporate/business unit goal into a sales objective** It is useful to take each corporate goal *individually* and translate it into a quantitative sales objective. A typical goal – 'improve operating margins to competitive levels' – can usually be translated directly into a sales objective, such as 'reduce selling costs by five per cent'. It is a good idea to establish a single, focused quantifiable sales objective in support of each high-level strategic goal of the enterprise.
- **Think of corporate goals as falling into three categories: revenue growth, profit growth, and customer loyalty** For all their diversity, most corporate goals fit comfortably into one of these three categories. It is well worth taking a step back and thinking about how the goals of the corporation might fit into these categories, because this simple typology can bring a lot of focus to the task of designing good sales objectives.
  - A growth goal generally requires that sales objectives be focused on new account acquisition, broad-based growth in the customer base, increased penetration into new markets, and increased penetration of existing key accounts.
  - A profit goal requires sales objectives that focus on increased customer retention, a reduction in transaction costs, better targeting of the most profitable customers, and more efficient usage of selling resources.
  - A customer loyalty goal generally requires sales objectives that emphasize improved customer service, more extensive post-sale support, and more flexible provision of sales resources and channels to key accounts.

  Of course, these three types of goals are not mutually exclusive. In fact, most companies have at least a little bit of all three in mind when they set their overall performance expectations. Yet by thinking about corporate goals in terms of these three basic flavours, companies are usually able to bring more clarity to the task of setting their sales objectives.

- **Aim for three to five key selling objectives** One industrial client recently listed for the authors seventeen separate objectives for its sales force and inbound call centres. Surprised at the sheer volume of channel objectives, we asked another client a week later to go through the same exercise. The result: fourteen separate objectives, many of them in conflict, including:
  - Grow overall sales by nine per cent;
  - Grow sales in key accounts (greater than $750 million) by fifteen per cent;
  - Acquire twenty new construction/engineering clients;
  - Reduce SG&A (selling expense) from twenty-six per cent of revenues to twenty-four per cent;
  - Increase average call volume per rep from eighteen to twenty-five calls per week;
  - Increase average revenue per sale from $16,250 to $22,000;
  - Improve customer satisfaction (no metric specified);
  - Decrease sales support from nine per cent of sales rep time to three per cent;
  - Etc.

  It is impossible to do anything useful with such a confusing, large slew of sales objectives. A much smaller handful of well-chosen sales objectives can do the job much more effectively. Indeed, three to five key sales objectives are often more than enough to serve as effective guideposts for developing channel performance targets.

This first step should be considered complete when a coherent set of sales objectives has been articulated. Sales objectives serve as the foundation for establishing *channel performance targets*, the key tools that companies have at their disposal to shape the direction of their channels' activities.

2. Establish channel performance targets

Performance targets are a central part of effective channel management, and it is easy to understand why. A clear and articulate performance target – 'increase channel sales by ten per cent this year' or 'increase call volume by ten per cent per month' – provides a benchmark for measuring channel success, monitoring its performance, and, if necessary, taking remedial action to bring its performance in line with expectations. Good channel performance targets are based on two inputs:

- **Sales objectives** As discussed earlier, sales objectives define the overall purpose of *all* selling activity. It only makes sense that an individual channel's target performance levels should be oriented toward helping to achieve those objectives.
- **The role of the channel in the sales process** Performance targets should be designed to reflect the unique role of each channel in the sales process. For instance, there is no sense in giving a channel a revenue target if its responsibility involves customer support or service. Similarly, customer satisfaction is not usually

a helpful performance target for a channel tasked only with generating leads. Performance targets – the expectations you set for each channel – need to reflect the specific responsibilities of the channel in the sales process.

As an example of how sales objectives and channel roles both influence the design of performance targets, consider the case of Orchard Park Logistics, a $40 million inventory management and warehousing subsidiary of a US-based shipping firm[2]. Back in 1996, the parent company put pressure on Orchard Park to grow revenues – then at $32 million – while also making a healthy reduction in the cost of sales. Orchard Park's board met and set three key sales objectives:

- Increase revenues from $32 million to $40 million by 1998 (approximately ten per cent growth per year).
- Reduce the cost-of-sales from thirty-two per cent of revenues to twenty-seven per cent, also by 1998.
- Reduce customer complaints by thirty per cent by 1998 (a key source of lost sales opportunities).

If Orchard Park Logistics had only one channel, its channel's performance targets would have been pretty clear. In fact, the lone channel's targets would have mirrored the company's sales objectives: grow revenues from $32 to $40 million, reduce the cost of sales by fifteen per cent, and reduce customer complaints by thirty per cent.

Orchard Park, however, has three channels: an outbound call centre, a field sales force, and a business logistics team. Its call centre is responsible for generating and qualifying new sales leads and sending them over to the sales force. The sales force is responsible primarily for taking leads from the call centre and closing them[3]. After sales have been completed, the business logistics team provides on-site project implementation and client support. Figure 12.3 displays the roles of these three channels in the company's sales process.

It should be obvious that although each of Orchard Park's three channels should be working toward the company's overall sales objectives, they each need to do so by working toward their own unique performance targets. For example, a target of twenty per cent revenue growth may be an appropriate one for the sales force, but it is an inappropriate target for the call centre – which deals in leads, not revenue. Twenty per cent revenue growth is just as inappropriate a target for the business logistics team, which enters an account only after a sale has been completed and therefore has no role in closing deals. Figure 12.4 shows how Orchard Park set its channels' performance targets in light of their unique contributions in the sales process.

As suggested in the figure, the process of setting performance targets involves comparing a set of sales objectives against a channel's specific respon-

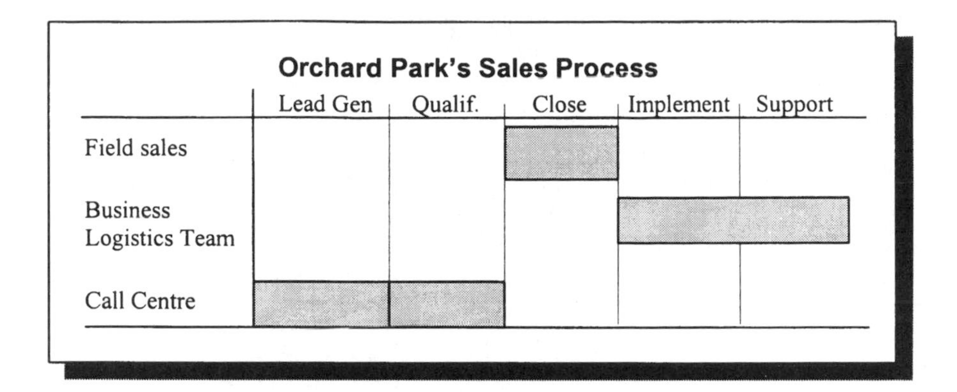

Figure 12.3 Orchard Park Logistics – channel role definition

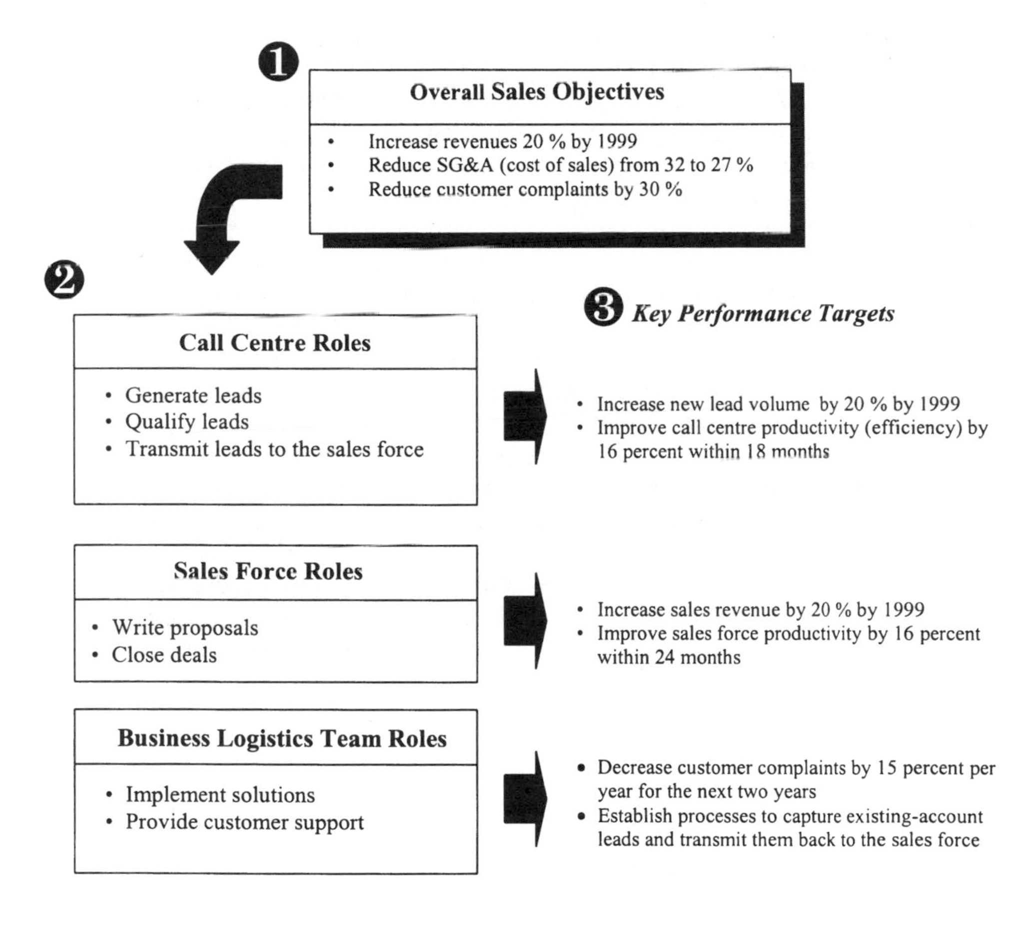

Figure 12.4 Orchard Park Logistics – developing channel performance targets

sibilities. For example, Orchard Park's objective of twenty per cent revenue growth must be translated into a call centre performance target. While the call centre doesn't directly generate revenue, what it does contribute is leads, which are the source of most of the company's sales. As a result, growth in sales leads is a reasonable – in fact, necessary – performance target for the call centre.

The challenge in establishing performance targets is thus to consider carefully what each channel is responsible for doing in the sales process and how each can best contribute to the achievement of the company's sales objectives. The outcome should be a set of performance targets for each channel that are:

- **Specific and quantified** Channel performance targets should be specific and, where possible, numeric. It is easier for a channel to work toward a goal of ten per cent sales growth – and it is easier to monitor how the channel is doing against that target – than it is for a channel to achieve 'growth in key vertical markets'. Channel performance almost always improves immediately when channel targets are made more specific and quantifiable.
- **Timed** It is a good idea to put a deadline on a performance target. Besides increasing the sense of urgency, time limits establish a finite period in which target performance levels must be achieved. 'Ten per cent growth within a year' is a better target than 'ten per cent growth'.
- **Forward-thinking** It takes most channels at least eighteen months to make significant changes in performance levels. A sales force, for instance, cannot be expected to grow revenues ten per cent overnight. Reps must be hired, trained, assigned to accounts, and given time to bring sales to fruition. It is important to recognize the time lag and plan for it. Channel targets should be set with an eye to the levels of performance required eighteen to thirty months out into the future.
- **Manageable in number** As mentioned earlier, there is no point in establishing an endless list of performance expectations for a channel. Most channels have two to four key things they need to achieve to contribute to the success of a go-to-market system. Orchard Park Logistics, for example, was able to define two to three targets per channel, each of which established an important corporate expectation for channel performance. As a rule of thumb, four performance targets is usually more than enough, and five is often a sign that the channel is being unnecessarily micro-managed.

So what do you do once you've identified good channel performance targets? Performance targets alone do not deliver performance, unfortunately; they only establish expectations. To get *actual performance* out of sales channels, you have to be able to see how they're doing against those targets and take corrective action. The next step looks at the key tool for doing just this – *performance measurement*.

3. Develop channel performance metrics

Performance measurement is one of the trickier areas of channel management. It requires a little explanation.

Everyone understands the measurement of, say, individual employees. Sales reps have to make a certain amount of sales per month. Secretaries have to be able to type a certain number of words per minute. Factory workers have to produce a certain amount of parts per hour. CEOs are measured on shareholder return and growth. These kinds of metrics provide a basis for monitoring individual performance and for ensuring that people meet the expectations of the organization.

Performance measurement is just as important with sales channels. Measurement enables managers to keep track of a channel's performance, ensure that it achieves its performance targets, and uncover any performance problems. Unfortunately, measuring a channel's performance is rarely as easy or simple as measuring an individual employee's performance. Channels are complex; they consist of many people, activities, and initiatives. The average channel could probably be measured on well over a hundred performance factors – which would constitute a management reporting and analysis nightmare. As a result, a big part of the art of good channel measurement involves narrowing down the field of possible performance metrics to a handful of particularly useful and informative ones. That is what this step is about.

The central concept in good performance measurement is the *key performance driver*. A key performance driver is a channel activity that directly and forcefully impacts the channel's overall performance. For example, in the long distance services business, a VP of sales might decide that *making more sales calls* is the most direct source of growth for a call centre. In fact, there may be no other single activity in which a call centre could engage that would have as much impact on sales growth. Increasing the number of sales calls, therefore, would be a key driver of the call centre's performance – if the goal is sales growth. If the goal is cost reduction, however, a key driver of performance for the call centre might involve *reduced time spent on each outbound sales call*. Key performance drivers are the activities or actions that most impact a channel's ability to achieve its performance targets.

Key performance drivers serve two purposes:

- They help identify the specific channel activities that need to be emphasized by the channel – and monitored by its managers – as it works toward its performance targets.
- They provide the basis for setting up metrics that measure and assess a channel's execution of its highest impact and most critical sales activities.

A simple illustration of how key performance drivers affect the design of channel metrics is shown in Figure 12.5.

Sales Force Performance Target
"Increase sales revenue by 20 percent within 24 months"

Key Performance Drivers	*Performance Indicators (Metrics)*
✓ Make more sales calls	Sales calls per month (per rep) Sales calls per month (by region # of sales reps
✓ Make more $$$ per sales call	# of calls per closed sale Average order size ($$$ per sale)
✓ Call on larger prospects	Avg. market capitalization per prospect
✓ Call on better-qualified prospects	Sales made divided by sales lost (by rep)
✓ Spend more time selling	Avg. selling hours per week (per rep) % of work-week spent in sales calls (per rep)
✓ Find more new accounts	New account closes per month (per rep) New account sales divided by existing account sales

Figure 12.5 Orchard Park Logistics – Identifying key performance drivers and setting metrics

As the figure illustrates, a company – in this case Orchard Park Logistics – should begin with a channel performance target, and then identify the key activities – the key performance drivers – that will contribute to the achievement of that target. For instance, Orchard Park's executive team decided that in its type of sale – complicated logistics management services – one key driver of sales volume was the size (market capitalization) of its prospects. A customer with $10 billion in sales would need more logistical and warehousing support than a customer with $300 million in sales. With that realization, Orchard Park was able to define a simple and clear metric – average market capitalization per new prospect – to monitor the types of accounts the sales force was pursuing and put pressure on its sales reps to increase the size of their average new customers.

As Figure 12.5 also suggests, performance metrics can become unwieldy. The time required for Orchard Park's sales reps and managers to accumulate, collate and report just the information shown in Figure 12.5 – which only con-

Key Performance Drivers ➡	*Performance Metrics*
✓ Make more sales calls	Sales calls per month (per rep) Sales calls per month (by region # of sales reps
✓ Make more $$$ per sales call	# of calls per closed sale **Average order size ($$$ per sale)**
✓ Call on larger prospects	**Avg. market capitalization per prospect**
✓ Call on better-qualified prospects	Sales made divided by sales lost (by rep)
✓ Spend more time selling	Avg. selling hours per week (per rep) % of work-week spent in sales calls (per rep)
✓ Find more new accounts	**New account closes per month (per rep)** New account sales divided by existing account sales

Figure 12.6 Orchard Park Logistics – Performance metric prioritization

cerns one of the sales force's three objectives – would have been excessive and unnecessary. The next part of the step thus involves *prioritizing* the metrics by focusing on the ones that count the most. Figure 12.6 shows the results from Orchard Park's prioritization process.

Orchard Park's reasoning was as follows. With the company committed to rapid business expansion, what really mattered the most was the ability of the sales force to bring in lots of new high-potential and high-revenue customers. Orchard Park determined that just three metrics – the average order size per sale, the average market capitalization of new customers, and the number of new accounts closed per month – provided a good overall snapshot of just how well the sales force was doing this. Some of the other metrics – sales calls per week, etc. – were deemed relevant, but at the same time, less indicative of whether the sales force was focused on the right types of new customers and selling opportunities. Thus, by asking itself 'what really matters the most?' Orchard Park was able to narrow down a field of eleven metrics to a highly-focused group of three.

Like Orchard Park, most companies benefit when they take a disciplined and focused approached to the selection of performance metrics. In general, three to five thoughtfully chosen performance metrics can provide a comprehensive view of a channel's ability to achieve its performance targets. It is worth keeping in mind that fewer metrics means less data collection and reporting on the part of the channel – and more time for what the channel and its managers are supposed to be doing: selling.

4. Identify performance gaps and create the channel action plan

This last step raises an important question: once you've defined channel performance targets and metrics, what do you *do* with them?

There are two primary uses for channel metrics. First, they can serve as powerful tools for managing channel performance in the field on an ongoing basis. For example, if a key sales force metric is 'sales calls per week', then collecting this information on a weekly basis can pinpoint where sales are strong and where they're weak – on a company, regional and sales rep level. This data can then serve as a sound and empirical basis for moving additional sales reps to fast-growing (and resource-deprived) regions, adjusting corporate sales expectations based on actual channel performance, rewarding high-performing reps, and dismissing or retraining under-performing personnel. Ongoing performance measurement, in short, is the basis for managing channels dynamically and for realigning expectations in 'real time' with the realities of the market place.

Second, and just as importantly, channel metrics provide an opportunity to identify the gaps between a channel's current performance levels and the future performance levels required to achieve its sales targets. The fact is that channels – except in the rare instance of a company with a zero-growth objective – never perform at the levels required to reach their targets two or three years out into the future. The key is to figure out what each channel needs to be doing to get to its future performance levels. Channel metrics play a crucial role in figuring this out. Figure 12.7 provides an illustration of how this works.

The channel action plan can be a powerful management tool for identifying the specific actions needed bring a channel up to target performance levels. Building one involves the following steps:

- Start with a channel's performance targets as well as the key metrics that will be used to measure channel activity against those targets (first two columns in the figure).
- Record *current* channel performance for each metric (Column 3).
- Identify the necessary performance levels eighteen to thirty months out for the channel to achieve its targets – thus establishing a *performance gap* (Column 4).
- Identify a set of tangible and specific actions that will assist the channel in bridging the gap from current performance to future (desired) performance levels (Column 5).

The real power in a channel action plan of this type is that it takes full advantage of the potential benefit of performance metrics. Metrics should be used not only to catch performance problems *after* they happen, but more importantly, to pre-empt problems and establish a proactive agenda for high performance. The channel action plan helps do this by translating a company's

Performance Target	Key Metrics	Current (1998) Performance	Year 2000 Target	Action Steps
Grow sales 20 %	Sales Calls Per Month	400	480	Hire 4 reps Increase per-rep calls/month from 20 to 24 Reduce sales rep admin time from 12 to 6 hrs/week
	Average Order Size	$26,000	$30,000	Launch mktg campaigns for higher-priced products Integrate products into larger 'solutions' Redesign comp plan: no credit for sales < $15,000
	Average Customer Size	$300 million	$1 billion	Increase prospecting activity in Fortune 500 Eliminate commissions on customers < $500 million Designate National Account Managers to focus exclusively on growing/penetrating large existing accounts
Reduce transaction costs by 6 %	Cost-per-sale	$1,500	$1,410	Instruct reps to qualify prospects over phone prior to site visits Instruct reps to ask for order by third contact Reduce customer payment terms to net 30 days Work through travel agent to reduce travel expenses Reduce sales management ratio from 1:6 to 1:8

Figure 12.7 The channel action plan for a field sales force

selling objectives and channel targets all the way down to the specific actions required from a channel to achieve those objectives and targets. It is an essential part of the channel management process.

Summary...and the end of the book

It is impossible to overstate the importance of sound performance management when a portfolio of multiple channels is involved. A guidance system – a set of thoughtful targets and metrics – provides a basis for ensuring that sales channels support the larger goals of the enterprise and do what they're supposed to do in the sales process. Targets and metrics also enable managers to identify the specific actions required to bring the performance of channels in line with corporate needs and expectations.

As most channel executives know all too well, performance management is not a simple process with a pat, easy answer. The tuning of channel performance over time, with the right mix of metrics and targets, is always an iterative learning process. However, it is possible to put some stakes in the ground and lay the foundation for a strong performance management system. This chapter defined a process that involves four steps:

- **Define/confirm overall sales objectives** The first step involves developing a clear and articulate set of overall (cross-channel) sales objectives.
- **Set channel performance targets** Here, channel performance targets are set, based on corporate sales objectives as well as the unique role of each channel in the sales process. The purpose of this step is to establish channel expectations that:
  (a) align with the goals of the company, and
  (b) are suitable for the channel's specialized role in the sales process.
- **Develop channel metrics** In this step, channel performance targets are translated into key performance drivers: actions and activities, such as 'increase the average order size' or 'make more sales calls,' that will drive a channel toward its target performance levels. These key performance drivers then provide a basis for identifying metrics – or quantitative measures of performance – that will guide and monitor the channel's activities as it works toward its performance targets.
- **Identify channel performance gaps and create channel action plan** Here, channel metrics are used to build the channel action plan. The action plan defines and articulates the gaps between current channel performance and desired future performance levels – and in so doing, establishes a sound basis for taking proactive steps to improve channel performance.

A performance management system is the last building block of a strategic channel initiative, and this topic brings to a close the journey that began twelve chapters ago. Unfortunately, the wide range of issues involved in a channel initiative – customers, markets, products, economics, channels, budgets, management techniques, etc. – are well beyond the scope of any single book. In fact, this book was not intended to include every conceivable channel design and management issue. Rather, it was written to bring clarity, structure, and a comprehensive sense of the 'big picture' to the task of building a high-performance system of multiple channels. We hope, in particular, that the reader benefited from our decision to focus on detailed, rich examples and practical suggestions, at the cost of occasionally omitting or only gently touching on some of the complex underlying theories.

It is always worthwhile to return to the basics at the end of a long journey. The book began with a straightforward and yet fundamental premise: namely, that executives must think not only in terms of *what* they sell, but *how* they sell it. The fact is that there are just too many innovative companies competing with new channels and clever go-to-market systems for the old philosophy – 'make a good product and they will come' – to work effectively anymore. Today, the question is less about *whether* to take a fresh, creative look at sales channels than about *how* to do so in a way that extracts the maximum possible value in terms of revenue and profit growth.

There is clearly a window of opportunity as organizations struggle over the next decade to understand, emulate and build on the experiences of leading channel innovators. We hope this book has instilled some confidence that a high-performance multiple-channel system is an attainable goal. Most of all, we hope this book has put some fire in the bellies of our readers to take a fresh look at how they can win new customers, sell more products, and make more profit faster through a more innovative and systematic use of sales channels.

Notes

[1] *Source*: Oxford Associates industry study, 1997.
[2] The name has been changed at the request of the client.
[3] The sales force actually has a more complex role than is indicated; the example has been simplified for clarity.

Index